In Search of Salt

Cameroon Studies

General Editors: *Shirley Ardener, E. M. Chilver,* and *Ian Fowler,*
Associate Members of Queen Elizabeth House, University of Oxford

Volume 1
Kingdom on Mount Cameroon: Studies in the History of the Cameroon Coast, 1500–1970
Edwin Ardener, edited and with an introduction by Shirley Ardener

Volume 2
African Crossroads: Intersections between History and Anthropology in Cameroon
Edited by Ian Fowler and David Zeitlyn

Volume 3
Cameroon's Tycoon: Max Esser's Expedition and its Consequences
Edited by E. M. Chilver and Ute Röschenthaler

Volume 4
Swedish Ventures in Cameroon, 1883–1923: Trade and Travel, People and Politics
Edited and with commentaries by Shirley Ardener

Volume 5
Memoirs of a Mbororo. The Life of Ndudi Umaru: Fulani Nomad of Cameroon
Henri Bocquené, translated by Philip Burnham and Gordeen Gorder

Volume 6
In Search of Salt: Changes in Beti (Cameroon) Society, 1880–1960
Frederick Quinn

IN SEARCH OF SALT

Changes in Beti (Cameroon) Society, 1880–1960

FREDERICK QUINN

Berghahn Books
NEW YORK • OXFORD

Published in 2006 by
Berghahn Books

www.berghahnbooks.com

©2006 Frederick Quinn

All rights reserved.
Except for the quotation of short passages
for the purposes of criticism and review, no part of this book
may be reproduced in any form or by any means, electronic or
mechanical, including photocopying, recording, or any information
storage and retrieval system now known or to be invented,
without written permission of the publisher.

Library of Congress Cataloging-in-Publication Data

Quinn, Frederick.
 In search of salt : changes in Beti (Cameroon) society, 1880–1960 / Frederick Quinn.
   p. cm. — (Cameroon studies ; v. 6)
 Includes bibliographical references (p.) and index.
 ISBN 1-84545-006-X (acid-free paper)
 1. Beti (African people)—Social conditions. 2. Beti (African people)—History.
I. Title. II. Series.

DT571.B47Q56 2006
305.896'396—dc22

2006042749

British Library Cataloguing in Publication Data

A catalogue record for this book is available from
the British Library.

Printed in the United States on acid-free paper

To the memory of

The Abbé Theodore Tsala, Englebert Mveng, S.J., Beti scholars, and Bernard Fonlon, founder of *Abbia* magazine, and Cameroonian Minister of Postes et Télécommunications, in deepest appreciation for many hours spent re-creating an African past

V. May the souls of the faithful departed rest in peace.
R. And rise in glory.

Contents

Introduction		1
1	Traditional Beti Society	13
2	Social Organization and the *Sso* Rite	30
3	"In the Time of Major Dominik": The Beti and the Germans, 1887–1916	43
4	The German Presence: Traders and Missionaries	61
5	The Beti and the French	74
6	Times of Expansion: The Inland Railroad, Cocoa Production, the Catholic Church	86
7	The Beti from World War II to Independence	101
Conclusion		116
Appendix A: Traditional Beti Literature		119
Appendix B: Aspects of Traditional Beti Society, by Abbé Theodore Tsala		126
Appendix C: English Translation of Appendix B		140
Annex		
	Abbia Stones, by Frederick Quinn	154
	Eight Beti Stones, by Frederick Quinn	157
Bibliography		159
Index		174

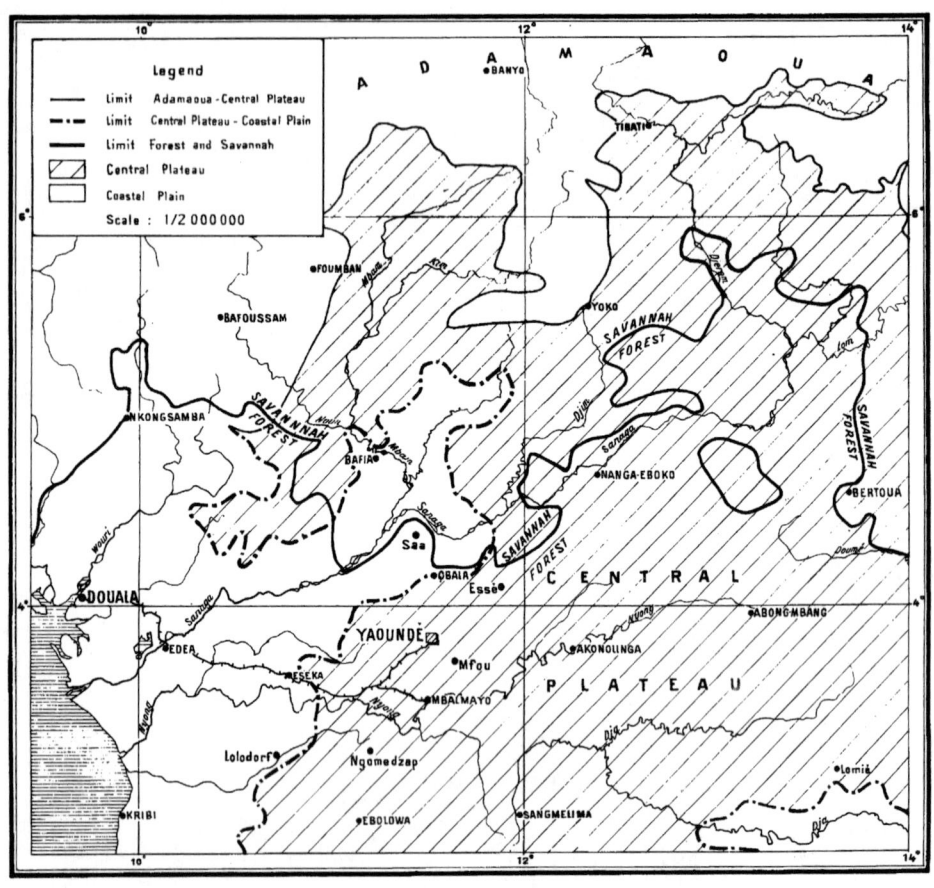

Central Plateau, Forest and Savannah Zones in South Cameroon

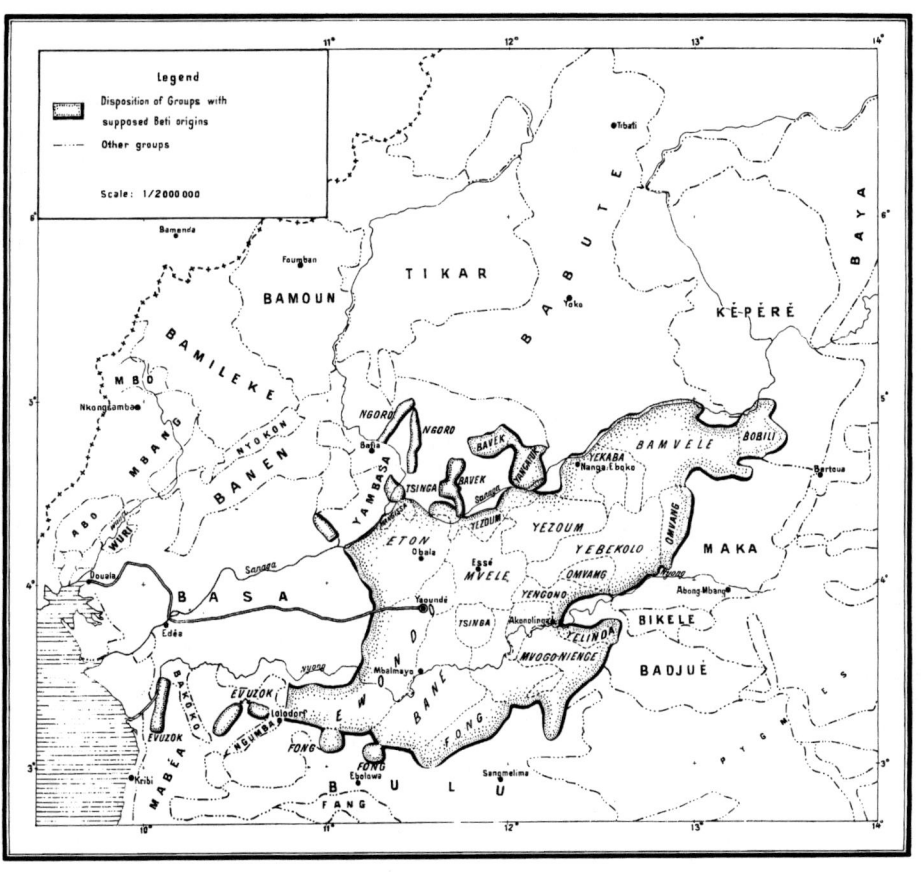

Ethnic Map of South Cameroon

Introduction

This book describes an African society and the changes it experienced, primarily during the first half of the twentieth century. The Beti of Central Cameroon, who number about a half-million people, are considered in four periods: (1) the 1880s, when they were one of several tribes in the interior of Cameroon whose politics were unaffected by contact with Europeans; (2) the German period (1887–1916); (3) the French administration (1916–1960); and (4) the early days of Cameroon's independence.

The group is called "Beti" because that is how its members knew themselves. They were all descendants of Beti, a proto-ancestor who founded the Eton and Mvele clans. His son, Kolo, fathered the Ewondo and Benë groups. These are the four principal extended Beti lineages, but other, smaller, more distantly related groups migrated to the central Cameroonian rainforest as well. Together these Beti groups shared descent from a putative ancestor and a common language and culture.

This study begins in the 1880s and consequently does not deal with the origins and early migrations of the Beti. It is difficult to reconstruct Beti history much earlier than the 1880s because there were no written records before the German arrival and because oral traditions are difficult to date with any certainty before that period. Moreover, Beti accounts of their history stress the recent past. The cut-off point in almost all genealogies and oral traditions is the period of migration across the Sanaga River and into the lands around Yaoundé, the Cameroon's capital. Most of the genealogies are eight generations deep or less. Allowing thirty to forty years for a generation and an overlap between generations, the period of migration would have been during the mid to late eighteenth century and later, since the Beti always seemed to be in motion in these accounts.

By ending the study in 1960, several questions of contemporary African political history are treated only in passing, such as the rise of Paul Biya to Cameroon's presidency. Biya is a Bulu, a Bantu-speaking ethnic group to the south of the Beti. Moreover, in dealing with the period 1945–1960 and the independence movement in Cameroon, this book comments only briefly on several important parties, ethnic groups, and leaders so that the Beti role at that time could be established in more detail. For the period 1887–1960, I do not examine in detail colonial or imperial history or the differences in German and French policies toward overseas territories. This is partly because differences between the policies of one colonial secretary and another, or between doctrines such as "assimilation" and "association," were often

---

Notes for this section are located on page 11.

little more than historical anagrams and *jeu de mots* that meant little by the time they reached the rainforest. The powerful European presence was always there, using Africans as laborers to systematically extract the region's natural resources in exchange for education, improved health conditions, and opportunities for personal advancement in institutions like the administration, schools, commercial enterprises, and churches.

As much as evidence will allow, this study will present a picture of how one African society was organized before colonial contact, how that society saw itself and the world around it, and how the structure and outlook of the Beti changed during the eighty years that followed their first encounter with the Europeans. I will not elaborate in detail on Beti relations with neighboring or competing Cameroonian societies, since the task of reconstructing Beti society itself is sufficiently difficult, given the lack of systematic studies of the Beti at the time I originally undertook my research in the 1960s and published the results, mainly in the 1970s. This work was originally written in the late 1960s, with some updating as later material on the Beti became available. Few such works appeared, beyond those published by Jane Guyer and Philippe Laburthe-Tolra, which are included in the bibliography. The exercise was like sitting in front of the scattered pieces of a puzzle; trying to connect names, dates, institutions, and beliefs and give them coherence; and then examine from where they might have come and to where they might be headed.

This study incorporates material from both archival sources and oral interviews. The archival material available in Cameroon represented a rich but scattered collection of documents and publications from the German and French periods. The National Archives in Yaoundé, then situated in a decrepit, garage-like building, contained some monthly and situational reports written by regional administrators of the German colony; although most of the important German records at the Yaoundé station had been burned during World War I, though, shortly before the Germans retreated from their former colony.

But extensive German sources were otherwise available, principally from published memoirs and the numerous geographic and colonial journals that flourished between the 1870s and 1916, such as *Globus, Koloniale Monatblätter,* and *Mittheilungen von Forschungsreisenden und gelehrten aus den Deutschen Schutzegebieten.* From 1908 to 1916, the journal *Amtsblatt für die Kamerun Schutzgebiet* published most of the German government's decrees concerning Cameroon. These publications contained explorers' reports, ethnographic surveys, colonial regulations, and detailed accounts of skirmishes and "pacification" missions, frequently including maps and illustrations. This researcher found the journals endlessly interesting, filled as they were with details about the latest cure for malaria, portable rubber tents, and bathtubs that "only took six bearers to carry."

Besides these printed accounts, there were descriptions of the Beti written by German colonial administrators, such as Curt von Morgen, Hans Dominik, O. Zimmerman, and Georg Zenker. These sources suggest that, while Germany had fewer colonies than did France or England, and acquired them late in the race for overseas territories, it still produced an extensive body of valuable colonial literature. My application to visit the German Colonial Archives in Potsdam was turned down by officials of the German Democratic Republic (why would an American diplomat in

Cameroon want to visit Potsdam during the Cold War?), and by the time the Berlin Wall came down, this study had been completed. Likewise, I did not visit the French Colonial Archives; their thirty-year access rule in the 1960s would have eliminated most of the files applicable to this study; besides, much French colonial historical and anthropological material on the Beti was already available in Cameroon.

Useful for the French period were the archives remaining in Cameroon, including monthly, quarterly, and annual reports from the administrative districts into which the Yaoundé prefecture was divided. There were reports of *passation du service*, the end of tour statements prepared by an outgoing prefect for his successor. These usually contained a statement about the local political climate, comments on African issues and personalities, biographical notes on Beti chiefs, some tax collection data, and population and health statistics for the district to the extent that they were available. Several other important accounts existed, including annual statements to the League of Nations, of which Cameroon was a mandate territory. These documents showed the lamentable conditions in which inland railroad African laborers worked.

Documents reflected the persons who wrote them, as well as the times in which they were written. The authors were usually soldiers or officers in the colonial service who saw their mission as bringing to the small corner of Africa they administered order, progress, and, during the French period, that nebulous, glittering goal of *la mission civilisatrice*. Progress also meant tax collection, road building, and public works. The civilizing force in this later period was French education, law, and culture. A few administrators also wrote ethnographic reports commenting on local customs or "the African family," which they compared to the Greek and Roman institutions described by Numa-Denis Fustel de Coulanges (1830–1889), the Strasbourg academic, in *La Cité Antique*, the one ethnographic work that many French administrators read before going overseas.

Further complicating matters was the inaccessibility of the National Archives in Yaoundé. Cataloguing was incomplete, and access procedures were not user-friendly. The director, Marc Etende, a Bulu, was sympathetic to my research project, but the French advisor who sat in the office next to his was a gatekeeper who viewed me suspiciously for over a year. However, when I learned he was a Protestant from La Rochelle, I told him about my earlier research on the Huguenots. He immediately became friendly and extended an invitation to his home in France. Originally, only one file could be requested from the archives at a time, and sometimes the task of retrieving files took a day or more to complete, for there was one clerk and several readers. Since I was reading files during my lunch or siesta hour, I wanted to move more quickly. Fortunately the clerk, Daniel Zé, was a Beti and a former secretary to an important chief. After he learned of my work, he would occasionally bring me piles of folders; he once took my wife and me to an all-night *mvet* sing in his village where for several hours a solitary singer-story teller recalled the past history of the assembled Beti lineage groups. Additionally, reproducing research materials, once they had been located, always posed a problem. This was the 1960s; the archives had a reproduction machine called a thermofax. A document was pressed against a page of photosensitive reproduction paper, and if the temperature was right, it produced a copy. If there was too much heat, the paper turned purple; not enough heat, and it turned as brown as a dead leaf. Daniel and I would patiently try various settings until we reached the right one. For some longer works, I contracted with a local photographer to shoot copies of pages with his 35 millimeter camera.

Apart from the National Archives, another valuable depository of manuscripts was the library of the Institut de Recherches Scientifiques du Cameroun (IRCAM), which also had an excellent collection of German and French books and periodicals about Cameroon. One day, after having gone through what I thought was most of IRCAM's material about the Beti, I was returning an old volume to its shelf in the librarian's office, when he glanced up from his desk and said, "There is something over there that might interest you." He pointed to a long row of thick folders, one of which contained perhaps two hundred pages of uncataloged material on Beti customs, social organization, and history. Shortly before independence, a member of the IRCAM staff had culled most of the National Archives, attempting to gather everything of ethnographic interest in order to store it in one place. The project was later abandoned and the material left in a pile of folders in the IRCAM library.

An additional source of archival material was the documents kept by the Beti themselves. Frequently an informant in a rainforest compound would interrupt our conversation and go to a metal trunk under his bed and return with a genealogy, a school notebook filled with writings about local history, a faded copy of a long out-of-print local periodical, or some official papers belonging to a father or grandfather. The largest collection of such documents came from a retired rural medical assistant, Ambroise Onana, who spent more than twenty years moving among different Beti groups between the Nyong and Sanaga rivers. During the day he treated patients, and in the evenings he recorded genealogies, proverbs, fables, and local histories. The results filled several notebooks, which he lent to two Beti researchers and myself for copying. Onana, like several Beti headmen, was a collector. Among the documents he and others retained were German and French medals, birth and school certificates, and, in one case, a German beer glass, the sort of object Germans collected before World War I. Engraved on it was a photo of the Beti chief, Karl Atangana, framed by a garland of vine leaves.

Thus, from both colonial and African sources, the unshaped substance of Beti history emerged: the names of leading headmen and chiefs of the late nineteenth century and first half of the twentieth century, and the outlines of how traditional society was organized; significant dates, such as 1933, when the administration substantially reorganized the *chefferie,* the order of chiefs; and important themes, such as the Beti effort to reconcile traditional values with Christianity. The next step was to assemble this raw information into some sort of order and to use it in oral interviews to discover how the Beti interpreted their own past, and to see how and why Beti history changed in the span of roughly three generations.

No less important than the written sources were the findings derived from oral interviews conducted during 1968 and 1969 with over twenty Beti elders, many of them active participants in events of the German and French eras. It was not difficult to find people to interview. (All have long since died; I was fortunate to spend time with a generation of Beti who knew the German and French colonial representatives firsthand.) Several names were suggested from the archives, and many prefects, priests, and rural schoolteachers put me in contact with elders in their districts who were especially interested in the past. Beti whom I knew in Yaoundé invited me to their villages and gathered kinsmen together for me to interview. The problem became not one of finding informants but of limiting their numbers. Absent from my list are interviews with women, which I regret. The role of women was important in the evolution of Beti history, but little was written about women in the German and French sources, and I was a product of the period in which I wrote, the mid to late 1960s, before gender studies and the perspective they provide had emerged.

Generally, interviews lasted an hour, and two sessions were usually enough to cover the topic, although with some informants, I held weekly interviews for longer periods. Interviews were conducted in French or in Beti (with the help of an interpreter). Most began with one person, but, especially in the bush, the room would gradually fill, with most participants listening to the principal informant, but occasionally providing illustrative material of their own. I tried to avoid group interviews, partly because the Beti elders were practiced conversationalists and would often take over the discussion and partly because informants in groups usually deferred to elders and added little on their own.

Originally, some rural governmental administrators wondered why a diplomat from the US Embassy would spend his spare time collecting material on the Beti past. They imagined an ulterior political motive. I obtained a letter of introduction from the Foreign Ministry, which allowed for unhindered passage in the rainforest. But after a few interviews, some of the administrators, and Beti in government posts in Yaoundé, wanted to discuss at length both their own views and my findings. The impact of the German and French presence and changes in Cameroonian society were subjects that did not lack for commentators.

Oral interviews were conducted as follows. At first I explained my intent, sought approval to tape record the discussion, and began to ask questions. Things moved slowly for the most part, because I was initially not sure what to ask. At this point, I assembled numerous photographs of early Beti chiefs reproduced from colonial publications and other photographs representing scenes from daily life. I placed the photographs before informants and asked, "Did you know this person?" or "Can you tell me what is happening here?" With this approach, the interview was off and running. At first I had only a vague outline in my head of what I wanted to cover. My intent was to let informants talk about aspects of Beti society that most interested them. For example, one person who had participated in the *Sso* initiation rite, which was the central Beti ritual act, might describe it in vivid detail, while another person of the same age who had not been a *Sso* candidate might have little to say about it. Some people knew the important Beti chief, Charles Atangana, well, others had opinions about him, without knowing him. I tried to keep the original interviews nondirective, which meant that many were long and rambling; but as I learned more about Beti personalities and society, I asked specific questions, and a fuller picture of Beti life began to emerge.

Of course I committed every possible error. Batteries went dead in the tape recorder deep in the rainforest, or late in an interview I recorded over the valuable first half-hour. But the Beti were patient and accessible. One elderly chief said, "Our own young people are not interested in these things." Originally, I had planned to deposit my research materials with the new University of Cameroon at Yaoundé. Once, while in London, I had a cache of Cameroon-related documents copied from the Public Records Office and gave them to the University of Yaoundé's librarian, a French technical adviser, explaining they were for access to researchers studying Cameroonian history. A year later, I visited the librarian, and the papers were still sitting on a shelf near her desk. I decided to deposit my additional research materials elsewhere.

The first person with whom I talked in detail was François Atangana, secretary of a cocoa grower's cooperative several hours' drive south of Yaoundé. Like many cocoa growers, he came to Yaoundé on occasion to find seasonal workers for the plantations. We covered Beti warfare and agriculture, and concepts of time, space, and distance, and my informant made some references to the *Sso* rite. François Atangana, then in his forties, was born several years after the *Sso* rite had been outlawed by the Germans. I asked if there were still men living who had participated in the rite and could describe it. He thought so, but most of the old men from his region who had take part in the ceremony were now dead. He took me one night, however, to the compound of a kinsman, Pierre Mebe, a retired schoolteacher and catechist whom several Beti had described as having a special interest in the Beti past. Possibly he would know if there were any men still living who had experienced the *Sso* rite.

We arrived late, arousing the compound after most of its inhabitants were asleep. Dogs barked, flashlights shone from windows, and we set up a time for a proper meeting. To these interviews Pierre Mebe summoned a kinsman, Joseph Essono, about eighty years old, who had the three incised lines on the nape of the neck that marked a *Sso* graduate. Joseph Essono described the *Sso* rite at length, and with Pierre Mebe, I began to unravel the pattern of Beti kinship. Pierre kept a large genealogical chart, and in purple ink and with a schoolmaster's careful hand, he traced his family's descent from Beti, the putative ancestor, through eight generations, to the present.

When it did not appear that much new information would be forthcoming from these initial interviews, I moved to other informants representing principal Beti lineages. With the help of four Beti interviewers (who were Roman Catholic seminarians looking for summer jobs), I asked more specific questions about personalities, dates, and themes of Beti history of the past century. During this phase of interviews, I talked with Max Abe Foudda, the last living Beti *chef supérieur* of the colonial period. Born around 1874, he belonged to the first generation of Beti educated by the Germans and, as a close associate of Charles Atangana, was the highest ranking Beti chief in both the German and French periods. Foudda had built a large house of European construction after the Beti chiefs had returned from Spain at the end of World War I. By the time of our interviews, Foudda was old and lived in a simple traditional dwelling on his compound. Our time together produced one serendipitous interview moment. It was 23 December 1967, just before Christmas.

We had just exchanged gifts; he gave me the leg of a young antelope and I was heading for the car when he said, "Would you like me to tell you what really happened?" "Of course," I said, not having an idea of what was coming. We had been talking about the time the Beti chiefs had spent in Spain. The Germans had sent them there at the end of World War I. It was assumed that, during the Versailles peace talks, the question of restoring its colonies to Germany would come up, and the Beti would be called on to testify what humane colonizers the Germans were. But the colonies were never restored, and the Beti went home, excluded from the peace talks. While in Spain, they observed that country's form of cabinet government at work and decided to establish a similar form of government when they returned to Cameroon. It didn't work, Foudda explained, Beti chiefs were unwilling to relinquish their traditional powers and were unexposed to European public administration based on specific functions, like separate departments responsible for roads and education. The two ways of governance were vastly different, the Beti saw no way to combine them. I never located any evidence of discussion of this plan in written sources; indeed, I would not have learned of its existence had I not left some silent spaces at the end of our interview.

Another Beti of this older generation was the Abbé Theodore Tsala, a Beti linguist and one of the first Beti ordained as a Roman Catholic priest. A former rural schoolteacher, he had published a dictionary of Ewondo, the chief Beti dialect, and several articles on Beti history and culture. Tsala lived in retirement at the Roman Catholic mission at Mvolyé, near Yaoundé, and I visited him often. We went over my research findings, and he generously shared his large library of German and French sources with me. Then, and later, after I had returned to the United States, I asked him to write brief commentaries on various aspects of Beti life and history, commentaries that became the unpublished articles "Le Gouvernement des Beti" and "Principales Valeurs Sociales des Beti."

My first encounter with Hubert Mbida Onana at Ayéné-Ngomedzap extended over six hours and resumed the following morning, lasting until noon. Subsequent meetings were only slightly shorter. In his later letters to me, Onana (ca. 1876–1976) signed them "Doyen de connaissances spécifiques des myths," or "dean of the specific knowledge of myths," which he certainly was. Onana was an engrossing storyteller with an encyclopedic mind. And if the discussion moved to the activities of a kinsmen, for example, the whole family would be described in detail. Onana wore a red stocking cap, a mark of chiefly authority that had replaced the leader's headpiece of red parrot feathers of an earlier era. At our final meeting, the headman stood up from the comfortable lawn chair in which he usually sat and, with both hands, presented me with his woven flywhisk. Tsala uncharacteristically interrupted, "Oh you young people," he said, "Don't you see, he's naming you his successor." The flywhisk was a symbol of a chief. I thanked him and said that, while I would soon be leaving Cameroon, I would do my best to preserve the traditional he was sharing with me for others.

Not all such encounters went so smoothly. Once I showed films in a cocoa growing region of southern Cameroon and interviewed some of the cocoa planters. At the trip's end, I told the Beti chief, "If you are ever in Yaoundé, come see me." (My wife, Charlotte, had not yet arrived.) Several weeks later, Gabriel, our houseboy, nervously announced, "Some people are outside to see you." It was the chief and two crowded taxis full of his family members. After exchanging greetings, he said, "I want you to have my daughter," and presented me with a frightened two year old, who cried and wet the tile floor. Not knowing how to respond, I asked Gabriel, sotto voce, "What do I do?" "He wants you to take the daughter so he will be part of your family," Gabriel explained. I thanked the chief, but said that, in the absence of my wife, I could not accept such a gift. "Keep her," the chief replied, pushing the frightened tot toward me. I declined again, but he insisted. Exchanging children and brides among rainforest societies was a common way of making alliances and solidifying ties among rainforest societies. But this knowledge came to me in the future; I had to extricate myself from the present situation. Gabriel whispered, "Give him a bottle of whiskey," which I did. A hurried exchange took place among family members. "That's not enough," the chief said. I added a new wash-and-wear shirt and a tie, and he looked pained. Two more ties and bottles of whiskey went on the pile, and the chief appeared satisfied, gave the signal for his party to leave, and in parting handed me a choice stock of bananas.

Two valuable informants on a more recent period of Cameroonian history were Benoit Bindzi and Jean-Faustin Bétéyene, both former foreign ministers of Cameroon. Bindzi, a youthful activist in the Cameroonian independence movement, had first-hand knowledge of the African ideas, personalities, and associations important in Cameroon in the period 1945–1960. Bétéyene participated in many of the African associations of the French period, was an important figure in the colonial administration, and later became president of the Société Nationale d'Investissement du Cameroun, the National Investment Company, a Cameroonian government agency formed to encourage large-scale economic investments from multiple local and overseas sources.

In 1968, toward the end of my time in Cameroon, Tsala asked if I would like to interview a relative of his, André-Marie Mbida, the most important Beti in Cameroonian politics until then. Mbida, active in the centrist Bloc Démocratique Camerounais party, had been selected on 10 May 1957 by French High Commissioner Pierre Messmer to be Cameroon's first prime minister. But his government lasted only nine months. Those early years of African rule in Cameroon were a politically tumultuous time, requiring finesse and balance from a leader; but these qualities were beyond Mbida, whose stubborn, blustery personality and intransigence contributed to his quick downfall. Our meeting was scheduled for 28 July 1968, a week before I was scheduled to leave Cameroon. Beforehand I had spoken with US Ambassador Robert Payton. The interview would require delicate handling; I was the US Embassy's cultural attaché, and I planned to interview the country's former prime minister, a figure who remained critical of the present government and who longed to return to office after a decade's absence. It was agreed that the meeting should have a low profile, and the interview was scheduled as a Sunday afternoon invitation to tea. At about 4 PM, while awaiting our guest, the grating sound of heavy metal was heard on the road outside our Bastos residence. I ran to the gate. An ancient Ford was making its way up the road, with something having gone wrong with its moving parts. In the front passenger seat was a large elderly man, ceremoniously doffing his homburg to the growing crowd of roadside gawkers. The former prime minister arrived, dressed in a heavy, blue double-breasted suit, the public uniform of French politicians of the early postwar period. His wife, who wore a tailored French dress from the 1950s, accompanied him. Soon the smell of mothballs filled the room. We talked at length about Mbida's days as a seminarian and schoolteacher, and of his role in French and Cameroonian politics. Finally, I folded my pad and thanked him for a valuable interview. Then Mbida announced that he had questions of his own. Was the real purpose of my invitation to express American discontent with the present government of Cameroon? Would we be willing to help him return to office? "No," was my short, nervous answer to both questions, as Mbida began his fulminations against his rivals. It was time to end the interview. Gifts were exchanged; Tsala, who had attended the interview, left a large captured bird for me, and we said goodbye. Shortly thereafter, we heard the screech of the worn-out brake pads of their departing car.

After I completed research and initial writing on the Beti, I deposited my collected research materials with the Hoover Institution Library and Archives at Stanford University. This came about because the Hoover Institution curator, Peter Duignan, and I both happened to be reaching for a glass of wine at an African Studies Association meeting in Los Angeles in the late 1960s and struck up a conversation. I knew of Duignan's work on African colonial history but did not yet know of the Hoover Institution's effort to collect documents on African history of the modern period. So one day in the early 1970s, after my doctoral thesis had been completed at the University of California at Los Angeles, and several articles had been sent off to scholarly publications, I packed my collected documents and working papers into two metal French army trunks and sent them off to Palo Alto. Duignan, who served as the Hoover Institution's African curator until 1995, and Karen Fung, assistant curator from 1966 until 2002, carefully catalogued and annotated the documents, with the assistance of Harold P. Anderson, who completed the catalogue in 1976. The materials are contained in sixteen boxes, three microfilm reels, two envelopes, an expanding folder, and four tape recordings; the entire collection is available on seven reels of microfilm.[1]

This study is a product of its times, the late 1960s. Much of its content has been published in individual journal articles, but the launching of this series of works on Cameroonian studies provided an opportunity to present the study as a whole. Several theoretical works listed in the bibliography, informed my writing, although I do not follow any school of historical or anthropological writing. Robert Mandrou's *Introduction à la France Moderne, Essai de psycologie historique, 1500–1600,* provided a point in medias res for my own framing of the question of how an essentially nonliterate society saw itself and its history. My initial chapter on the organization of Beti society profited greatly from a reading of M. G. Smith's "Segmentary Lineage Systems" and the theoretical sections of *Government in Zazau, 1800–1950,* and from several conversations while Smith was still at the University of California at Los Angeles. Several other works on segmentary lineage systems also proved useful, including Marshall Sahlins's "The Segmentary Lineage: An Organization of Predatory Expansion" and his book *Tribesmen.*

In writing about the *Sso* rite and other aspects of traditional Beti beliefs, I considered Clifford Geertz's important essay "Religion as a Cultural System" and the writings of Victor Turner, in particular his theoretical constructs in *The Forest of Symbols, Aspects of Ndembu Ritual*. The discussion of the Beti economy gained from Manning Nash's study, *Primitive and Peasant Economic Systems*, John Middleton's *The Effects of Economic Development on Traditional Political Systems in Africa South of the Sahara*, and several important articles by Jane I. Guyer on the Beti economy. Philippe Laburthe-Tolra and I both worked in the Cameroonian rainforest at the same time in the mid 1960s, and I enjoyed contact with him then and in later years. Laburthe-Tolra, who went on to a distinguished career at the Sorbonne, spent nearly four decades working among the Beti from the mission station of Minlaaba, producing a steady flow of detailed ethnographic studies, novels, and articles on traditional religion and symbolism, a magisterial and unparalleled research effort meriting him a place among the leading Africanists of his generation.

Claude Tardits, Labuthe-Tolra's predecessor at the Sorbonne, was a leading figure in Cameroonian studies of the time. Often he would stop by our house in Yaoundé in the evening for a conversation, and would stay on for dinner and a thorough discussion of local politics and ethnography. Professor Hilda Kuper, a social anthropologist, originally from South Africa, was most helpful as a teacher and thesis advisor at the University of California at Los Angeles, as were Professors Eugen Weber and Jere C. King, both of whom taught French history at UCLA.

This history of the Beti provides a case study of political change in an acephalous, segmentary society over roughly a century. The period was marked by contact with the Germans first, then with the French, and finally by incorporation of the Beti in the Cameroonian state. Internally, the Beti experienced the deterioration of traditional means of political equilibrium and the rise and decline in importance of a class of chiefs. These chiefs were named by the colonial powers as the legitimate leaders of the Beti but were regarded by the Beti as the tax-collecting and labor-recruiting agents of the Europeans. In this study I focus on the institutions of the headmanship, the structure of appointed local leaders during the German period, and later the *chefferie*, councils, and institutions, like the *Sso*, that brought independent lineage segments together in closer contact. Where such material was available, I added sections on the Beti economy and on the impact of Christianity on the Beti. When I completed the initial study, a colleague asked, "Why did you concentrate on the Beti alone, it would be a much more interesting work if you had discussed the Beti's interactions with other neighboring groups." I fully agree, and an important study remains to be written on the internal expansion and interaction of Cameroon's many ethnic groups, their competition for land and trade, and their patterns of warfare and alliance making. But such a work is for another scholar, at another time. My goal was to reconstruct Beti society and to follow its changes across several decades. At the time I began my research, very little English-language scholarship existed on the Beti, and most of what was available in German and French was episodic in nature. Little had been done with oral interviews, and almost no material existed documenting the Beti's perspective on their own history. It took over two years of fieldwork and more than four years of intermittent writing to produce this work, which I hope will serve others in advancing Cameroonian studies.

Acknowledgements

The Cameroonian National Archives in Yaoundé proved rich stores of documentation on the colonial period. I thank its director, Marc Etende, and two members of his staff, Daniel Ze and Marcelin Mboa, for their assistance. That all three were Beti and took an interest in my project gave the breath of life to many of the names and events that otherwise would have likely remained lifeless entries in faded archives folders. The library of the Institut de Recherches du Cameroun and its director, Martin Njikan, were no less helpful in providing many valuable documents on the Beti and other Cameroonian societies. My thanks are due to the Royal Geographic Society, London, and to the Bodleian Library and Rhodes House, Oxford University, for the use of their excellent collections and facilities. The graduate library of the University of California at Los Angeles and the Library of Congress in Washington D.C. were of considerable assistance as well.

I am grateful to the many individuals named in this introduction for their assistance, and to two young Beti scholars, Pierre Betene and Apollinaire Ebogo, for their help. I am indebted to the late professors Michael G. Smith of Yale University and Hilda Kuper of the University of California at Los Angeles for their comments on earlier versions of the ethnographic material I gathered on the Beti. Mrs. Lucian B. Heichler translated sections of some German explorer's accounts on Cameroon for me. Professor Henri Brunchweg read and commented on the original outline for this study. Professor Peter Geschiere of the University of Leiden read the updated manuscript and made several valuable comments.

In Oxford, Elizabeth M. Chilver, who is a leading figure in Cameroonian studies, provided valuable advice, as did Shirley Ardener and Ian Fowler. Over the years I have profited from conversations with Philippe Laburthe-Tolra and from his extensive writings on the Beti. The same is true for the work of Jane I. Guyer on Beti women, bride-price, and the Beti economy. Written after my own work was completed, they are included in this book's bibliography and cited in several sections of this work.

My debt is also to my late wife, Charlotte, who read and commented on the various versions of this manuscript while writing her own book on nineteenth-century Senegambia and raising our son, Christopher, and daughter, Alison.

Portions of this material were published in *Africa, African Arts, Cahiers d'Études Africaines, Griot,* and the *Journal of African History,* all of whom have kindly extended rights to use the material here. Other articles were published in *Abbia, Tarikh,* and *Afrika und Übersee,* all of which have ceased publication.

Notes

1. A complete inventory of the collection is contained in the Online Archive of California, Hoover Institution Register of the Eugene Frederick Quinn Papers, 1882–1991. The inventory is included as part of the bibliography of this volume.

CHAPTER 1

Traditional Beti Society

For the Beti, the earliest recollections of their history begin with the flight across the Sanaga River, the main body of water traversing Beti lands. According to one version of this myth, small bands of the Beti were driven southward by better-armed northerners, some of whom were mounted on horses. Their passage was blocked by the Sanaga River, a fast-moving stream cut frequently by rapids and infested with crocodiles. Suddenly, a fabulous serpent, *Ngan Edzaa*, rose from the river and with its back formed a bridge, allowing Beti, the proto-ancestor, to lead his followers, the founders of the Ewondo, Benë, and Mvele groups, across to safety. When most of them had crossed, one of the warriors tapped the serpent's back with the butt of a spear, and the serpent plunged, leaving several Beti groups stranded in enclaves on the river's north bank. Those who crossed the stream continued southward "in search of salt." The crossing probably dates to the mid eighteenth century, although some groups were moving southward much earlier, and some continued their slow migrations toward the coast until the late nineteenth century. This working date for the principal migrations is reached by allowing thirty years for a generation and, with some overlap, projecting back the eight to ten generations Beti groups recall in reconstructing genealogies.[1] Philippe Laburth-Tolra's reconstruction of Beti genealogies suggests two migratory strains--an earlier one coming from the east or south, and a smaller, later one composed of warriors moving through the Yaoundé region in the late eighteenth century.[2]

The fragmentary, episodic nature of the gradual Beti push toward the sea was described by Abbé Théodore Tsala:

> Do not represent these migrations like the exodus of the Children of Israel across the Desert. They were more like the successive bands, following a general axis, of small family groups or villagers. One could speak of such migrations as one route leading to another [*saut-de-mouton*, or piggyback]. Family A is settled, family B founds a village more to the south, family C occupies the former territory of B. A then heads for a village south of B. A¹, then B, could do the same, while A, with pressure from C, once more moves toward the sea, which remained the final goal. This, multiplied a hundred times, resulted in the widespread movement of family groups, extended families, and clans, at

---

Notes for this chapter begin on page 27.

the same time, [representing] the stirred up, agitated movement [of peoples] explicable by its disordered result. Entire groups have reversed their steps following a military loss or to avoid contact with the European administration.... The migration was exclusively by land, even when the axis crossed a navigable waterway. The Pahouins did not use canoes and the routes customarily taken were established footpaths rather than (routes) through valleys. The settlement of people was essentially linear, installed along trails, and now, roads, long ribbons separated by empty spaces.[3]

Who exactly was a Beti? No geographical or political definition was possible, for the Beti were a mobile, migrating people who never formed any state-sized political organization. A Beti was first of all a member of an immediate family, then of an extended lineage, then of one of the four main composite lineage subgroups, and, finally, a Beti. Such definitions were elastic, subject to expansion and contraction, depending on the individual's situation. In meeting a Hausa, a headman might say, "I am a Beti"; in encountering someone from the next compound, the statement might be, "I am so-and-so's son."

Accounts of the Beti creation myth differ depending upon the person recounting the story. The degree of hostility of the northerners is subject to variation; so is the point of origin from which the Beti came. Some versions speak of quarrels that broke out or alliances formed during the exodus, which explain subsequent Beti enmities or friendships. Old men, each with their supporters, have argued at length over details of the crossing, such as whether or not the serpent was struck with a club or a spear.[4] Despite understandable variations in the telling, this myth of origins provides four ingredients important to all Beti accounts of their past: an involuntary flight and migration, a heroic ancestor, a sense of Beti uniqueness vis-à-vis neighbors who did not share this exodus, and a genealogy linking all Beti through kinship ties to all other Beti. Such myths of origin, and the inventions of tradition that follow them, are common elsewhere. They allow people to explain their origins and reinforce their identities; they also provide people with a means to explain their histories to themselves, to others, and to their children.

The Beti speak a common Bantu language, with dialectical differences. A Beti linguist has suggested the language evolved from *Ati*, a proto-language. Linguist Joseph Greenberg included the Beti in the language groups of the northwestern Bantu border, which belong to the Benue-Congo subgroup of the larger Niger-Congo subfamily of languages. In Malcolm Guthrie's linguistic classifications, Ewondo, Eton, Mvele, and Benë all belonged to the Yaoundé-Fang group of Bantu language.[5]

Ewondo was the Bantu dialect of the large Beti group near Yaoundé. Its characteristics are described in detail in an unpublished manuscript, the *Grammaire Ewondo*, written by the Abbé Tsala, a Beti linguist. It is a tonal language, with a present and three future tenses. There was no past tense, but past action was indicated by such phrases as "in the time of the ancestors," "in the time of the great dry season," or "in the time of my father's youth." Past time was also established through approximating the event to be dated with an epidemic or *Sso* initiation rite.[6]

Counting was by series of six, seven, eight, nine, ten, or one hundred. A Beti hunter could thus say, "I killed four series of nine birds." Distance was judged by the number of days a journey took or by the number of rivers crossed. Shorter distances were measured by finger, arm, or lance lengths, or stones' throws. Time was told by the passage of the sun during the day or through the use of bird and animal sounds like "when the cock crows" or "when the small bird stirs."[7]

The Geographical Setting

Geographically, the Beti occupy part of the central plateau in the modern state of Cameroon. This region falls within the northwest extremity of a vast rainforest plateau covering much of the Congo River Basin and Central Africa. It is generally flat terrain, dotted with inselbergs and etched by sharply eroded ravines. Heavy rainfall during two rainy seasons a year has contributed to the gradual washing away of fertile soil, leaving laterite in many places.

The combination of dense rainforest and simple Beti technology resulted in small-scale shifting agriculture. Small farming plots, laboriously cleared from the thick growth, were cultivated by herdsmen for several years, after which new fields were cleared, and the original soil lay fallow for several years. If his land was unproductive, or he had difficulty finding vacant land, a Beti headman simply moved elsewhere in the sparsely settled rainforest.

North of Yaoundé, the capital of the modern state of Cameroon, the land becomes savanna. Most likely, much of this region was still rainforest two hundred years ago, but advancing Beti migrants, moving southward and westward toward the coast, cleared it to establish their compounds.[8]

The central plateau is intersected by the Nyong and Sanaga rivers, and the approximately 800 square miles between them is the Beti heartland. Falls and rapids frequently interrupt both rivers, especially where the plateau drops sharply to become a coastal plain about 125 miles inland. Thus, neither river allowed transportation to or from the coast, although the Nyong is navigable for a stretch of approximately 100 miles inland between Mbalmayo and Abong-Mbang, which allowed in the 1880s access to the rich rubber regions farther east. Both streams have banks generally covered with thick growth, and both empty into coastal mangrove swamps. No developed land corridor to the coast existed until the 1880s, when the Germans cleared long-distance trails inland from the important port town of Douala and nearby Edea, strategically located for the passage inland. Until then, the main communications routes used by the Beti were a web of paths between compounds.

The lands where the Beti settled were almost equidistant from the coast and the Adamaua Mountains. This left the Beti for much of the nineteenth century on the fringes of two centers important in Cameroonian history. Coastal societies, like the Duala, a Bantu-speaking group, were gradually being transformed by expanding European trade during that time, its members developing skills as traders and becoming increasingly dependent on European goods, including canned foods. In the north, the early nineteenth-century Muslim revival movement in Sokoto triggered the spread of Islam across Adamaua and gradually toward the savanna and upper margins of the rainforest, where its arrival coincided with that of the Germans. Trade came later to the Beti, however, and Islam hardly at all.

Thus, Beti contact with neighboring groups was influenced in precolonial times, by the fact most groups were recent migrants to the area, their numbers small, and the possibilities of conflict with other ethnic groups real when, in the Beti case, territorial expansion pushed on the borders of more established societies like the Basa and Vute. Finally, long-distance trade, the catalytic force for much intertribal contact elsewhere in Africa, was of minimal significance in Beti history at this point. The Beti were rarely traders, and except for a dwindling supply of ivory, they had few products of interest to other African traders. An advantage the Beti possessed, however, until the proliferation of metal guns and farm implements from coastal traders, was demonstrable skill as metal workers. From locally constructed hard mud furnaces fired by locally cut wood, came spears, knives, hoes, metal bars used as currency, and tools for hunting and farming.[9]

Neighboring Groups: The Vute

The expansionist-minded Hausa to the north had two choices: to move directly southward through the relatively healthy and easy-to-traverse Cameroonian highlands along a well-known route to the coast, or headlong through the Nyong Valley rainforest, which was unfamiliar to them, had questionable commercial benefits, and was occupied by an inhospitable people. The Hausa chose the former route and did not enter Beti territory in any numbers until after the French were installed in 1916, and they received official encouragement to do so.

Of the four major groups that surrounded the Beti, the most formidable was the Vute, which occupied the area north of the Sanaga River. They spoke a Sudanic language and were Muslim, at least from the time of the Sokoto revival, if not before. In their lands north of the Sanaga River was a large Hausa trading community, which represented a well-known slave and ivory market for the southern Adamaua.

The Vute were well-armed and organized into three chieftainships under suzerainty of the Sultan of Tibati, to whom they delivered 500 slaves yearly as tribute. Most of the slaves came from the Beti. The Vute also demanded elephant tusks as tribute from the Mvele, a nearby Beti group, and pressured the latter to adopt "Hausa" dress and Sudanic house construction, which consisted of circular buildings with mud walls instead of the rectangular bamboo and palm-thatch dwellings characteristic of Beti construction. At the same time, the Mangisa, a small Beti group living on the banks of the Sanaga River, were driven by the Vute into isolated settlements on some of the small islands of the Sanaga River for protection.[10]

The Vute conducted raids deep in Beti territory with little opposition, except for ambushes of the raiding parties. Their expansion was gradual, as the Vute chiefdoms were split by dynastic quarrels and internecine warfare. Moreover, the Vute were accustomed to a Sudanic environment and unfamiliar with the rainforest. If Vute penetration of the Beti had not been checked by the Germans, the Vute probably would have demanded some sort of tribute rather than actually settling in or conquering Beti lands.[11]

The Basa and Bulu

The principal group to the west of the Beti was the Basa, which until German times successfully blocked Beti access to the coast. The Basa, sometimes called Bakoko by early writers, also speak a Bantu language and are organized through headmen, each ruling his compound. The Beti were pushing into the frontiers of Basa lands, and border friction was constant between the two groups, although the Basa do not appear to have tried to acquire Beti territory. This is probably because their own lands, which included sections of the rich littoral, easily sustained their populations and the Basa became increasingly interested in the advantages presented by coastal trade.

The Beti lands bordered on the territories of two other sizable groups. The Bulu, a tribe that bore many structural and linguistic resemblances to the Beti, occupied the Nyong River valley to the southwest.[12] Farther to the southeast were the Maka, another Bantu-speaking, acephalous society. There are a few passing references to feuding between the Beti and these groups, but otherwise there was little noted contact between them. No one of the three groups dominated the other, probably because none had sufficient organizational or numerical strength to expand the area of its control over the others. Thus, the two main external pressures on possible Beti expansion came from the north, where the Vute conducted slave raids freely into Beti lands, and from the west, where the Basa blocked Beti expansion toward the coast.

Beti society was a work in progress in the mid nineteenth century. The population traveled lightly, gradually approaching the coast. Compound construction was mobile, with local woods, bushes, and leaves providing the basic ingredients. Anthropologist Jane Guyer has written, "Attracted toward the sea by trade in guns, ivory, and salt, and repelled from the savanna by Fulani slave raiding, they were moving into the forest as conquerors, armed with superior metal technology and a highly productive farming system."[13]

Beti agriculture employed a two-field system. The first field was the *Esep,* a large field cut from the forest and named for the long December–February dry season. Here plantain, taro, melon seeds, and sugar cane were grown (mostly by males), as well as smaller crops such as yams and maize. The second smaller field, the *Afub owondo,* was cultivated with short hoes by women; here groundnuts, maize, cassava, yams, and vegetables were grown.[14]

A Beti Genealogy

Table 1 shows the genealogy of the Beti, as reconstructed by a French colonial official in the 1930s. The genealogy was gathered from oral interviews with Beti elders and does not differ from other genealogies collected among the principal Beti groups approximately thirty years later.[15]

Nanga is mentioned only as a figure in the legendary past, and little more is said about Beti, the founding ancestor, except that he led his people across the Sanaga River and established the Eton and Mvele, the two largest Beti groups north of Yaoundé, and three smaller groups, the Badzu, Omvang, and Ntumu. Another of

Table 1: The genealogy of the Beti

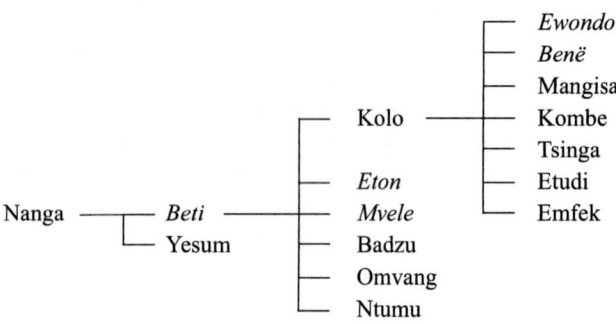

Beti's sons, Kolo, did not found a lineage himself, but fathered the Ewondo and Benë peoples. Kolo also established some smaller groups, the Mangisa, Kombe, Tsinga, Etudi, and Emfek.

The most conspicuous units of Beti society were several thousand minimal lineage core segments, each operating autonomously and each a structural replication of the others. These lineage segments were composed of a headman, his wives and children, the headman's unmarried brothers, clients attached to the household, and slaves. Each of these Beti cellular units was an autarchic enclave, ruled by its headman, while retaining political independence and residential autonomy for most of its existence. At times, units combined temporarily into larger groups for warfare, hunting, or ritual activity, but these unions dissolved once their limited purpose was achieved. In short, the headman was the key agent in Beti society. Elders played an important role as agents of consensus, brokers between disputants, and the uniter of lineages for ritual actions, such as warfare of the *Sso* rite; but they never represented a distinct, permanent social group within Beti society. A German ethnologist-explorer suggested that a map of the region with each sovereign compound given its own color would be as kaleidoscopic as a map of German principalities of the Middle Ages.[16]

The Beti *Mvog* (Lineage)

Political and kinship terms overlapped in Beti society. The basic kinship institution was the *mvog*, literally "line," an exogamous patrilineage traced to the founding ancestor.

When two Beti met, a man first identified himself as an Ewondo, or Eton, Mvele or Benë. Next he named one of his best-known ancestors to further establish his lineage. A Beti, whose family identified itself by using the name of a prominent ancestor six generations removed, explained, "If someone is a small man and gives his name, no one will know him. He must give the name of kinsmen who are well-known." Following this, a person's father and his parents, and mother and her parents, would be named. In this way, any possible tie of kinship between the people meeting was explored.[17]

Within his own minimal lineage core, a man was first of all designated as the son of his father. If the father was polygamous, the mother's name might be added by the son to distinguish him from collaterals. If Fouda, head of the minimal lineage segment, had several sons, they would be "Fouda Mengue," to which the individual's name, such as "Mbida," might be added. Consequently, the name "Fouda Mengue Mbida" would identify the father, as head of the lineage segment, and would indicate which of his wives was the mother, and then would name the son.

The Other People of a Minimal Lineage Core

The Beti used two words in speaking of their social units: *mvog* meant "lineage" or "line" and was used with lineages of any depth or span. Another word, *nda bod*, meant "dwelling" or "house and family" and usually was restricted to the people of a minimal lineage core segment, which included the headman, his wives, their unmarried children, and possibly his unmarried brothers until they acquired wives and founded their own *nda bod*. Clients, called *mintobo*, and domestic slaves, called *olo*, completed these residential units. *Mintobo* (which comes from the word *tobo,* meaning to stay, live) were male clients of the headman who, unable to establish their own households, offered services as hunters, field workers, and warriors in return for food and lodging. Sometimes *mintobo* were individuals who needed help raising bridewealth and stayed as clients until this was possible or who had left their own *nda bod*.[18]

Mintobo lived in the headman's dwelling, in their own huts, or were assigned by the headman to various wives, but all children engendered by the *mintobo* and the headman's wives belonged to the headman. These clients were free to marry, provided they could raise bridewealth, and could leave when they wanted to or when the headman died. *Mintobo* were sometimes thought of as parasites, and visiting strangers living temporarily in the compound did not want to be considered *mintobo*.

Olo were slaves, either taken in warfare or inherited by the household. There were no offices among the slaves. They usually lived apart from the compound in huts of their own, although male slaves might stay in the headman's dwelling, and some might be assigned to the hut of one of the headman's wives. Usually the headman left the regulation of his slaves to his women. If a male slave had a child by a headman's wife, the child belonged to the headman. A slave could be given freedom and a wife by the headman and could found a family; sons of the male slaves gained freedom by participation in the *Sso* initiation rite. Some slaves kept their names, others were given names by their owners. Many of the slaves had an ear cut off as a symbol of their status.[19]

The Headman's Powers

A *nda bod* was controlled by a headman, whom the Beti called *mie dzala*, literally "molder of the compound" (*mie* = molder, shaper; *dzal* = compound). A *dzal* was the equivalent of the *nda bod*, and the words could be used interchangeably.

A headman's authority was limited to his own *nda bod*, and here his control was virtually complete. The land was his, and a portion of anything grown or killed by hunters in his territory went to the headman. When trade with the coast developed, he received payment of the goods moving in both directions across his land. His symbols of office were a flywhisk, which other men also carried, and a headpiece of red parrot feathers, which hunters also wore. He possessed an ebony pipe, a twin-bladed hand-axe used in warfare, a bouquet of palm leaves, a bundle of spears, and a basket of herbs symbolizing the protection of the ancestors (*nted nnam* = basket of the country). At his installation, neighboring headmen sent lances as a way of recognizing the headman's new office. Taken together these symbols suggested the headman's role in Beti society as an elder, warrior, and dispenser of justice, who ruled his compound as the ancestors wished.

In principle, a *mie dzala* was succeeded by his oldest son by the first wife, but he could be followed by another son if the father thought the first son incompetent. If there was no eligible son, succession passed to the father's next senior brother by the same mother, or to another brother.[20] Sometimes the father announced his successor before his death, in which case the Beti might say, "The leopard is reproduced in his offspring." In other cases, a headman confided the choice to a confidant. If there was no successor, or if the heir was a minor, a council of the headman's brothers could appoint one of their number guardian of his descendants and property.[21]

Like succession, inheritance of goods among the Beti passed agnatically. If the headman had no sons, his goods went to his brothers, who otherwise were not included in the inheritance and would be expected to move away and found their own compounds.[22]

A Beti commentator has written of the *mie dzala*'s power: "A *dzal* compound had but one *mie dzala*. The other members, married or not, were *bongo be dzal*, children of the village, in a word, minors. That is why any self-respecting person would want to build his own place where he would be *mie dzala*." All women in the *nda bod* were either his wives or daughters, and he could assign or deny other men in the *nda bod* access to their huts.[23]

The *nda bod* had no fixed size. A prosperous headman might have thirty or more wives and as many as 100 children and retainers, but many compounds were limited to a few persons. Compounds were larger where there was fairly continuous warfare or growing trade with the coast, as in the regions near the Vute and Basa frontiers. German travelers noted that the Mvele, the Beti cluster of linked lineages nearest the Vute, were frequently organized into large compounds for protection and warfare. Günter Tessman calculated the upper limit of wives per headman in the south at about thirty, but near the savanna-forest the number could be as high as 100.[24] Likewise, the three other largest Beti groups, the Eton, Ewondo, and Benë, who lived on the western rim of the Beti frontier with the Basa, were organized into large compounds. There were several reasons for the large size of these compounds. First, the inhabitants were among the first migrants to the area and could occupy their land with little pressure from later Beti migrants. Second, they needed the protection afforded by large groups. Third, once the coastal trade reached the Beti, who received goods to allow traders passage through their lands,

Beti headmen could acquire additional wives and attract additional clients, thus increasing the size of their compounds. Many other Beti groups, however, especially those in the relatively untroubled and isolated eastern section of the Beti lands (which were relatively unaffected by trade or large-scale feuding), tended to retain smaller settlement and household units.

The intelligence and acumen of an individual headman could be important in determining the size of a Beti *nda bod*. A *mie dzala* might skillfully build his household through marriage alliances, his success as a warrior, or participation in the gradually growing inland trade. His skills as an orator helped win the headman a following, as did the degree to which he extended hospitality or provided gifts. Likewise, his following could diminish if the compound was decimated by disease, if the wives were infertile, or if the headman was unskilled as a warrior or inept in running his *nda bod*. If a *nda bod* shrank to the point that it could no longer function effectively, its members might attach themselves as clients to a more powerful headman who was probably a kinsman as well.

Description of a Compound

The physical layout of its compounds reflected the organization of Beti society. The central building served as the headman's house, the *abaa*, a large, oblong structure possibly sixty feet long, with a pointed roof built of wood or bamboo poles covered with woven or plaited raffia or palm branches. The *abaa* was a gathering place for the *nda bod*. The men's meals were eaten in it, or in the nearby compound, and in the evening it was the place where tales, fables, and riddles were told, genealogies recited to children, or gossip exchanged. Sometimes it had as many as thirty bamboo beds, and the dwelling of one famous Beti headman was known euphemistically as "the *abaa* with a hundred roof beams." Skulls of animals, representing successful past hunts, decorated the interior of the *abaa*, lances were stacked in corners, and musical instruments, including the *mvet*, a stringed instrument, hung from the walls. Near the *abaa* the Beti kept a large drum, made from a hollowed log, that was used to communicate news of wars, visitors, births, and deaths to other compounds. The drum language was onomatopoetic; a Beti informant estimated that a network of drums could transmit news quickly over several miles. Not far from the clearing grew banana trees, vegetables, and tobacco. Domestic animals were kept in an enclosure made of tightly packed tree trunks, which was elevated to keep out marauding animals. The compound was surrounded by cactus or other densely foliaged plants to keep goats from wandering away.[25]

Extending in a straight or parallel row from the headman's house were the houses of his wives. These huts were usually between twenty to forty feet long and ten to fourteen feet wide. The most distant house from the *abaa* was occupied by the first wife the headman had taken, called the *ekomba*. As senior wife, it was her responsibility to keep order and regulate disputes among the other wives. Sometimes the *ekomba* was a wife given to headman by the headman's father from among his own wives, which gave the father influence in his son's compound.

The next most distant hut belonged to the second wife in seniority, the *ebedan ekomba* or vice *ekomba*. Apart from these two, three other wives had titles in a Beti compound. The most prominent was the *mkpeg*, or favorite wife, the headman's "pipe-carrier." She was his confidant, prepared the headman's food, and lived in a hut built in the middle or to one side of the other huts. The headman spent most of his nights with her; other nights he would alternate between only a few of his wives (this was referred to as *lan melu*, "counting the nights"). The headman's valuable possessions remained with the *mkpeg*, and she mixed a soothing preparation of palm oil and red powder and rubbed it on his body when he was tired. However, the position of *mkpeg* was a fluctuating one, and the incumbent was subject to jealousy and witchcraft (or accusations of witchcraft) from the other wives.

Two junior wives lived near the headman's dwelling and performed chores, such as serving food and water at his gatherings. They were the *otongo* (from *ton*, to nourish) and the *nyedmendim* (*yed mendim*, to ask for water). The remaining wives were known collectively as *minlui* (from *lui*, to languish).

The number of wives a headman claimed represented an index of his wealth. They provided sons, who were potential warriors and workers, and daughters, a prime source of bridewealth and ties with other headmen. Some wives attracted *mintobo*, who joined the compound as laborers.

Role Differentiation

Clear distinctions could be observed between male and female roles among the Beti. Male work consisted of warfare, hunting, and tree-felling. Climbing high trees and bringing them to the ground, usually done by a headman's son, was risky, but it brought admiration for the climber's prowess. The "Song of the Woodcutter" (see Appendix A, *Traditional Beti Literature*, at the end of this volume) describes the woodcutter's bravery: "My war is against that giant ... for one of us the war will be fatal," but "I have inherited ... the legendary strength of my Father."[26]

Gender roles were clearly differentiated in Beti society. The male setting was the forest, the site of warfare and the hunt, the place where animals were sought for their meat or land claimed to settle a compound or clear a field. "Women's milieu was, by contrast, the earth itself," Guyer has written, "the open clearings or the savanna.... A woman worked the fields, bending over the earth with her short-handled hoe.... She cooked in earthenware pots, bending over the fire, fished by building earth dams across streams, bending into the water to trap the fish, and she 'cooked' babies in her womb." The binary opposites are thus forest and savanna, the lengthy digging stick used by men and the short-handled hoe used by women, standing upright (males) and bending (females). For Guyer, these contrasts "gave the opposition of male and female both enormous power and concrete content. The sexuality and fertility of marriage brought sets of oppositions together, conceptually, but also organizationally."[27]

Many years later, a female Australian teacher, who spent considerable time with women in a Beti village, wrote:

When I said I'd rather have a long-handled hoe, Angeline was scandalized, "Women don't use them," she said with complete finality. So we stooped, or rather Angeline did, in a graceful arc, with legs quite straight and her body bending over from the hips.... Cameroonian women stoop for everything—in the fields for planting and weeding, by the river for washing the clothes, in the house for stirring the pots on the cooking fire, or washing the dishes on the floor. It is ... a graceful movement, the body sweeping in a fluid line like a round triangle, with the up-ended bottom as the apex and the long curve of the torso to the floor. But it helps to lead ... to all those backaches in old age.[28]

Beti Religion

Another feature common to all Beti groups was a religion and set of laws governing human conduct. The Beti believed in a high god, Zamba (*za*, he who; *mba*, plants or builds), who created the universe, but the most important element in Beti religion was not the high god but respect for the ancestors and their teachings. The ancestors were venerated, and headmen and elders communicated with them before making decisions of any importance. Old men were respected because they were closest to the ancestors, in communication with them, and were the most able to interpret an ancestor's will, through which the society was governed. One indication of the respect paid to old men is that the best meats, such as viper, were reserved for them. Contact with the ancestors was achieved through *bewu*, spirits of the lineage dead, who appeared in dreams, suggesting remedies for illness, offering opinions on current problems, forewarning of deaths and catastrophes, or advising on the division of goods following a death. All such spirits, the Beti believed, emitted vibrations that could be interpreted by individuals who came in contact with them.[29]

Likewise, the Beti religion included the belief in evil spirits, sent by sorcerers, that could be defeated by powerful preventative magic, the correct observation of food interdictions, and the use of amulets and herb preparations. The Beti employed several forms of divination, including rolling small, marked stones and reading the patterns in which they fell, or interpreting the manner in which a spider, on leaving its hole, disarranged straw sticks that had been placed in front of it. Almost anyone who wanted to could be a diviner; no caste groups or corporate offices were formed by such persons, who usually added divining to their ordinary work for the payments and prestige it gave them.

Often Beti wisdom was expressed in religion through the character of a wise spider, Abodo. In one parable, the spider responds to the query of Otende-Nka, an iguana that suffered deep adversity. The omnipotent, harsh nature of the high god Zamba is disclosed when the spider probes for a fuller explanation of the problem of good and evil. Zamba replies that, when the spider dies, it will have no burial; its remains will be left hanging in its own web until they crumble into dust. The spider story discloses the distant, detached characteristics of Zamba, seen by the Beti as the creator of good and evil:

> Zamba, the living God, is the cause of all things, the good as well as the evil. Nothing happens without him. God gives us life and then takes it back. Health comes from him, but so does sickness. Inborn infirmities also originate from him. Zamba allows us to live

from the fruits of the forest, and when it pleases him, Zamba burns it to ashes. Zamba allows us to live from the animals in the fields, and when it pleases him ... diseases destroy them. And how can we not understand that men also are sometimes very good and sometimes very bad![30]

Regulatory Groups

Beti could belong to two regulatory groups. The first, the *Melan,* was an association of approximately twenty members, including women and slaves drawn from several neighboring compounds. Candidates paid the organizer a small fee, such as a chicken, to join. Dances and sacrifices were held in front of a collection of ancestor skulls, especially during times of war, epidemics, or witchcraft accusations. The group had no political, judicial, hunting, or work responsibilities. *Melan* sacrifices did not supplant those of the headman but frequently supplemented such sacrifices.[31]

The second group, the *Ngi* (gorilla), was a male regulatory group that came to the Beti from the neighboring Ngumba. The *Ngi* usually consisted of about ten men from the same lineage. The functions of the group's members overlapped with those from Beti lineage councils. One of the objectives of the *Ngi* was to combat sorcery; in case of famine or poor harvest, members burned leaves and scattered the remnants over fields; for infertility, they held a container of leaves over the woman. The leader of the *Ngi* group was called *Nya Moro,* or "dean," as a Beti informant later translated it, and members addressed one another as *Tsida,* "intimate brother" or "counselor," and sometimes "descendants of the same father." Neither of these associations was widespread among the Beti.

The Beti made no clear distinction between religion and law. One Beti has said, "The natural and the supernatural, or perhaps 'preternatural,' was so intermixed that it was seen everywhere together."[32]

The Beti often described the main laws, which governed their *nda bod* as a set of nine commandments, as following no special order; indeed, the content of the laws varied somewhat with the reporter. The Beti frequently used the number nine because they believed it to have a power above other numbers. The Beti's nine commandments were as follows:

1. Do not kill a kinsman, friend, age mate, or stranger
2. Do not lie
3. Do not take the goods of others by force
4. Do not disclose the secrets of a council meeting
5. Do not steal
6. Do not touch a sacred object
7. Do not destroy someone else's property
8. Do not commit incest or have sexual relations with a *Sso* candidate
9. Do not violate the food interdictions[33]

Beyond this, Beti laws dealt primarily with four areas, the *Sso* rite, warfare, martial and kinship disagreements, and land and property disputes. There were interdictions against non-initiates entering the *Sso* compound or interfering with a man on a journey to organize a *Sso* rite or stealing from a compound protected by the *Sso* sign. In warfare, it was forbidden to kill a man from a position of ambush without announcing, "I, son of so-and-so, am firing" or "throw this spear." Such a public announcement displayed the bravery expected of a Beti warrior.

In personal relations adultery was forbidden, and should a man be convicted of it, he could be required to pay the husband of the woman the entire sum of her bridewealth or a fine. A father, whose obligation was to help a son raise the initial bridewealth for a marriage, could warn the son, "If you go off with a woman your bridewealth goes with you."[34]

The elders could order stolen objects returned or their replacement by objects of comparable value. They could direct someone to hold a rite, like the *Sso* ritual, and levy fines, such as payment of a certain number of goats. These penalties were usually assessed for offending an elder. A Beti commented, "It was not advantageous to seek judgment against an elder, for you were always obliged to pay him something, as damage if he were judged in the right, or for him to save face if he was wrong."[35]

Exclusion from the *mvog* was the most severe possible penalty. It was an extreme sanction, which could be levied against any man who refused to follow a decision made by the council of elders. The man was visited by the elders, who told him, "We are the closest to the ancestors and their representatives in the lineage they founded. Because you have ignored us, in our turn we ignore you. You are no longer in the *mvog*. We even leave behind you the dust from your house that has rested on our skin." Then the elders stood up, quickly flapped the dust from the rolled-up animal skins each had carried with him, and disappeared.

From that moment the recalcitrant Beti was isolated from his lineage. He could not call on *mvog* residents for aid. He was vulnerable to raids from other groups and could be sold into slavery, unless he approached the elders and asked for restitution.[36]

Two frequent subjects of disputes among the Beti were questions involving land and animals. Even so, quarrels over land never became as grave a problem for the Beti as they were for larger groups with limited land; the territory into which the Beti migrated was sparsely occupied, except for pygmy bands in the southwestern regions and the lands to the south held by the neighboring Bulu, Maka, and Ngumba groups. All Beti land was controlled for the collectivity by the headman, who established his homestead by cultivating it or marking off a border of fruit trees or plants. The land, however, was not considered a headman's personal possession. Land disputes usually concerned boundaries, water rights, or trespassing and were settled among headmen or by their asking for arbitration from a third headman or an elder whom both sides respected for his judgment.[37]

Disputes over animals were numerous because household animals were allowed to run freely, and there were frequent Beti palavers over possession of the animals, chiefly goats, and demands for recompense for damage caused by goats to gardens.[38]

Beti hunting groups often disagreed over how to divide their take; additionally, numerous disputes arose about damage to cultivated fields caused by the hunting groups when they crossed the fields. Hunters did not form a caste group. They could be drawn from one or several compounds and had no special officers. They hunted with guns, spears, nets, traps, pits, and by bush burning.

In principle, the hunt's organizer received the front legs of the animals. The stomach and sides went to the beaters and other hunters. Hunters also gave a portion of their take to the headman on whose land the animal was killed and to other headmen whose lands were crossed. Should the hunt be a daylong affair, the man who killed an animal could cut off its tail and take it with him, leaving the animal, which no other hunter could rightfully claim.[39]

Beti Social Norms: *Akab, Ayong,* and *Akuma*

In addition to accepting a common set of laws through which the society was governed, the Beti also distinguished themselves from other groups by observing a set of values in their relations, which produced a distinct Beti lifestyle. Beti men should practice *akab*, which meant showing generosity and hospitality, liberally giving gifts and graciously receiving visitors; *ayong*, or bravery, which the Beti described as "never walking with one lance, but with five"; and *akuma*, riches translated into wives, children, animals, and food. The possession of land was not a sign of wealth in precolonial times because land was abundant. If a man displayed these virtues, he was fulfilling what was expected of him as a Beti. The word "Beti" has been translated as "noble."[40] Work as traders or storekeepers was incompatible with such a Beti self-image of nobility, and most headmen limited their economic activity to taking compensation from traders who crossed their lands. Headmen profited from the sale of ivory or slaves, but usually the exchanges were carried out by their sons or brothers.[41]

The hierarchy of virtues also helped create a pronounced sense of individualism among the Beti men, for they were virtues that individuals would display. Courtesy was extended by one man toward another; bravery was always described as a personal act, and riches were accumulated by a headman's own efforts and were not the property of his office or lineage segment.

Thus, a strong sense of a headman's independence was an important aspect of Beti culture; it also meant that a wider sense of community beyond the headman and his compound was difficult to develop. The most inclusive Beti concept was of an *ayong*, which meant "all the Beti," but it never became a geographic or political reality.[42]

Notes

1. T. Tsala, "Géographie et Populations," 1 June 1968, pp. 7–9. *Ngan Edzaa* = Conqueror of magic spirits.
2. P. Laburth-Tolra, *Les seigneurs de la forêt (Minlaaba I)* (Paris: Publications de la Sorbonne, 1981), p. 125.
3. "Il ne faut pas se représenter ces migrations comme l'exode des Enfants d'Israël à travers le desert. Elles seront plutôt par bands successifs, suivant un axe general, par petits groupes familiaux ou/et villagois. On a pu parler à leur propos de migrations en saut-en-mouton: une famille A s'installe; une famille B fonde un village plus au sud; une famille C occupe l'ancien territoire de B; A essaime alors un village au sud de B. A une, puis B pourra en faire autant, alors que A, sous le pression de C, se sera de nouveau déplacé *mfa'ya man*, vers la mer, qui reste le but final. Ceci, multiple des centaines de fois, entraîne une dissémination extrême des groupes familiaux, familiaux-étendus et claniques, en même temps que des remous, des tourbillons qui expliquent l'enchêvêtrement actuel. Des groupes entiers sont revenus sur leurs pas, à la suite d'un échec militaire ou pour éviter le contact avec l'administration européene.... Les derniers groupes Beti à franchir la Sanaga, bloqués par ceux qui les avaient precedes, ont dévié perpendiculairement ou obliquement à l'axe general de la migration.

    L'ensemble de la migration s'est fait exclusivement par voie terrestre, même quand son axe suivait le cours d'un fleuve navigable. Les Pahouins ne sont pas des piroguiers et les pistes coutumières empruntées était plutôt les lignes de crête que les vallées. Le peuplement est essentiellment linéaire, étalé le long des pistes et, maintenant, les routes, en longs rubans séparés par des zones vides" (Tsala, "Geographie et Populations").
4. The oral interviews conducted by the author were as follows: François Atangana, Yaoundé, 2 May 1967; Pierre Mebe, Yaoundé, 17 May 1967; Hubert Onana, Ayéné, 5 August 1967 and 18 March 1968.
5. Tsala, "Géographie et Populations," p. 6; T. Tsala, "Grammaire Ewondo," Mvolye, 1970. Joseph H. Greenberg, "The Languages of Africa," Part II, *International Journal of American Linguistics*, vol. 29, no. 1 (January 1963); Malcolm Guthrie, *The Bantu Languages of Western Equatorial African* (London, 1953). Guthrie includes Mangisa with the neighboring Sanaga group of Bantu languages.
6. Tsala, "Grammaire Ewondo." Ewondo lacks technical terms, but it is rich in words for animals, plant life, and minerals, and terms describing people's occupations in the rainforest. It is equally well-endowed with kinship terms. There are many verb phrases describing the minutiae of Beti daily life. For example, there are at least twenty expressions that might be translated as the English verb "sit," such as "to sit," "to sit indifferently," "to sit like a bird on its eggs," "to sit, ready to spring," or "to sit in a small and isolated manner."
7. Tsala, "Grammaire Ewondo."
8. One of the most useful descriptions of the geography of Beti lands is presented in André Franqueville's "Le Paysage urbain de Yaoundé," *Les Cahiers d'Outre Mer* 82 (1968): pp. 113–54. Other valuable sources are Pierre Billard, *Le Cameroun Physique* (Lyon, 1962); J. A. Ngwa, *An Outline Geography of the Federal Republic of Cameroon* (London, 1967); and Pierre Vaast, Henri Bala, and Roger Gineste, *La République Fédérale du Cameroun, Géographie à l'usage des Écoles Primaires, des Collèges et des Candidats aux concours Administratifs* (Bourges, 1962). Another important geographical study is J. Champaud, *Atlas Regional sud-ouest 2* (Yaoundé: Institut de Recherches Scientifiques du Cameroun, Yaoundé 1965).
9. Joseph-Marie Essomba, "La fer dans le Development des Societes traditionelles du Sud-Cameroun," *West African Journal of Archeology*, no. 16 (1986): pp. 1–24.
10. G. Zenker, "Yaoundé," *Mittheilungen von Forschungsreisenden und Gelehrten aus den Deutschen Schutzgebieten*, vol. VIII (Berlin, 1895), p. 38.
11. A commentary on the Vute, which includes a review of earlier literature, is Eldridge Mohamadou, "For a History of Central Cameroun: Historical Tradition of the Vute or 'Babute,'" *Abbia* 16 (1967): pp. 59–129. I. Dugast, *Inventaire ethnique du Sud-Cameroun, Memoires de l'Institut Français d'Afrique Noire, Centre du Cameroun*. Populations series, no. 1 (Yaoundé: IFAN, 1949); pp. 147–50 include a discussion of the internal rivalries in Vute society. Several German

explorers of the Yaoundé region, such as C. von Morgen and H. Dominik, deal with the Vute in their memoirs. C. von Morgen, *Durch Kamerun von Süd nach Nord* (1893), pp. 78–80, 85. H. Dominik, *Kamerun*, (1901) 134ff.

12. A description of Bulu society can be found in Pierre Alexandre and Jacques Binet's *Le Groupe Dit Pahouin (Fang-Boulou-Beti)* (Paris, 1958). I. Dugast discusses the Maka in *Inventaire ethnique*, pp. 95–100.
13. J. Guyer, *Family and Farm in Southern Cameroon*, no. 15 (Boston: Boston University African Research Studies, 1984), p. 11.
14. J. Guyer, "Female Farming and the Evolution of Food Production Patterns amongst the Beti of South-Central Cameroon," *Africa*, vol. 50, no. 4 (1980): p. 344.
15. The genealogy of the Beti prepared by Cournaire, who served as an administrator in Yaoundé in the 1930s, is contained in I. Dugast, *Inventaire ethnique*, pp. 57ff. A resume of such genealogical literature as is available on the Ewondo is contained in Henry Ngoa, "Situation Historico-genalogique des Ewondo, Étude Critique," *Abbia* 22 (1968): pp. 65–88. See also Pierre Mebe, interview with author, Yaoundé, 22 February 1968, and interview with Hubert Ondana Mbida, Ayéné, 5 August 1967 and 18 March 1968.
16. G. Tessman, *Die Pangwe, Völkerkundliche Monographie eines westafrikanischen negerstammes*, vol. I (Berlin, 1913), p. 48.
17. T. Tsala, interview with author, Mvolye, 14 May 1968. Henri Atangana Amengue, interview with author, Mpou, 26 May 1968. Beti greetings were not elaborate. A man might hail another with the cry "A vuma al," which translates as "Does a kinsman pass?" The other man would answer with a deep, throaty sound of agreement, after which they shook hands in silence. Friends might rub foreheads, and then genealogical inquiries were begun. Tsala, "Grammaire Ewondo," p. 263.
18. Tsala, "Géographie et Populations," p. 41. Martin Mballa Foe, interview with author, Mbalmayo, 14 March 1968. Martin Heepe, "Jaunde-Texte von Karl Atangana und Paul Messi, nebst Experimentalphonetischen untersuchungen über die Sprache," *Abhandlungen des Hamburgischen Kolonialinstituts*, XXIV (Hamburg, 1919), pp. 96–97.
19. T. Tsala, interview with author, 17 February, 19 March, and 26 March 1968, Mvolye; Pierre Mebe, interview with author, Yaoundé, 30 June 1967.
20. Heepe, *Jaunde-Texte*, p. 60. Interview by author with Marie-Jean Ze and Henri Atangana Amengue, Mfou, 4 April 1968. Laurent Ondoua Awoumou, Ebogo, 14 March 1968, and Hubert Ondana Mbida, Ayéné, 6 August 1968.
21. Tsala, "Géographie et Populations," p. 41.
22. Heepe, *Jaunde-Texte*, pp. 60–61. Interviews by author with Etinne Ahanda Ayissi, Ngomendzap, 18 March 1968; Laurent Ondoua Awoumou, Ebogo, 14 March 1968; Jean-Marie Ze and Henri Atangana Amengue, Mfou, 4 April 1968. If the eldest son by the first wife was incapacitated and the headman's post went to another person, the first son still was given his father's dwelling. If the eldest son was an old man by the time his father died, the headmanship could pass to a younger brother, but the older brother would share in any honors connected with the post, such as receiving a larger portion of meat than other men.
23. T. Tsala, "Le gouvernement des Beti," 7 June 1968, pp. 1–2, and "L'Organization judiciare," 2 March 1968, p. 2. Details of the structure of Beti society were corroborated in oral interviews with T. Tsala, as cited, and Hubert Ondana Mbida (Ewondo), Ayéné, 3 March 1968; Philibert Ateba (Eton), Obala, 19 April 1968; Gotefried Bisso Medza (Mbidambane), Dzeng, 18 March 1968; and François Atangana (Ewondo), Yaoundé, 2 May 1968.
24. Quoted in Jane I. Guyer, *Family and Farm in Southern Cameroon*, no. 15 (Boston: Boston University African Research Studies, 1984), p. 19.
25. Zenker, "Yaoundé," pp. 38–40, for description with illustrations of a Beti compound in the 1890s. For photographs and sketches of a Beti compound, and other rainforest dwellings, of the colonial period, see T. Tsala, interview with author, Mvolye, 14 June 1968, and Tsala, "Géographie et Populations," pp. 1ff.
26. This song, and the others presented in Appendix A, were collected by Pierre Betene, a researcher and seminary student, during the summer of 1967.
27. Guyer, *Family and Farm in Southern Cameroon*, p. 11.
28. S. Deane, *Talking Drums from a Village in Cameroon* (London: John Murray, 1985), p. 32.

29. T. Tsala, interview with author, Mvolye, 1 June 1968. An important early article dealing with Beti religion and ethnology is Hermann Nekes's "Jaunde und seine Bewohner (Südkamerun)," *Kolonialen Rundschau* 8 (1912): pp. 468–84. A comprehensive work on traditional Beti religion is Philippe Laburthe-Tolra, *Minláaba, Histoire et Societe Traditionelle chez les Beti du Sud Cameroun*, tomes I–III (Paris: Publications de la Sorbonne, 1977, 1985, 1991).
30. B. Fouda, "Philosophical Dialogue and the Problem of Evil amongst the Beti (Southern Cameroun)," *Journal of African Religion and Philosophy*, vol. 1, no. 2 (1990): pp. 43–52. His basic material on Zamba, the high god, was collected in 1958 at Otélé by the Abbé Sylvain Atangana of the Beti *mvog* Atangana-Mballa of Ngomedzap.
31. T. Tsala, interview with author, Mvolye, 6 June 1968. The *Ngi* rite had neither the transcendent national character ascribed to it by Alexandre in *Le Groupe Dit Pahouin*, p. 63, nor was it in any sense "le principal, sinon le seul élément de cohésion tribale sur le plan politique." (It had a limited membership, was most prevalent in the region near the Beti-Ngumba frontier, and while it was an anti-sorcery group, it did nothing to promote tribal cohesion.)
32. T. Tsala, letter to author, 1 November 1969.
33. T. Tsala, "L'Organization Judiciare," 2 March 1968, p. 1.
34. T. Tsala, "Nian Mesin," letter to author, 8 April 1969.
35. Pierre Mebe, interview with author, 8 November 1967.
36. Tsala, "L'Organization Judiciare," pp. 4–5.
37. Pierre Mebe and Joseph Essona, interviews with author, Yaoundé, 1 November and 30 November 1967.
38. T. Tsala, "les Moeurs et Coutumes des Ewondo,"*Etudes Camerounaises*, no. 56 (1958) p. 40. Pierre Mebe, interview with author, Yaoundé, 21 December 1967.
39. T. Tsala, letters to author, 15 February 1968 and 5 May 1969. Heepe, *Jaunde-Texte*, pp. 62, 68–69. T. Tsala, interview with author, Mvolye, 6 June 1968.
40. T. Tsala, "Principales Valeurs Sociales des Beti,"(MS Mvolye, June 1968) pp. 1–5; T. Tsala, letter to author, Mvolye, 21 September 1969.
41. This suggests a similarity in outlook to the French nobility of the Ancien Régime, who could not envision the prospect of commercial careers and allowed others to profit from the growth of French overseas trade, in contrast to the British nobility of the same period, many of whom participated actively in commerce or married into commercial families.
42. This political individualism is demonstrated in the career of André-Marie Mbida, whose movement in and out of national politics is described in Victor T. LeVine, *The Cameroons from Mandate to Independence* (Los Angeles, 1964), pp. 162–66, *passim*. The idea of *Ayong* was discussed by Pierre Mebe in an interview with the author, Yaoundé, 6 July 1967.

CHAPTER 2

Social Organization and the *Sso* Rite

Although for most of its existence traditional Beti society functioned as several thousand autonomous *nda bod* operating independently of one another, there were several ways in which these units combined for ritual action, such as through marriage alliances, warfare, and the *Sso* initiation rite. No central hierarchy existed among the Beti and marriage alliances provided the means for headmen to gain wealth through bride-price, solidify their positions, "trade up" with more powerful headmen, and extend influence with other headmen. Other forms of interaction helped groups reinforce their identity and solve practical needs. Feuds with other lineages or wider warfare with neighboring peoples brought several lineages together for the conflict's duration. Leadership was an ad hoc affair, agreed to among the participating headmen. The *Bilabi*, a Beti form of potlatch, and periodic wrestling matches provided rallying points for different Beti groups to assemble, sing, dance, and eat at someone's expense, and have fun, but with no lasting implications. All of these forms of interaction were subsidiary to the great *Sso* rite which, as discussed below, brought young men and their male sponsors together from several lineages for an ordeal whose symbolism was central to Beti society.

Lineage Councils

One of the most important forms of interaction was through meetings of an informally constituted lineage council, whose composition varied depending upon the issue being discussed. The council usually included a headman, his brothers, elder sons, male kinsmen living nearby, and neighbors whose opinions were valued. If the matter being discussed affected them, wives, clients, and slaves also participated.

There were also councils that united headmen from several *nda bod*. These meetings could range from several headmen discussing fishing rights on a river, to a meeting of most members of an extended lineage to plan warfare against a common enemy or to organize ritual action to ward off crop failure or disease. Such meetings were ad hoc, and the units represented were those particularly affected

---

Notes for this chapter begin on page 41.

by the question under discussion; permanent institutions or offices were never created beyond the minimal lineage segment.

These larger lineage groupings were presided over by one of the headmen with limited powers. This headman, called *mie nnama* (*mie* = to shape; *nnama* = the country), was also *mie dzala* or headman of his own minimal lineage segment.[1] The headman was usually the senior living lineage member who linked the group with its founding ancestors; there were exceptions to this, however. The office of *mie nnama* could pass from a headman to his brother instead of his son if the brother was considered a more able leader.[2] This type of council, which was called an *esie* (*sie* = to revive, restore), was primarily designed to maintain harmony between related lineages and the ancestral will and to restore contact with the ancestors where this harmony had been broken.

Council members might include the *mie dzala* of several *nda bod*, all of whom had completed the *Sso* rite, men of some riches or whose opinions or skills as orators were valued. The elders, who formed no permanent office, were sometimes called collectively *mengi-mengi* (gorilla-gorilla), a title of respect. They were "the old men of the country, nearer the tomb than the cradle, representing the union between the living forces in the country and the departed ancestors."[3]

Women, children, or slaves attended portions of the meetings and could speak if the question being discussed affected them directly. However, a woman would not assist at a council session dividing the inheritance of a headman if she was a potential inheritor. Sometimes persons with special skills in debating or conciliation were asked to come from a distant *mvog*. Such a person, noted for his ability to regulate quarrels among brothers or spouses, might be named a *ntsig medzo* (*tsig* = to cut; *medzo* = a palaver), a designation indicating that he was respected as an advisor.[4]

Frequency and Duration of Councils

Council sessions were not held regularly, and membership was not permanent. There were no fixed sites for assemblies; most often they took place at the compound of the headman desiring the meeting. Such gatherings were scheduled several days in advance if many people were involved or if some participants would have to travel considerable distances. When a large lineage council convened, it might last for several days. The person requesting the council meeting usually spoke first. "The man whose legs are wettest speaks last," the Beti observe, meaning that those who walked the longest distance would be the last to speak. When all who were concerned had spoken, the elders retired to reach a decision.[5] Sometimes one of the elders disclosed it, but the summing up might be delegated to a person with ability as a speaker, such as the *zum loa*, whose orations closed the *Sso* rite. Here his main role was to solicit enthusiasm for the council's decision. Such oratory was important in Beti council deliberations, for unless decisions were presented in such a way as to gain general acceptance among all parties, there was a danger of splitting the group into contending factions. These councils had some authority to levy sanctions such as demanding fines, prescribing sacrifices, or as a last resort expelling a member from an *mvog*, but otherwise they had little power to enforce decisions. There was no police force, and councils depended on popular acceptance to carry out their will. Thus, the orator was important in mobilizing support and helped strengthen the fragile ties between Beti groups.

Most lineage assemblies closed with a sacrifice, usually a goat or a lamb, prescribed by the elders, after which participants took an oath to abide by the decision that had been reached. The council always decreed that a sign would follow, which would confirm their decision as the right one. Such a sign might be that, on the next hunt following the council meeting, hunters would return with two birds.[6]

Marriage Alliances

Another form of interaction among Beti *mvog* was through marriage alliances. Marriage represented one of the most important means by which an *mvog* increased its influence, enlarged its size, and stabilized its relations with other groups. Beti marriage was exogamous, and marriages were prohibited within the fifth degree of relationship. Polygamy was frequent. Plural marriages provided insurance for the successful man against high infant mortality, low life expectancy, and frequent sterility. They increased the headman's possibilities of having sons who would work and fight for him and daughters who were important as future sources of marriage payments. It also allowed a headman to strengthen ties with neighboring headmen.[7] There were no warfare, work, or other obligations entailed between the two lineages linked by marriage beyond a possible temporary work obligation incurred as part of the bridewealth payment. A father was, however, likely to send male and female workers to help his daughter if she needed them, and he, or one of his brothers or sons, was expected to take a familial interest in her during her lifetime, reimbursing the bride-price if the woman left her husband.[8]

A woman retained ties with her mother and usually returned to the mother's hut for the birth of her children, after which the husband ceremonially "bought" his wife back by giving a chicken or a goat for the medical/magical herbs used by the mother in assisting at childbirth. The daughter's visits to her mother were frequent; so were the husband's gift to the latter. A Beti proverb states, "The basket of the wife's mother is never filled."

The Beti practiced several forms of marriage, including the widespread exchange of daughters and sisters. Sometimes the bride was accompanied by a sister, real or classificatory, or servant, who was incorporated into the headman's compound. If a bride was assisted by servants or slaves from her patrilineage in this manner, they were for her use and could not be assigned by her husband to another woman. Sometimes a man offered one of his daughters to a friend without bridewealth to cement an alliance. Such a gesture was common among the headmen of relatively equal means but might be discouraged if made toward a prosperous headman by a less affluent headman. Infant betrothals were common. A man might say of a friend's pregnant wife, "If the child is a daughter, she will be my wife." Child brides were placed with other wives until they were nubile and given huts of their own.[9] Except in exchange marriages, bride-price was high. The Beti called bride-price *meveg*, meaning "estimation" or "appreciation." It completed the transfer of a girl from one lineage to another.[10]

Some of the items included as bride-price were *bikie*, iron bars made by Beti smiths and counted in bundles of tens or hundreds, an occasional piece of ivory, agricultural products, palm oil, palm wine, domestic animals, and European goods when they became available. A representative bride-price in precolonial times might be two guns, a small keg of powder, a hundred small iron bars, and several goats, but there are also reports of a thousand or more iron bars being given in the transaction. Increasingly, as trading goods were more widely available, they became desired objects in the bride-price transfer. Seen as an economic event, marriage was an occasion for the headman with a daughter to gain a windfall of goods for himself and his immediate relatives.[11] Jane Guyer wrote, "The ultimate aim of *bikie*, and of wealth in general, was marriage.... For most senior men, already married at least once, the bridewealth of their daughters, ivory and guns from trade, and herds of goats constituted their most important sources of wealth, leaving agricultural products less as a source of bridewealth than as the basic necessities for feasting and entertaining."[12]

Some headmen preferred not to take bride-price for their daughters, insisting instead on a provision by which the husband did fieldwork, cut and delivered wood, or provided similar services over a period of several seasons. No bride-price was given for women coming to an *nda bod* from lineage segments accused of recent sorcery, or for women given as compensation for an offense or for women lost to another man through a gambling debt, such as one incurred through the rolling of *Abbia* stones, for example.[13] Wars often ended with the exchange of one or more women between the combatants, and women taken in warfare became the property of the headmen or of warriors who seized them and were taken as wives with no subsequent ceremony or bride-price payment.[14] The status of children in a Beti marriage was determined by the following formula: *mon a ton nso bikie*, or "the child goes to him who paid the mother's bridewealth." Thus, the man who had given bridewealth for the child's mother was its father, whether or not he was the genitor. If a male child was born before the transaction was completed, he would have inferior status within the *mvog*, would be regarded as a *mintobo* (client), and would not inherit from his father.

The Beti marriage ceremony took place in the courtyard of the bride's father. The headman chewed a mixture of maize and pepper and spat it in the bride's face. Then he anointed her stomach and back with the blood of a freshly killed goat, placed the bride's hand in that of her husband and admonished them to leave and not look back, at least until after they had crossed a stream. The maize symbolized fecundity for the Beti, the pepper the eventual hardships that should be supported with patience. The goat was an expiatory sacrifice, and the prohibition against looking back was to indicate that the marriage was definitive.[15]

Marriage alliances were concluded between headmen, who could also terminate the contract if the agreed upon bride-price was not delivered. If a wife was found guilty of infidelity, serious quarreling, or witchcraft, the headman could return the woman and demand a return of bridewealth. A woman could leave her husband if he had a contagious disease such as leprosy. A council of both lineage segments decided whether or not her reasons for leaving were valid.[16]

Temporary Alliances for Warfare and Feuding

Mvog also came together through alliances for warfare or feuding. Beti conflict generally consisted of armed disputes among male kinsmen or with neighboring groups. *Ndum* was a form of limited fighting usually between close kinsmen when clubs were used instead of lances and opponents were struck with the side of a machete instead of the blade. The causes of such disputes included adultery or theft of a woman, sorcery accusations, avenging attacks on kinsmen who were insulted or robbed while traveling through another headman's territory, and disputes over land, animals, or hunting and fishing rights.[17]

Before any attack began, the headmen and councils of the two sides consulted diviners to determine a propitious time and place for the battle and appointed one of their own as war leader for the conflicts. They also arranged alliances with nearby groups by sending a loosely knotted palm branch to neighboring headmen: if the branch was returned with a knot pulled tight, the headman supported them; if it was returned as it was sent or was loosened, the headman declined. Another method of making alliances was to send an emissary to neighboring compounds. If the headman gave him a red pepper, it meant support; a green pepper meant opposition. The messenger returned with a string of peppers that showed by their colors the positions of the neighboring *mvog*.[18]

The decision to open hostilities came by sending the enemy a baton covered with white clay. If they accepted, they returned a similar baton, or if they sought reconciliation, an emissary was sent instead. Another way of opening conflict, usually reserved for small-scale feuds, was to set dogs on one person's compound. If the dogs were chased away with threats, it was the beginning of a conflict.[19]

Beti warfare, as conducted by the larger lineage divisions, differed little from conflicts between the smaller units, except for the number of persons involved. It was characterized by ambushes and raids, for example, by surprising a small party of opponents on a path or in their compound. Sometimes groups met in direct confrontation; at other times, each side named an individual to fight for it. Headmen led their groups in warfare or could appoint someone with skills as a warrior in their place.

The main weapons used in disputes between Beti lineages or with another tribe were lances, axes, machetes, crossbows, and bows and arrows, sometimes with poisoned arrows. The presence of European flintlocks, sounding "like the popping of dried corn in a fire" when discharged, appears to have been widespread by the 1880s. Also, the Beti devised a method for firing spears from rifles modified for that purpose, but they were as unsafe as they were inaccurate.[20]

At the outbreak of hostilities, women, children, and the elderly usually retreated into the forest or to a friendly neighboring compound, where they were safe from attack or capture. Some women served as lance-bearers for the men. The main objects of intergroup conflict were to kill or capture the headman of an opposing group, destroy or seize crops and animals, and loot and burn compounds. Raiding groups do not seem to have been larger than a hundred people and the most commonly used strategy was ambushing a party or village, pillaging and withdrawing. Although there were sometimes efforts to dislodge a settlement, the Beti never tried to establish control over another group.

Taking prisoners was incidental during Beti conflict. Prisoners were questioned and, if they could establish kinship ties with their captors, were exchanged or held for ransom. Otherwise, they were sold as slaves to another tribe, such as the coastal Basa, or were killed. War captives were sometimes slaughtered at the graves of important headmen. Sometimes the head of a rival headman killed in warfare was left at the grave of his dead adversary.[21]

When one or both sides decided the conflict should stop, an envoy was sent to the other side. If conflict was between several Beti compounds, usually this emissary was a *man ka*, a "sister's son" (uterine cousin), whose mother had married into one of the disputing groups and whose father came from the other. The *man ka* had safe conduct in both camps but was not entirely trusted by either as he had kinship ties to both sides. His drum name was "He who is against you should explain the reason," meaning that the *man ka*'s reluctance to commit himself to one group came from his kinship ties with its opponent.[22] When peace was arranged, the losing group paid an indemnity in animals or goods and a reconciliation meal was held. If the dispute was between Beti groups, several brides might be exchanged among the two parties as a guarantee against further hostilities.[23]

Short of conducting warfare or convoking the lineages involved, there were other procedures for regulating disputes, such as the settlement of debts with non-lineage members or kinsmen. These included *mimbog* (to seize). Should Fouda from one lineage be in debt to Noah of another lineage, and the two were not otherwise related, Noah might seize a kinsman of Fouda who wandered near his land and keep him with a foot fixed in a wooden block until the debt was settled.

A second procedure was *Asan Ayanga* (to cut and wait). If a non-lineage man would not settle his debt, the person to whom it was owed might suddenly appear in the compound of the influential headman from another lineage and, without saying anything, begin cutting his plants or killing his animals. When asked for an explanation, he would answer, "I am furious at someone who will not pay me this debt." The influential headman would send a drum message, "Everything I have is cut down, all my plants are chopped down. These people arrive armed to the teeth. They must have compensation." Next, the neutral headman and the man who claimed the debt was owed to him visited the debtor together, requesting him to pay both his debt and the damage done to the influential person's plants and animals, or risk being taken captive.

A third device was *Evuson* (from *son*, an oath to the dead). A petitioner, stating he was owed something by another man, visited an influential headman known to both, saying, "I implore you on the name of your ancestor to help me recover this debt" or "I implore you, on what remains of your father's corpse, to help me." The influential person and his kinsmen then visited the debtor to demand payment and costs of the journey. As in the cases of *Asan Ayanga* or *mimbog*, should the claim prove false, the instigator would have to indemnify all involved. Obtaining recompense from anyone who was not a kinsman required considerable skill, for the Beti had no leverage outside their own society. As the Beti proverbs stated, "It does you no good to swear by your father's body in someone else's village" and "The large mouse, when it crosses a stream, becomes very small."[24]

Beti Potlatch: Dancing the *Bilabi*

A frequent form of interaction between *mvog* was through "dancing the *bilabi*," a Beti form of potlatch. The contact between lineages provided by the *bilabi* frequently resulted in marriage and friendships, but it also served as a way for a headman to gain prestige and material advantage at the public expense of a rival. *Bilabi* contests, which were usually held annually until one side defaulted, were accompanied by much surface camaraderie and good humor, but they could bring near ruin to the loser. One Beti informant described the contests as examples of "fraternal love that could lead to war or marriage."[25]

The contest began when one headman notified another that, at a given time several weeks later, he and his kinsmen would arrive "to dance the *bilabi*." When they arrived at the appointed time, perhaps a hundred strong, it was with fanfare and elaborate gestures of courtesy. Then the visiting headman started to dance and began insulting his host: "I have great pity on you, poor and unhappy that you are.... Your family has never had salt to eat. I will take you today into my family so that you can work on my plantations." At this point he produced several bars of salt and presented them casually to his host, while his own followers vigorously applauded.[26]

As the dancing continued, the host would rise and begin a dance of his own, singing to his challenger: "Here are ten baskets of fish for you and your kinsmen. I doubt if you have ever eaten them before because your men are such poor fishermen." The gifts became successively more elaborate, and the insults and feasting continued for three to five days. Almost any object, including wives, could be given in a *bilabi*. Representatives of both sides kept an exact tally of what had been given. During the next year the host and his *mvog* would visit the headman who had started the *bilabi*, ridiculing him and his position with song and dance, trying to surpass the previous year's *bilabi* by giving more gifts. These *bilabi* might take anywhere from three to seven days and involve at least 100 participants on each side. The contest ended when one headman could not assemble resources enough to hold a more extensive *bilabi* than his rival last offered. The defaulting headman had then to reimburse his opponent for his outlay at the last *bilabi*, and the series ended.

Among headmen, the exchange was both a means of flaunting the prestige of his *mvog* at the expense of another and also a way of creating marriage ties with that *mvog*. In addition to the wives given among the *bilabi* gifts, others could be exchanged or contracted for work during the festivities. Brides could even be seized by young men of one side from the other without bridewealth. If a daughter was seized in such a manner, her father was not allowed to show indignation. "The fish that remains in the basket does not leave," she might explain.[27]

At another level, the *bilabi* was a leveling device among *mvog*, which prevented headmen from accumulating what they and their peers might regard as too much power and wealth. In a society that depended on elaborate and careful balance among its member units for equilibrium, several ways of leveling out accumulations of wealth between *mvog* were employed. One was that headmen were expected to extend hospitality to visitors, and use up their wealth in the process. Another was through the *bilabi* potlatch, and a third device was through the outlay of foods and gifts expended in the Beti *Sso* rite. If several headmen watched a peer grow increasingly wealthy and wanted to bring him down to size, the simplest way to do it was to pay him a number of visits, challenge him to a *bilabi*, or encourage him to hold a *Sso* rite. He, in his turn, would return the favor.

Wrestling Matches

Like the *bilabi*, wrestling matches were also used by headmen to establish superiority over rivals. Such matches were usually held during the dry season and were arranged between the headmen of the two *mvog* several days or weeks in advance. In late afternoon the wrestlers, elders, women, and children of one *mvog* appeared at another *mvog* with whom the match had been arranged. The rival groups sat at opposite sides of the compound, dances were held, and taunts exchanged. The match began when one of the men from the visiting side danced over to the host's wrestlers and touched one of them on the shoulders. The winning side was determined by the number of falls it accumulated. A fall took place when a wrestler was thrown on his stomach, not his back. A skilled wrestler could throw as many as twenty opponents in a day, according to one report. There were some matches between women of the two sides, during which the men sang and cheered.[28]

Each of these forms of interaction among *mvog* had different purposes and participants. Council meetings determined the ancestors' will and could attract more than a hundred participants from several lineage units meeting for several days if required. On the other hand, marriage alliances affected only two *mvog*. Warfare might bring several lineage units together, but this was a temporary union that dissolved once the conflict was ended. *Bilabi* potlatches and wrestling matches were between two *mvog* and served the limited purpose of asserting the prestige and power of one headman at the expense of another.

The *Sso* Rite

The *Sso* rite provided both a way for Beti men to expend their ties across several lineages and, at the same time, provide Beti culture with root imagery from which the Beti derived many of their eschatological explanations. The Sso rite provided Beti life with its core ritual; from its symbols, Beti society derived many of its explanations about life and proper conduct.

Apart from its religious significance and the deep psychological imprint it left on participants, the *Sso* ritual was also a way of extending contacts among lineages, whether or not they were already related by marriage. Through the *Sso* rite, young men of several lineages were united in a school for warriors. A marriage united two *mvog*, but a *Sso* rite, frequently involving as many as sixty candidates, created ties between several *mvog*. These ties took place at many levels, principally between the sponsor and the candidates, between the sponsor and the candidates' fathers, and among the candidates themselves.

The ceremony was named for the *Sso* antelope, a prized kill for hunters, a swift animal that supposedly never slept. "Killing the *Sso*," or completing the rite, symbolically meant that the young men aged fifteen to twenty-five had made the passage from *ebin* (uninitiated) to *mkpangoss* (warriors), were now considered adults and could sit as council members, and eat select meats previously forbidden them. It also assured them of passage to the land of the ancestors at their death. Finally, a successfully completed *Sso* rite gave its sponsor and his *mvog* considerable prestige. Only headmen of means could provide the outlay of food and hospitality required to sponsor a *Sso* gathering. A successfully completed *Sso* also meant that the sponsor had satisfactorily expiated some secret sin such as incest that had caused him or his lineage misfortune.[29]

Sso rites, usually held during the dry season that began in November, were organized in several sponsors' compounds, taking place at the same time in the same region. They attracted candidates from *mvog* related to the sponsor's lineage and from other Beti groups as well, including those several miles away. Before the ceremony began, the sponsor held a preliminary gathering, a small feast called the *efeb nsen*, "approving the court." This gathering was attended by fathers who wished for their sons to participate in the rite; it provided an opportunity for them to ascertain if the sponsor had sufficient means to provide for the several feasts expected during the six-month period that would follow and whether the sponsor had recruited the proper ritual figures who went from *mvog* to *mvog* conducting the rite. The sponsor's paternal and maternal kinsmen were expected to assist him by providing goats and various foods. Anyone who contributed in the preparations would share the prestige of the successfully completed rite.[30]

Among the candidates (*mvon*), three people stood out. First, there was the *asu zoa* (the elephant), a strong youth who was picked by the sponsor to lead the group ("Where the elephant has gone there is a path for others," a Beti proverb states). Usually the *asu zoa* came from the sponsor's family. Second was the *dib koa*, "the line closer," who brought up the end of the candidates' line when they were hunting. These two candidates were responsible for order among the *mvon*. A third figure was the *zogo*, or "weakling," the butt of compound jokes. Each candidate has an *Esia Sso*, or *Sso* father, someone who had completed the rite and who helped arrange its various ordeals. Candidates kept friendly ties with their *Sso* fathers in later life and could use this tie of quasi-kinship to ask the *Sso* father for assistance in accumulating bride-price, but they could not marry his daughters.[31]

The *Sso* candidates did not form clearly delineated age sets. There was no distinction between different groups of candidates, and they did not have collective obligations for warfare, hunting, or farming assistance either toward the sponsor, or among themselves. Although candidates spent as long as six months in seclusion during the *Sso* rite, living in special barracks called the *essam Sso*, no elder stayed with them, and no one was assigned as a teacher for the candidates. They were left with few instructions about relations toward one another, except that sexual relations with a *Sso* brother's sister were forbidden, and they were told not to let a calumnious statement be made of a *Sso* brother. Their continuing ties, once the rite was completed, were those of men who had shared an important common experience over a prolonged period, and they addressed each other as *avus* (spiritual brother).

Two important ritual figures completed the list of persons necessary for the rite. The first was the *mbegë Sso*, who organized the ceremony, supervised its conduct, and decided when the different ceremonies would be held. He was "holder of the *Sso* sack," which contained herbs and leaves later mixed with food and drink ritually consumed during the ceremony.[32] The second, and most important, ritual figure was the *zum loa*, whose orations closed the rite. The *zum loa* appeared at the rite's termination, when he delivered an oration, enumerating the faults of the sponsor, which occasioned the rite. A striking figure, dressed in an antelope skin, carrying a lance and wearing iron bracelets and a red cap, a costume unique to his office, the *zum loa* was known as a skilled orator, and people bowed before him, deference not accorded an ordinary headmen. The *zum loa* was also in demand as an arbitrator between lineages or to close council meetings by announcing the decision and soliciting its favorable reception. The office was not hereditary within a lineage, and the *zum loa* had no other functions. His skills as an orator and arbitrator, within the limit of the powers delegated him by the disputants, made the *zum loa* one of the most important figures in Beti society. "To speak like a *zum loa*" was a high tribute to a Beti man's forensic skills.[33]

The Rite Begins

The most important of the opening rites was the *Ekpe ndzom Sso*, "cutting the *Sso* tree." Three days before the *Sso* rite began, the elders from several compounds felled a tree, and the candidates cleared off its branches. It was carried to the sponsor's compounds and decorated with carvings of guns, snakes, birds, and animals, and its trunk leveled so that the candidates could dance on it. A feast was held, and praises were sung about the candidates and their parents, marriage contracts were sometimes negotiated, and palavers settled. Following this ceremony, candidates began a series of tests and ordeals. There were frequent contests of bravery, endurance, and strength, such as jumping over fires, being beaten by elders and engaging in mock conflict with them, or being surprised and beaten while on a hunting trip.[34]

Some of the exercises were no more than a mild form of hazing. Candidates crawled through wet tunnels after an itching powder was thrown on them or climbed trees for kola nuts but found driver ants instead. The period was one of license, and candidates often raided compounds and seized animals and made off with unguarded meals left on the fire. "To steal like an *mvon*" was a Beti expression.[35] During this time *Sso* candidates from different localities exchanged insults and fought with one another. Sometimes such clashes were violent, causing deaths among the candidates. In such a case, the candidate's death was hidden from his parents until the rite's end, when they were told he had become a *Sso*, the legendary antelope from which the rite took its name.

After about five months of hunting tests, ordeals, and living together, the *mfek Sso*, who organized the rite, gathered the candidates together and fired his gun from the *Sso* tree, declaring, "the *Sso* dies in ten days." This was the signal to begin final ceremonies. The village was cleared of women and children, and the elders dug a tunnel or trench from the *Sso* compound to the sponsor's compound.

The trench, which was covered with leaves, had three exits and was only wide enough for a single person to crawl through at a time. During the final ceremony the candidates danced several times around their dwelling and then were steered into the trench by their *Sso* fathers, who tossed ants or itching powder on them. The candidates were told to crawl through the trench and exit only at the last opening, otherwise a slave armed with a hand-axe would slay them. Musicians played on drums left with the skins untightened, which the Beti say made a menacing sound as the *mvon* crawled through the dark passage.

When they emerged into the light each raised his hand and shouted, "*Tara*, my father, I have killed the *Sso*," after which he placed his hand on the entrance of the sponsor's *abaa* and rolled in the dust and leaves to assuage the effects of insect bites. Finally, the sponsor began to dance, and disclosed the offense that had prompted him to hold the rite. A goat, called symbolically *Sso*, was brought into the compound; it had been fattened and fed a plant called *akon*, which coated its vocal cords and prevented it from making any sound. The goat was progressively dismembered by the *Sso* elders and finally its throat was cut. If it made no sound, a great cry went up, "*Sso wu mben*," the *Sso* is dead. If it did make a sound, the rite was invalid and had to be repeated.

Next the *zum loa* began his peroration. After recalling the sponsor's offenses and saying they had been expiated, he warned that in the future anyone who mentioned the sponsor's fault would be guilty, as the sponsor once had been, and might have to sponsor a *Sso* rite himself. He also declared that the candidates and their parents had atoned for their sins through the rite, and extolled at length the virtues and duties of Beti warriors, which the *Sso* participants had become.

When these ceremonies were finished, the candidates retired to the *essam Sso* until any wounds sustained during the ordeal were healed. However, restrictions on them were less rigorous than before, and they could move about more freely. If a *Sso* participant showed himself skillful in warfare and hunting, he could leave the *Sso* compound early. If he had accidentally killed another person in one of the mock raids of the *Sso* ordeal, his bravery was recognized and he could leave shortly after the final ritual. Candidates went on a final hunt, the *ekulu mvon*, and then returned to their homes instead of to the *essam Sso*. The rite had finished.[36]

The Sso Rite's Importance

The *Sso* rite illustrated several important aspects of Beti institutions and culture in the period before colonial contact. There was something in the *Sso* for all Beti, participants or not. For the candidates, it marked the transition from youth to manhood; for the sponsor, it was a means of gaining prestige, stabilizing relations with peers, and extending influence. For those whose participation was marginal, it provided entertainment and a meeting place for the exchange of conversation.

For the whole society, the passage of time was reckoned by the interval between *Sso* rites; metaphors from its lore provided the most common idioms in Beti thought. If some of its ordeals were more in the nature of hazing, the ultimate purpose of the *Sso* ritual—expiation and the assurance of eventual safe passage to join the ancestors—spoke to the deepest aspirations of Beti society. And in its interplay of personalities between those who gave and those who received, those who sought expiation and those who accorded it, the delicate balances maintained throughout the *Sso* ritual reflected the state of Beti society itself.

It was a paradox in traditional Beti social organization that the same traits that helped strengthen the headman's control of its smallest units were a block to forming any more inclusive permanent social groups. Headmen enjoyed complete control over their autarchic *nda bod*, and among them the sense of individualism was pronounced. Yet the Beti never established a political structure equating with the lineage at its extended level and had no corresponding idea of a wider political community.

The Beti were at a juncture in the 1880s where their society could have developed one of several ways; but the direction their society ultimately took was dictated by circumstances over which the Beti had no control. They could have moved toward government by strong headmen who extended their power through military or economic influence if Beti headmen had become conquerors or traders. If the *Sso* group had ever consolidated into age sets, it could have provided a base for wider political institutions, drawing the disparate lineage clusters together. Ritual figures such as the *zum loa* or diviners could have become politically important, or ties between headmen and their wives' patrilineages might have assumed a political dimension. There were ways the Beti could have united. But none of these things happened. A new set of circumstances affected Beti history; migrations were cut short and relations with the Vute, Basa, and other groups were sharply altered when, in 1887, the Germans sent their first expedition from the coast toward Beti lands.

Notes

1. T. Tsala, "Grammaire Ewondo," 1970, pp. 256–63; T. Tsala, "Le Gouvernement des Beti," 7 June 1968. Jean Fouda Ngono, interview with author, Ngomedzap, 18 March 1968.
2. T. Tsala, interview with author, Mvolye, 19 March 1968.
3. T. Tsala, "L'Organization Judiciare," 2 March 1968, p. 2.
4. Martin Mballa Foe and Cyprian Owona Nde, interviews with author, Mbalmayo, 14 March 1968. Tsala, "L'Organization Judiciare," pp. 1–3.
5. Laurent Ondoua Awomou, interview with author, Ebogo, 14 March 1968.
6. T. Tsala, "Principales Valeurs Sociales des Beti," p. 4. Interviews were conducted by the author with Laurent Ondoua Awomou, Ebolo, 14 March 1968; T. Tsala, Mvolye, 15 February 1968; François Atangana, Yaoundé, 2 May 1967; Martin Mballa Foe, Mbalmayo, 14 March 1968. Some men had their tongues vaccinated with a viper's fang as a way of gaining eloquence that would hopefully match the viper's sting.
7. G. Zenker, "Jaunde." *Mittheilungen von Forschungsreisenden und Gelehrten aus den Deutschen Schutzgebieten* (Berlin), no. 8 (1895): pp. 49–52. Interviews were conducted by the author with Pierre Mebe, Yaoundé, 6 July 1967; Etienne Ahanda Ayissi, Ngomedzap, 18 March 1968; Abbé Frédéric Essomba, Mbalmayo, 14 March 1968. A Beti has written, "Chez les Beti la polygamie n'avait pas pour principal la concupiscence de la chair mais l'orgueil de la vie: on voulait avoir beaucoup d'enfants, on voulait grossir son hameau, ses plantations, pour avoir de quoi être genereux" (among the Beti, polygamy did not have the principal purpose of fleshly concupiscence,

but fulfilling the will to live, one wanted to have many children, to expand his compound, his plantations, to have what was needed to be generous). T. Tsala, "Charles Atangana Ntsama," 25 August 1968.
8. Jean-Marie Ze and Henri Atangana Amengue, interview with author, Mfou, 4 April 1968.
9. Laurent Ayissi Nsimi, interview with author, Ngomedzap, 18 March 1968.
10. M. Heepe, *Jaunde-Text*, in *Abhandlunger des Hamburgischer Kolonial-Instituts*, Band XXIV (Hamburg: L. Friedrichen & Co.) p. 61. Pierre Mebe, interview with author, Yaoundé, 6 July 1967.
11. Oral interviews conducted by author with Fabian Okah Mbana, Ngomedzap, 18 March 1968; T. Tsala, Mvolye, 7 April 1968, 1 May 1968; Gotfried Bisso Medza, Dzeng, 18 March 1968. Tsala, "Grammaire Ewondo," pp. 8–9.
12. J. Guyer, "Female Farming and the Evolution of Food Production Patterns amongst the Beti of South Central Cameroon," *Africa*, vol. 50, no. 4 (1980): pp. 341–56.
13. T. Tsala, interview with author, Mvolye, 7 April 1968; Laurent Ondoua Awomou, interview with author, Ebogo, 14 March 1968.
14. T. Tsala, interview with author, Mvolye, 7 June 1967; Laurent Ondoua Awomou, interview with author, Ebogo, 31 March 1968; Zenker, "Jaunde," p. 49.
15. T. Tsala, letter to author, 11 January 1971.
16. Ibid.
17. Heepe, *Jaunde-Text*, pp. 313–15.
18. Hubert Ondana Mbida, Interview with author, Ayéné, 14 March 1968.
19. Ibid.
20. Zenker, "Jaunde," pp. 44–45; Heepe, *Jaunde-Text*, pp. 70–72. An illustration of Beti weapons is contained in Morgen, *Durch Kamerun von Süd nach Nord* (Leipzig, 1893), opposite p. 54.
21. T. Tsala, "La Morte de Zibi Ngomo et les sacrifices humains," Mvolye, 1968, p. 3.
22. Heepe, *Jaunde-Text*, pp. 66–67, 74; Max Abe Foudda, interview with author, Nkolbewa, 7 January 1968; Hubert Ondana Mbida, interview with author, Ayéné, 14 March 1968. The *man ka* inherited nothing from the headman. Sometimes he had developed a friendship with some of the deceased headman's wives, and they were given to him at the headman's death.
23. Hubert Ondana Mbida, interview with author, Ayéné, 14 March 1968. Martin Mballa Foe, interview with author, Mbalmayo, 14 March 1968.
24. Pierre Mebe, interview with author, Yaoundé, 8 November 1967; Pierre Mebe and Joseph Essono, interviews with author, Yaoundé, 6 August 1967. T. Tsala, Interview with author, Yaoundé, 7 June 1967.
25. Laurent Ondoua Awomou, interview with author, Ebogo, 31 March 1968.
26. Martin Otyam, "Institution des *Bilabi* chez les Boulous," 1937, p. 3, Institut de Recherche du Cameroun (IRCAM), Yaoundé, File N. Laurent Ondoua Awomou, interview with author, Ebogo, 14 March 1968.
27. Laurent Ondoua Awomou, interview with author, Ebogo, 31 March 1968.
28. Heepe, *Jaunde-Text*, pp. 44–48.
29. Tsala, "Le Gouvernement des Beti," p. 2, and "L'Organization Judiciare," pp. 3–5.
30. Tsala, "L'Organization Judiciare," pp. 4–5.
31. Pierre Mebe, interview with author, 1 November 1967.
32. T. Tsala, interview with author, Mvolye, 6 June 1968.
33. Ibid. Laurent Ondoua Awomou, interview with author, Ebogo, 14 March 1968.
34. Pierre Mebe, interviews with author, Yaoundé, 1 November 1967 and 8 November 1967.
35. Pierre Mebe, interview with author, 8 November 1967; Pierre Mebe and Joseph Essono, interview with author, Yaoundé, 6 August 1967.
36. T. Tsala, interview with author, Mvolye, 7 April 1968.

CHAPTER 3

"In the Time of Major Dominik"
The Beti and the Germans, 1887–1916

The chronology of German-Beti political contact is not difficult to periodize. What is more difficult to assess is the extent of change this contact brought to Beti society and to discern how and why change took place.

The period 1887–1916 falls logically into three parts: the time of initial Beti-German contact, from 1887 to 1894, when the small Yaoundé post was established and when the Beti groups had only initial contact with the Germans. The second period is what the Beti called "the time of Major Dominik," from 1894 to 1910, the time in which "pacification" was completed, locally recruited troops and clerks were employed by the Germans, and a local administration structure was created. In the final six-year period, from 1910 to 1916, World War I abruptly ended the German colonial presence; the Germans devised an order of appointed chiefs who had responsibilities for collecting taxes and recruiting workers and who were rewarded with money and power.

During the quarter century of Beti-German contact the Germans first improvised, selecting scattered local agents to recruit workers and collect taxes, but then, as the German presence expanded, a more elaborate network of chiefs were appointed; this resulted in two sorts of alterations in Beti social organization. First, the headman's traditional role diminished as the latter's role as compound head and protector of his people conflicted with increasing demands from the administration to find laborers and collect revenues of various sorts, such as money, when it became available, foodstuffs, or rubber. Some individual headmen who sided with the colonial power gained handsomely for their efforts through tax rebates and support from the administration; they gained wealth, and their plantations grew. Still, they were not and never could be Germans. Moreover, their new roles conflicted with their place in traditional Beti society. What ultimately happened was that the structure of Beti society was disrupted, beginning in the German period and continuing in almost the same manner through the French protectorate. If the workings of traditional Beti society could be compared to the delicate

---

Notes for this chapter begin on page 59.

balance of a chemical compound, the colonial presence injected a foreign solution that destroyed the equilibrium of the original mixture.

Cameroon became a German colony on 14 July 1884, when Dr. Gustav Nachtigal, a peripatetic German consul-explorer acting on his own volition, signed several treaties with the coastal Duala people and raised the German flag over a number of coastal factories. At that time, there were more British than German traders around Douala, and the British and French traders had already been in active contact with the coastal chiefs for several years. However, a British representative who hoped to ally the coastal people with Great Britain arrived in Douala five days after Nachtigal distributed his treaties and flags, and Cameroon became a German colony.[1]

The initiative for Germany to acquire colonies came primarily from German traders and colonial societies rather than the government. The German chancellor, Otto von Bismarck, hoped the traders would provide revenues from the colonies and help govern the lands from which they profited, and that only a minimum of government participation would be necessary. He was wary of sending troops and money to the colonies, as he believed the French were doing to their ruin.[2] The resident traders, however, though loathe to assume the burdens of administration, still wanted protection from a governor, who they hoped would establish an administration supported by gunboats. The traders made constant demands on the government for protection, but gave the administration little support, frequently undercutting it through the sale of contraband arms and goods, and opposing almost every measure to levy customs or taxes.

The Move Inland

In the late 1880s, two different groups of German explorers moved inland along two main routes. The month-long trip overland to the Yaoundé region was undertaken in the period 1887–1890 by three German officers, R. Kund, Hans Tappenbeck, and Curt von Morgen, while in 1888 a civilian trader, Eugen Zintgraff, and his associates moved inland from West Cameroon toward Bali in the West Cameroon grasslands.

The primary concern of both groups was finding a route to the north, where the Germans hoped to capture what they believed was the lucrative British ivory trade along the Benue River in Nigeria and divert it to their own gradually expanding sphere of control. They also wanted to curb the spread of Islam from Adamaua to the savanna and rainforest. This was again for commercial as well as for religious reasons, as the progress of Islam was linked to the movement of Hausa traders, whose contacts with the British were already established.[3]

There was a sharp contrast in the methods used by the two German military and civilian administrations in their distribution of firearms and ways of dealing with native people. The military explorers were reluctant to provide Africans with firearms. The soldiers knew that they were outnumbered; because they occasionally traveled through hostile regions, monopolizing firepower was to their advantage. Zintgraff, on the other hand, was an independent trader who, in his role as explorer, frequently distributed European weapons to African groups he believed supported him. He also managed to lose quantities of firearms and ammunition through raids or pilfering of his supplies. Among the West Cameroonians, he found some powerful allies in the paramount chiefs of large groups, such as the Bali, with whom he quickly made treaties. No similar arrangement was possible in the Yaoundé region because the several thousand headmen had no paramount chiefs or territorial control beyond their own relatively small holdings. The nearest paramount chief was the ruler of the Vute, the Sudanic people who occupied the north bank of the Sanaga River, bordering on the Beti lands. In the absence of paramount chiefs in the Yaoundé region, the Germans initially appointed a number of agents with limited powers to convey their orders, whom the Beti called "mayors." Later they selected chiefs from among Beti headmen and other Beti males. There was one reported instance of the Germans appointing a woman as chief, but later Beti informants say that she exercised no actual power.

Initially, German interest was confined to Douala and the coast, and the Yaoundé region was not explored until 1887, three years after Cameroon had become a German colony. At that time, two inland routes were open to the Germans. The most traveled led through what would later be called West Cameroon, a hilly region conducive to agriculture and settlement. In 1901, the Germans moved the colony's capital from coastal Douala to hilly Buea in West Cameroon. Buea was located on the slopes of Mt. Cameroon, and stretching from it westward to the sea were plantations with rich volcanic soil that provided most of the colony's coffee and cocoa exports. A steady stream of Beti and other Africans came to this region from the interior to work as field laborers. From this part of West Cameroon a natural corridor to the north opened by way of the Bamenda-Foumban highlands, and it was along this route that most of the German explorers of the 1880s moved.[4]

A second, less frequently used path from the coast inland ran eastward from Douala toward the savanna, but this involved a laborious crossing of mangrove swamps, a heavy belt of rainforest, and frequent encounters with hostile tribes like the Basa, who menaced caravans and wished to monopolize trade with the interior. This second route was opened in 1887 but was not easily accessible until the turn of the century.

Before they decided to establish a post at Yaoundé, the Germans hoped to build a station farther to the south on the Nyong River. They abandoned this plan because the Beti headmen in that region refused to cooperate with them and provide food. Instead, a German post was established by Tappenbeck in February 1889 farther inland, on a hill near the settlement of an Ewondo headman named Zonu. It was the first German inland station in Cameroon. "Jaunde," as the word appeared in German documents, is a transliteration of "Ewondo," the name of the Beti clan living in that region.[5]

During most of its early existence, the Yaoundé station served principally as a jumping-off point for German pacification and trade caravans moving farther inland. German interest in the Beti region was always secondary to their fascination with northern Cameroon.

Beti Reaction to the German Presence

Several responses to the gradually growing German presence were open to the Beti, ranging from massive resistance to acquiescence and capitulation. During the period 1887–1905, scattered Beti groups engaged in sporadic and isolated-armed conflict with the Germans. Such resistance was usually limited to a clash between individual headmen or a few headmen and their followers and a German-led patrol. Headmen fought because they believed the Germans would end their lucrative practice of taxing passing commercial caravans; other feared the loss of lands or women, and some Beti headmen, used to conflict and feuding, regarded this as the proper way to deal with any interlopers.[6] Not all Beti groups resisted all the time; some extended their conflict for twenty years, opposing Germans and other Beti at the same time. But the Beti never mounted a massive resistance movement, like the *Maji Maji* in East Africa or the Bulu, who had attacked the German station in Kribi. A few Beti groups practiced noncooperation and passive resistance, but this again was usually at the level of a single headman.

A popular Beti proverb discusses how to resist a seemingly stronger adversary. A Beti man would say, "I will model myself on the lizard; swallowed partially by the chicken, he leaves his legs limp, and spread out." Many Beti headmen became allies of the Germans soon after initial contact, and numbers of their kinsmen worked for the administration, traders, and missionaries, quickly adopting German dress, language, and modes of thought. Thus, the most powerful elements in Beti society, those leaders from which a resistance movement might likely spring, came fairly quickly under German control. Moreover, there was no suprapolitical or religious organization among the Beti, which would have made a sustained and coherent resistance possible. The Beti *Sso* groups, despite their resemblance to age-sets, never formed permanent offices or created political ties across lineages.

Beti Perception of the Germans

It is difficult to ascertain the Beti perceptions of the Germans in the 1890s, but they appear to have evolved in three stages. Initially the Beti equated the Germans with their own ancestor spirits, *bekon*, which were pale. Hence, those Beti who held this view did not initially fire on Germans in warfare. When some of the Germans encamped at Yaoundé, it was a highly favorable sign, and the Beti provided them with foods, as would be expected from the living as gifts to ancestral shades. "The spirits that came from the sea," the Beti called them.

Soon the Beti interacted with the newcomers and their Edenic image of the visitors dissolved quickly. As one sign that the relationship had altered, the Beti left the Germans not eggs, as had been the case in the past, but a chicken. The message was, "Raise your own eggs." Also, a German whom the Beti had called "The Pretentious" died of natural causes and was buried publicly at the Yaoundé station. Some Beti interpreted this as a real death, hence the newcomers were not ancestral shades; others thought that he was simply a *bekon* returning to his country.

A third perception of the Germans--more lasting than the other two, which appear limited to the first few years of German control--was that the newcomers possessed power superior to what the Beti had, and the Beti would like to share this power. It was not only the presence of superior arms; the new power included traders' goods, German medicaments, a new religion, and schools that introduced a new culture and values. Part of this process was the Germans saying that African culture was primitive, savage, childish, unevolved, and inferior, and many Beti believing it, or at least having serious doubts about the worth and value of their own traditions.

Which of these aspects of German culture most affected Beti life, and among which Beti? Some tentative answers are suggested by what the Beti remember most about the German period, how the role of the headmen changed, how the influx of trade goods came to the interior, and how the new religion increasingly was accepted by the Beti. Each of these themes is treated in the discussion that follows. What will emerge is a picture of change in Beti institutions during a quarter century. But just as there was not a uniform entity called "the Germans," neither were "the Beti" an undistinguished mass. We can never establish how 500,000 people perceived an epoch. Such sources as remain in Cameroonian archives and the recollection of Beti elders present a truncated, selective record of what changes took place and why.

The existing archival records and remaining oral sources come largely from Beti headmen or the descendants of well-known headmen, identified with the colonial period. These leaders formed the power structure of Beti society and adopted German ways with little resistance. While it appears that most headmen were active cooperators with the colonial power, possibly other Beti figures, such as some of the healers and ritual figures associated with the *Sso* rite, may have been slower to absorb and accept colonial values and incorporate them into their own thinking. Such traditional figures were the repositories of traditional Beti culture and values, which provided a fairly complete world-view and value system that did not need a German overlay to complete it.

However, before examining the political, economic, and religious changes the Beti experienced in their contact with the Germans, it is useful to summarize the extent and character of initial armed contact between the Beti and the Germans in the period 1887–1905.

Beti-German Conflict at Yaoundé

During the first two decades of its existence, the German station's response to sporadic Beti attacks was usually slow. The German military presence at Yaoundé amounted at times to little more than five European troops and a hundred native soldiers with a territory of several hundred square miles to cover. Thus, a reprisal raid against the Basa in 1899 came about a year after the original dispute with the Germans; there are other examples of retaliation raids taken as late as six months after an incident.[7]

Beti resistance was sharpest in the first decade after the Germans' arrival, from 1887 to about 1900. Afterwards, there were few incidents of violence reported in the Yaoundé region, and armed resistance ceased being a significant theme in Beti history.[8]

The Ewondo groups around the Yaoundé station were generally friendly with the Germans. The Ewondo were threatened by neighboring groups, and the presence of a German station gave them protection they would not have otherwise enjoyed. Hostilities between the Ewondo and the neighboring Benë and the Eton continued until the turn of the century, and there were numerous Ewondo-Basa border disputes over possession of land and attempts by the Ewondo to travel to the coast without paying tolls to the Basa.

The only disputes of any length between the Ewondo and the Germans in these early years occurred late in 1895. The German station was manned at that time by a contingent of 50 to 100 African troops whom the Germans had brought to Cameroon from Dahomey to guard the station and accompany German commercial and military caravans. The Germans bought these troops from a Dahomian king who had captured them in warfare and was preparing to sacrifice them. Quarrels between the soldiers and the Beti were frequent, especially over women or payment for food. During such a disagreement near the Yaoundé station in December 1895, one of the colonial force members was killed and another kidnapped by an Ewondo, who sold him as a slave. The Germans demanded that the two soldiers be returned and those responsible for the incident report to the station, but the Ewondo answered by attacking the post instead.[9]

For the next six months, the Ewondo fought German patrols, ambushed caravans, killed or wounded porters, and took booty. The German station commander ordered the warring headmen and their followers to the compound as hostages until the dispute was settled and German control restored. The Germans also conscripted a number of workers without salary for a period, and the Beti paid an indemnity in ivory and livestock. In early May 1896, six months after hostilities had broken out, calm was restored.

The Benë, a Beti group living southeast of the Yaoundé station, continued to feud with the Ewondo during much of the period of pre-European contact, and after the Germans' arrival, they frequently raided or ambushed German patrols or caravans.[10]

In an attempt to stop these ambushes, the Germans sent an expedition against the Benë in November 1896. The African soldiers fighting on behalf of the Germans wore no shoes, and the Benë lined sections of the trail with sharpened sticks. A German who accompanied the expedition wrote: "The blacks always use the same cowardly trick: they pour out of an ambush, open fire on us, and quickly pull back. In such attacks the blacks disappear into the forest after the first shots, and while we are aiming our rifles, the object is no longer there."[11]

The Eton, a large Beti group north of the Yaoundé station, appears to have been relatively peaceful during most of the late nineteenth and early twentieth century. Within a few years after the Yaoundé station was opened, the Germans considered the Eton land safely under their control, although there were a few reports of the Eton attacking German caravans.[12]

The Eton's principal enemy during this period was the M'velle, another Beti group pushing westward into Eton lands. The M'velle, the most powerful Beti group north of the station, was well respected among the Beti as warriors. M'velle compounds were organized into larger settlements than was usually the case with the Beti, probably because the M'velle had to protect themselves against slave raids by the more powerful Vute, a Sudanic group controlling the north bank of the Sanaga River. Curt von Morgen, a German officer who explored the region, remarked in 1890 that the M'velle were pushing the Eton to the west and that in the interval of a year between his trips through the region, the M'velle had moved several kilometers westward into what had been Eton territory. At the same time, he said the Vute were pushing the M'velle south away from the Sanaga River.[13]

Resistance to the Germans: The Mbidambane and Mbida Menge

One of the most aggressive Beti groups was the Mbidambane, whose leader, Mbida Menge, was well known among the Beti as a headman and warrior. The Mbidambane lived southeast at Yaoundé and east of the lands occupied by the Benë. After they had dominated most of the smaller tribes around them, the Mbidambane attacked the Benë and Ewondo in three battles during the 1870s and 1880s. They also fought the M'velle and raided as far south as Sangmalima and north to Akonolinga.

In warfare Mbida Menge favored ambushes, after which he would take slaves, burn his opponent's compound and demand a number of women as the price of concluding peace. His raiding parties included at least 100 warriors armed with machetes and rifles made by the coastal Duala, who then traded them to inland tribes. Another technique was to move perhaps 100 of his followers near the compound of headmen whose lands he wanted. He would tell the headmen, "My brother, I have come here to build near you." Mbida Menge's people next settled on several sides of the original headman's compound, leaving the original inhabitant with the options of fighting or moving on to other land.[14]

In 1907, Mbida Menge took on the Germans. An African who accompanied a German expedition sent in retaliation said Mbida Menge attacked the Germans because "I was born to know combat and bravery, which is why I have always made war. Would you expect me to say something else?"[15]

The Mbidambane were subjugated by the Germans, and the German commander who had earlier given Mbida Menge a sword as a sign of faith now fined him 1,200 marks, ordered him to furnish 600 laborers, and to compensate the Germans for ammunition the colonial troops used during the campaign. Mbida Menge was sentenced to six months' imprisonment. His people paid the fine, and after three months imprisonment, the chief, gravely ill, was released. He died soon after in 1910 or 1911.[16]

After 1905 there were few reports of military activity among the Beti or among tribes within the ambit of the Yaoundé station, and warfare, until this time part of the fabric of Beti life, ceased being a theme of any importance in Beti history. There are several reasons for this. First, German military control of the interior of Cameroon expanded steadily during the early twentieth century, and military patrols could move more quickly as the system of roads and trails from the station through the hinterland gradually expanded. Beti resistance also subsided because it ultimately proved futile for the Beti who participated in it. They neither discouraged caravans or patrols nor gained new lands or conquests. Traditional Beti warfare was based on individual bravery or ambushes by small groups, and there was never any prospect of the Beti mounting the sort of military activity that would have been necessary to effectively combat the Germans.

Beti resistance also waned because the headmen of traditional society, the agents of warfare, were either placed on the German's payroll or were gradually replaced by an order of Beti functionaries employed by the Germans. As the older generation of militant headmen died, were removed by the Germans, or joined the government payroll, possibilities for resistance diminished sharply. It was in the interests of this new class, which by 1910 numbered some several hundred individuals, to discourage resistance and promote pacification. Alignment with the Germans brought them profitable jobs, education, and power.

Contact with the Germans also produced important alterations in political organization among the Beti. During the quarter century of German rule, administration of the Yaoundé district changed from one of ad hoc contact between Germans and individual headmen, with their traditional positions in the society, to the beginnings of a full-fledged colonial administration created to bring the area under military control, produce revenues, and provide laborers for public works such as roads and railroads.

The Administration

The linchpin of the German colonial administration was the district commander (*Bezirksamtmann*). In the Yaoundé district in the 1890s, the administrative problem, as the Germans saw it, was to devise a way to mobilize large numbers of Beti to perform functional tasks, such as road building and tax collecting, and to create some semblance of political control over a large geographic region. The Germans had no ready-made blueprint for colonial administration; Germany had little experience with overseas colonies until the 1880s. Attempts at creating local administrations were improvised in response to local conditions and often bore the stamp of the colonial administrators who created them. It is true that Governor Jesko von Puttkammer worked hard for German commercial interests in Cameroon, and little stood in his way of finding African laborers for them, until his removal from office in 1907; and Bernhard von Dernburg, state secretary for colonies from 1907 to 1910, favored a greater use of African intermediaries. But the reality was that, in the rainforest, local German commanders were relatively free to set their own policies with little possible recourse from the Africans affected by them.

Initially, German interest was chiefly in building the Yaoundé station and opening roads and trails to the coast and farther into the interior. No carefully considered policy of native administration was ever on the books, and much of what was later referred to as German colonial policy was locally improvised and reflected the personality and interests of individual station chiefs like Georg Zenker and Hans Dominik, the first two administrators of the Yaoundé station.

From 1889 to 1894, the station was directed by a civilian botanist, Zenker, who later retired with his African wife to a farm near the coast. Zenker was preoccupied with the difficulties of constructing the post, securing provisions, and clearing roads and trails. He was also a careful observer of life at the station and published two articles on the station and people near Yaoundé.

It was Major Hans Dominik, more than anyone else, who symbolized German policy for the Beti. He was chief of the Yaoundé station from 1895 to 1898 and again from 1902 until his death in 1910. Dominik arrived in Yaoundé in 1895 as the military replacement for Zenker. During this first tour, which lasted three years, he concentrated on bringing the Sanaga River area under control and further building the station and extending its routes. He also began the practice of sending Beti headmen's sons to German schools on the coast and replacing Dahomian slaves in the colonial forces with locally recruited troops.[17]

From 1898 to 1902, Dominik was in North Cameroon, and when he returned he brought with him cattle, which until then had not been kept in the Yaoundé region. In 1902, Dominik returned to Yaoundé, where he stayed for most of the next eight years. Twice he was taken ill and returned to Germany; on both occasions he was prematurely recalled in 1906 and 1910, to put down revolts among the Maka, a nearby Bantu language group not related to the Beti.

In 1910 the Yaoundé post became a full military district, incorporating Ebolowa and Dume. Dominik, now a major, was its commandant. In December 1910, though, he died en route to Germany to complete his medical leave.[18] The Beti called him "governor" and gave him the sobriquet *ebe Sso*, a *Sso* symbol, which meant that he had a strong sense of justice and could see everywhere. They also described him as "the fire that burns peppers" and "leopard-lion."[19]

The Beti say he spoke some Ewondo badly, was quick-tempered and loud, traveled a great deal, and knew the local groups better than any other administrator of the German period. The powers of summary justice were his, and Dominik hung several chiefs whom he thought were plotting against him. The Reichstag in Berlin investigated a charge that he allowed war prisoners to be mutilated by their captors without interfering. Despite his severity, Dominik was well liked by the Beti, who named many children "Dzomonigi," a transliteration of his name.[20] Unlike Zenker, whose detailed reports on the Beti rank him among the most observant of the Cameroonian colonial figures, Dominik rarely mentioned Africans in anything but clichés. He called the Beti a "childish folk, not to be trusted"; they were like the wild horse that obeyed only the rider who had control of the reins and knew how to use his spurs.[21]

His larger loyalty was to "mother, Fatherland, and regiment," and his idea of colonization was summed up in the following statement: "The real colonist in African should be a practical man; he should learn to leave his rank and understand manual work ... general rules can never be established for a colony, for the care of the land, the planting of potatoes, the layout of gardens ... all that should be decided locally, as should relations with the natives. This is very important in the practice of colonial policy."[22]

Dominik also had what appeared to be a set speech, which he delivered to the Beti and other Africans through an interpreter. Its essence was, "The white man has come to bring order to the country so that all men will live in peace, work, and build new houses and roads." Warfare and killing would cease, Africans would learn the white men's ways, and "everyone will obey the Kaiser, who sent the whites to the blacks. The riches of the whites will pass to the blacks, those of the blacks equally to the whites." Disbelievers risked exile, prison sentences, and fines.[23]

Dominik was first of all a soldier, and little of his Prussian sentimentality was ever translated into concern for the Africans. Nevertheless, he handpicked the rudiments of a new Beti elite, whom he sent for training to Buea, Douala, and Germany and did not hesitate to incorporate Africans into responsible positions in the administration. His quarters in Yaoundé were simple, and he received many visits from Africans. A few, like Charles Atangana, his interpreter who later became an important chief, were invited to dine with him.[24]

Compound "Mayors"

During the first fifteen years of their administration in Yaoundé, the Germans improvised a system in which local headmen were recognized as "mayors" (that is what the Beti called them) of compounds and surrounding lands. Such recognition was usually extended to headmen who had befriended a German caravan, sold the Germans food, or otherwise won their favor. Sometimes the Germans appointed men who were not headmen in traditional society, but were headmen's brothers or clients. This frequently resulted in conflicts of authority within the compound. The Beti tell stories of the Germans coming to compounds while the headman was absent, being entertained by a headman's brother or client, and giving him a paper naming him a chief. Headman created in this fashion by the Germans were called by their people *nkukuma ntanga* or "the white man's chief," as opposed to *nkukuma nnam*, which meant "chiefs of the country."

Duties of the German-appointed local agents included providing lodging for the workers, porters, and caravans employed by the German administration, providing hospitality to Africans, including chiefs, who were convoked by the administration from distant regions, assembling the interested parties in disputes, assuring the cleanliness of the administrative post, caring for the post's livestock and plantations, translating and interpreting drum messages, and reporting news to the authorities.[25]

One of the first Beti named to such a post was Essono Ela, a Beti headman. He had given land to Kund and Tappenbeck, the original German explorers, and had thus won the Germans' confidence; he was named head of Dzungola Village on the outskirts of the Yaoundé station. Other Beti headmen later blamed him for facilitating the white man's settlement among them.[26]

Another such Yaoundé German agent was Onambele Mbazoa. Exiled to Victoria for several years, he returned after his release and became a chief and assessor in the Yaoundé African court.[27] Mvog Otu, another appointee, was removed for laziness and drunkenness. Accused of plotting against the Germans, he was one of several Ewondo sentenced to death by hanging in 1907. The Germans next picked a candidate, Fuda Medzi, from the Mvog Fouda lineage. He was later asked to resign and went to live, in the words of an informant, as "*un grand bourgeois*" in a village forty miles south of Yaoundé.[28]

The Germans eventually concluded that their chiefly client system was not working. The Beti appointed to the position of mayor had little administrative experience, and tax revenues were not coming in. As German control expanded, a more disciplined element was needed, especially to collect taxes and carry out administrative functions, such as building roads and posts on the northern route to the ivory trade. Eventually the informal system of naming ad hoc Africans local agents was abandoned, and a network of appointed chiefs was named instead.

Beti Chiefs and the Tax Collection Problem

During the 1900s, an office of "chief" emerged that differed considerably in powers and duties from the headmen of traditional Beti society. Headmen inherited their positions, chiefs were appointed. Headmen and councils were the rulers of their compounds, responsible to themselves and their people, but chiefs were agents of the Germans. Headmen were accountable to the ancestors and were their representatives, but chiefs were first of all accountable to the colonial power.

Authority in the German administration was highly centralized. The Beti's system of autarchic kin groups living in continually fluctuating relationships with their neighbors was an untidy and unworkable institutional framework on which to base a colonial administration. The administrative problem, as the Germans saw it, was devising a way to mobilize large numbers of Beti to perform functional tasks and to create some semblance of political control over a large geographic region.

In 1903, the Germans established a direct tax, which was collected in kind by administrators and "mayors" from people living near the station. In 1904, they attempted to extend the tax to a wider area and collect it in German marks. This created problems, as marks were not widely circulated and the Germans had no desire to collect Beti iron bars. Also, the Germans had no idea of how many people lived within the station's jurisdiction.

On the African side, organizing the Beti for tax collection purposes fell to Karl Atangana, an Ewondo who had attended the Mission School at Kribi and who at that time was a clerk for the administration in Yaoundé. He was appointed supervisor of a group of Africans who took a census and arranged with headmen to collect the tax among principal Beti groups. He recommended a list of 300 headmen to serve as tax collectors. From this list the Germans selected 233 collectors who received a 5 percent rebate on whatever tax revenues they collected. Although Atangana did not have actual control of the tax collecting organization, the headmen were aware that his influence placed them in positions to receive the tax rebates. Already in favor with the Germans, he thus extended his influence with the Beti as well.

The first widespread tax among all Beti groups was established in October 1908. It required all grown males in Cameroon to pay six marks a year or perform thirty days of labor (*steuerarbeit*, or labor tax) on public works, for which they received neither pay nor food unless they had been sent a long distance. Students were exempted from this labor tax, but apprentices were not. The rebate for chiefs who helped collect the tax was increased to 7.5 percent.[29]

When the Germans appointed a Beti chief, they gave him a certificate on thick paper, bordered in red and black, and created with the imperial seal. It said the chief "has supported the German flag and is placed under the special protection of the Kaiser's government." A blank space followed in which special conditions were noted, such as the chief's agreeing to maintain roads in his district. The standard conditions applying to all chiefs were printed on the bottom of the certificate: the chiefs agreed to sell food to passing caravans, and if the caravans became lost or their members quarreled among themselves, chiefs agreed to inform the nearest Europeans.[30]

Chiefs kept tax receipt books, which became a sign of their authority. One colonial official advised an administrator against seizing the receipt books of chiefs who were in arrears. He said a chief's tax receipt book was an important sign indicating his tie with the administration, and taking it would be the equivalent of telling his people they were no longer under the post's protection.[31]

Chiefs were instructed to keep frequently traveled roads open and to maintain them; swamps and streams were also to be cleared and drainage ditches dug on both sides of the road, and the roads lined with citronella or palm trees to provide administrators shelter from the hot African sun. Another responsibility of the chiefs was to ensure that houses were grouped in units of at least six in a row perpendicular to the road, thus allowing for easy road repair. Chiefs could not move their compounds without authorization, and dwellers could not move without approval of the chief.[32]

Another important aspect of the German administration in Yaoundé was its efforts to build an African police force. The principal military force in the colony from 1891 to 1895 was the *polizeitruppe*, or police troops, composed mainly of Dahomians whom the Germans had bought from a Dahomian king who was preparing them for sacrificial slaughter. In December 1893, the Dahomians staged an uprising against the Germans in part because they did not receive their training stipends (but Cameroonians did) and in part because of repressive measures taken against them, such as a German order allowing their wives to be flogged publicly. The Dahomian troops were never popular among the Beti. Two were kidnapped after a dispute over payment for food purchases near Yaoundé. By 1895 most of the Dahomians had left the *polizeitruppe* and were replaced by Beti.[33]

A colonial force, similar to the force already in place in East Africa, was created in 1895, and in the following years the Beti joined it in great numbers. By 1914, the colonial force included 1,500 troops and 185 officers, while the police force numbered 1,200 men and 30 German officers.[34] Relations between the local populations and the colonial force were frequently marked by disputes. A 1915 list of rules for soldiers in the neighboring post of Ebolowa probably reflects the difficulties in Yaoundé and at other posts. Soldiers were allowed to have a woman or a serving boy live with them, station guards could keep both, but men who kept women were required to provide marriage certificates for them. Bride-price was fixed at 200 marks. Soldiers were prohibited from leaving the station without a European accompanying them, from going to villages to make purchases, and from bringing their serving boys with them on marches of less than one month in duration.

Strangers were not allowed to loiter near the post, and unemployed kinsmen of soldiers visiting their relatives at the station risked being conscripted to work on the railroad then under construction near the coast. Soldiers were instructed to keep their possessions in the caserne and not lend or rent them to people in nearby villages. Each soldier was issued sixty rounds of ammunition and was fined one mark for each bullet that disappeared without authorization. Hunting without permission was also forbidden.

In addition to the colonial forces, the administration also employed locally recruited messengers. The messengers were conscripted by a chief who was held responsible for their conduct. Each messenger received a starting salary of four marks a month, and ten marks after one year's service. They were not allowed to carry arms or to change their costumes to impersonate soldiers.

There was a second order of messengers, called route messengers, who delivered government communications and guarded prisoners. They received the same salary as other messengers but were armed and wore an insignia and a Roman numeral indicating the route number. Two were assigned to each road, usually covering a 10-kilometer stretch. Once a week the messengers reported to the station for new orders, which were written in two notebooks, one for them, the second for the station.[35]

German Justice

Many "palavers" or disputes between Africans, and between Africans and the administration, were settled by traveling German administrators, who served as itinerant judges. In an attempt to regularize the administration of justice, the Germans instituted a system of African courts in Douala in 1892. Such courts had jurisdiction in civil cases involving objects of less than 100 marks in value and in criminal cases with prison sentences of six months or less or a fine of 300 marks or less. There was also a second African appeals court.[36]

The most frequent penalty for minor offenses in German times was whipping, which had been permitted by decree since 1896. The decree limited the number of lashes that could be administered at any one time, and a physical examination supposedly preceded the flogging.

By 1911/12, the number of Africans punished for crimes was 11,229, including 2,781 crimes of property. Approximately 4,800 whippings were administered. There were 584 prison sentences of over six months, and 4,147 under six months; 943 fines were levied.[37]

A court of Native Arbitration at Yaoundé was organized by the Germans in 1911. It had an Ewondo president, a Benë vice president, eight assessors, including five Ewondo and three Benë, a clerk, cashier, registrar, and twelve police officers. The court had both a judicial and an administrative function. Its legal jurisdiction was limited to civil cases, and decisions were by majority vote. Two years was the limit for any sentences the court might give. Court decisions were reviewed and carried out by the administration. Appeals could be made to the appeals court within two weeks.[38]

Administratively the Beti court members had two additional functions: to announce German orders to the Africans and to win confidence for the administration. Their other function was to advise the Germans about what was happening among the Beti, and how the populace reacted to German orders.

Karl Atangana, "He Who Is Known by the Nations"

The office of highest political importance that an African could hold in the German administration was that of *Oberhäuptling*, or superior chief, a position that had not existed in traditional society. In the Yaoundé region, this position was held by Karl Atangana, a Beti headman's son who attended a German school and worked his way up in the administration as clerk and translator, until he was named superior chief in 1914, shortly before World War I.

Atangana was born in circa 1884 near Yaoundé, the eleventh of twelve sons of an Ewondo headman, which would have left him out of the line of succession to become head of his father's lineage segment. When Atangana was one year old, his father died, and he was raised by a father's brother. He worked as a houseboy for one of the Germans at the Yaoundé station, and in 1895 was among the first Beti to attend the Pallottiner Mission School in Kribi, where he remained for two years.[39]

Schooling and contact with the Germans shaped the future path Atangana followed. He spoke and wrote fluent German, and specimens of his handwriting and signature show a neat, almost engraver's script.[40] After two years' instruction, Atangana was baptized a Catholic on 31 October 1897 at the church in Kribi. He appeared to be unfaltering in his acceptance of the new religion, attended services regularly, gave the church land and gifts, and was quick to condemn such Beti rituals as the *Sso* rite as being pagan and uncivilized.[41] Look behind the veil of Atangana's newly accepted religious beliefs, and you find a devout convert. This was true of most Beti who became Catholics in large numbers and who became orthodox Christians with few traces of retained indigenous beliefs.

Atangana's rise to power was inseparable from his work with the German administration. His first post was in 1900 at Buea, the colonial capital, where he became a medical assistant and interpreter for the administration and the community of several hundred Beti plantation workers living there. Next he returned to Yaoundé to work as a clerk and interpreter.

In relations between Germans and Africans, an interpreter had considerable influence. There are numerous accounts of Atangana's mediating on behalf of the Beti.[42] An elderly Beti informant recalled that his brother, who was also an interpreter, once argued with a German soldier, whose gun fired accidentally during the scuffle. Instead of condemning the Beti to prison for fighting with a German, as would be expected, the African was told to carry a heavy load back to his village, a loss of face for an interpreter. Atangana's intervention, however, saved the man from a prison sentence.

It was Dominik who sent Atangana to school in the mid 1890s; a few years later, Atangana became Dominik's chief African assistant, a relationship that lasted six years until Dominik's death in 1910. Atangana accompanied Dominik on at least fifteen of his administrative tours and pacification missions through the Yaoundé region. He acted as an interpreter and negotiator between the Germans and other Beti groups, but he never served as a soldier. His writings suggest a conciliatory and pacific temperament; his greatest use to the Germans was as a negotiator with the tribes with whom they came into conflict.[43]

His relationship with Dominik was one of unusual mutual confidence and respect, considering Dominik's fiery temperament and his general distrust of the Beti. Atangana was invited to his house, ate at the table with the Germans, a rarity in that period, and was singled out for some of the infrequent praise Dominik gave to Africans in his memoirs.[44]

From 1911 to 1913, Atangana worked in Hamburg at the Colonial Institute for further training in administration. While there he compiled a long collection of letters, fables, tales, and historical anecdotes in Ewondo and translated them into German. They were published as the *Jaunde-Texte* by a German linguist, Martin Heepe, of the Colonial Institute and remain invaluable for the study of this period of Beti history.

The letters show aspects of Atangana's personality as well as shed light on his relations with the Germans. He wrote, "To dare to approach the Germans it is necessary to abandon the traits which displease them, to become their friend and then to be valued by them." Unswerving loyalty was a characteristic of his attitude toward the Germans, and there is no indication that he ever modified his commitment to European customs and religion. He was an inordinately sensitive and sometimes jealous man, careful of guarding his prerogatives and position. The *Jaunde-Texte*, which includes accounts of Atangana's stay in Germany, describes a visit by the Kaiser to the Colonial Institute in Hamburg while Atangana was there. Although he did not meet the Kaiser, apparently they did exchange glances. It was enough for Atangana to build an anecdote around, the conclusion of which was the exchange of looks was almost the same as a personal encounter.[45] In his written accounts, opponents or those who disagreed with him came to naught. At one point Atangana wrote, "A number of persons who associated themselves with Europeans and proved themselves useful to white people achieved positions in the native society through fraud and extortion. But the Europeans, having noticed it, stopped it. They could discern natives of the noble class by their loyalty and honesty."[46] The implication was clear: schemers would fall, but Africans who were loyal and honest, as he was, would be rewarded by the Germans.

Atangana's commentaries on Beti society are illuminating in most cases, but misleading in others. For example, his claims of noble birth are pure invention; he translated *nkukuma* as "king," a term that distorts the headman's traditionally limited role in Beti society. He also claimed descent from a royal lineage, but none existed among the Beti. He further stated that his father, Atangana Essomba, was Superior Chief of the Ewondo and Benë, when in fact he was one of several hundred headmen.[47]

Atangana received two appointments that moved him to the pinnacle of power in native administration. In 1911 he was named president of the local court of the

Ewondo and Benë. The court handled most property, marriage, and civil disputes between Africans, could levy fines and set prison sentences of up to two years, relayed German orders to the local people, and reported the people's reaction back to the administration. Criminal and political cases were left for the Germans.

From this powerful position Atangana moved to an even stronger one. Shortly after his return from Germany he was named *Oberhäuptling,* superior chief, of the Ewondo and Benë. The provisional appointment was made on 25 March 1914, to take full effect the following year if ratified by the two groups. In speaking of Atangana's new position, a Beti source said he thought it actually made little difference to the people because they knew they had to pass through him to have access to the white man in any case.[48]

Atangana was in his early thirties at the time. He had a position unparalleled in Beti history; his new post gave him virtual control over the Ewondo and Benë and, because of his closeness to the Germans, importance vis-à-vis other groups as well. His drum name at this time was "He who is known by the nations."

Atangana built a large house and furnished it in the German colonial manner with locally made European-style furniture. Set on the crest of a hill at Mvolye near the mission station, it was larger than the district officer's house and almost the size of the missionary building. Any important Africans who came to the region stayed with Atangana, who extended hospitality but could also kept track of their business.

Atangana also created a twenty-member band with instruments and uniforms from Germany. The musicians were sent to Kribi in order to learn German military and promenade music and played at public gatherings, religious holidays, African weddings, and other celebrations. There was no charge for their services, but only Atangana could tell them where to play. The band was one of the many devices employed by Atangana for rendering a service to others while simultaneously winning credit for bringing it about.[49]

A Changing World

The two decades of contact with Germans resulted in significant changes in Beti political organization. The major innovation was the imposition of a colonial administration with its numerous European and African agents on what had once been an acephalous society. A new sense of territoriality, the colony, was introduced, with accompanying demands for tax revenues, road work, and other forms of service. African agents of the administration intervened in the society in ways that would have not been traditionally possible.

It required considerable skills to have influence in both the African and European spheres, and among the Beti, only Karl Atangana emerged equally strong in both. He had begun his life in a situation comparable to that of any other Beti youth, but with the disadvantage that he was not in line to succeed his own father as headman. Atangana realized that his advancement dependent on his relationship with the Germans, and his record was one of both accepting increasing responsibility from the colonial administration and expanding his influence over the Beti, a process that continued uninterrupted until World War I.

Drawing a balance sheet on the extent of internal change within the Beti in the period 1887–1916 involves an element of speculation. What is certain is that free Beti migrations through the rainforest decreased sharply, armed feuding diminished to almost nothing, and an order of chiefs replaced headmen in most of the Yaoundé region. What is less certain is how this changing headman's role influenced other levels of Beti society. There is not much evidence that polygamy diminished among the Beti during the German period. The institution of compound slavery ceased; but in all likelihood most former slaves continued to live as before in the *nda bod* where they had been held captive but where they had food and lodging. The system of clients living with prosperous headmen continued, largely because bride-price remained high throughout Beti history. This meant that young men, unable to raise it, would offer their services as fieldworkers for headmen, and the headman would, after due service was rendered, provide bride-price.

Notes

1. H. Rudin, *Germans in the Cameroons: A Case Study in Modern Imperialism, 1884–1915* (New Haven, 1938), pp. 18ff. "Expedition von Hauptmann Kund," Freiherr von Dankelman, ed., *Mittheilungen von Forschungsreisenden und Gelehrten aus den Deutschen Schutzgebieten* (Berlin, 1889), pp. 61ff. "Reise von Lieutenant Tappenbeck von der Jaunde-Station über den Sannaga nach Ngila's Residenz," *Mittheilungen von Forschungsreisenden und Gelehrten aus den Deutschen Schutzgebieten*, vol. 2 (Berlin, 1890), pp. 109–13. H. Schnee, *Deutsches Kolonial-Lexikon*, vol. I (Leipzig, 1920), pp. 128–29. S. Passarge, "Die Geschichte der Erforschung und Eroberung Kameruns," *Zeitschrift für Kolonialpolitik, Kolonialrecht und Kolonialwirtschaft* (1908): pp. 557–75. C. von Morgen, *Durch Kamerun von Süd nach Nord* (Leipzig, 1893), pp. 49–50.
2. Rudin, *Germans in the Cameroons*, pp. 120 ff.
3. Ibid., pp. 235–36.
4. "Expedition von Hauptmann Kund," Freiherr von Dankelman, p. 61. Schnee, *Deutsches Kolonial-Lexikon*, pp. 128–29. Passarge, "Die Geschichte der Erforschung und Eroberung Kameruns," pp. 557–75. Morgen, *Durch Kamerun von Süd nach Nord*, pp. 49–50. Rudin, *Germans in the Cameroons*, p. 82.
5. Rudin, *Germans in the Cameroons*, p. 82. Pierre Mebe, interview with author, Yaoundé, 8 November 1966.
6. *Ewondo* is also the Beti word for "groundnut." The Ewondo referred to themselves as being "as numerous as groundnuts." Pierre Mebe, interview with author, Yaoundé, 22 February 1968. "Geschichte von Mbidemenge," in M. Heepe, *Jaunde-Texte von Karl Atangana und Paul Messi* (Hamburg, 1919), pp. 237–43.
7. T. Tsala, "Grammaire Ewondo," Mvolye, pp. 257–58. Morgen, *Durch Kamerun von Süd nach Nord*, pp. 173–78.
8. A chronicle of several of the most important incidents in the Yaoundé region is contained in Passarge, "Die Geschichte der Erforschung und Eroberung Kameruns," pp. 557–75.
9. O. Zimmermann, *Durch Busch und Steppe von Campo bis zum Schari (1892–1902)* (Berlin, 1909), pp. 52ff. Théodore Tsala, interview with author, Mvolye, 17 February 1968. Pierre Mebe, interview with author, Yaoundé, 10 May 1967. H. Dominik, *Kamerun* (Berlin, 1901), pp. 155–57. See also Rudi Kaeselitz, "Kolonialeroberung und Widerstandskampf in Südkamerun (1884–1907)," pp. 26–33, in Helmuth Stoecker, *Kamerun Unter Deutscher Kolonialherrschaft*, vol. II (Berlin: Deutscher Verlag der Wissenschaften, 1968), and Heepe, *Jaunde-Texte*, pp. 75–79.
10. Passarge, "Die Geschichte der Erforschung und Eroberung Kameruns," p. 569. "Kamerun, Bericht uber die Bane-Bulu Expedition," in *Deutsches Kolonialblatt* 16, 15 (August 1896): pp.

498–504. Cameroon National Archives (CNA) TA-39, "Rapport Dominik du 25.9.1885," p. 6. Dominik, *Kamerun*, p. 217.
11. Zimmermann, *Durch Busch und Steppe*, p. 89.
12. Morgen, *Durch Kamerun von Süd nach Nord*, pp. 60–61, 78–80, 85. Dominik, *Kamerun*, pp. 66, 237.
13. Morgen, *Durch Kamerun von Süd nach Nord*, pp. 78–80, 85.
14. T. Tsala, letter to author, 21 September 1969; Gotefried Bisso Medza, Interview with author, Dzeng, 26 March 1968.
15. Heepe, *Jaunde-Texte*, p. 241.
16. Gotfried Bisso Medza, interview with author, Dzeng, 26 March 1968.
17. See entry on "Dominik" in Schnee, *Deutsches Kolonial-Lexikon*, I, p. 471.
18. T. Tsala, interview with author, Mvolye, 3 March 1968. Schnee, *Deutsches Kolonial-Lexikon*, I, p. 471. *Amtsblatt für die Schutzgebeit Kamerun*, 14 October 1912, pp. 311–13.
19. T. Tsala, letter to author, 29 November 1969.
20. Interviews were conducted by the author with T. Tsala, Mvolye, 6 June 1968; Max Abe Foudda, Nkolbewa, 23 December 1967; Pierre Mebe, Yaoundé, 30 November 1967; François Atangana, Yaoundé, 2 May 1967.
21. H. Dominik, *Vom Atlantik zum Tschadsee, Kriegs-und Forschungsfahrten in Kamerun* (Berlin, 1908), p. 32.
22. Ibid., p. 38.
23. Max Abe Foudda, interview with author, Nkolbewa, 23 December 1967.
24. Gotefried Bisso Medza, interview with author, Dzeng, 26 March 1968.
25. C. Atangana, "Signification des Mots Politiques," MS, Institut de Recherches Scientifiques du Cameroun, pp. 6–7.
26. T. Tsala, letter to author, 21 November 1969.
27. C. Atangana, "Signification des Mots Politiques," pp. 4–5. T. Tsala, letter to author, 21 November 1969.
28. T. Tsala, letter to author, 21 November 1969. Fouda Medzi's rise in importance was translated in his drum name as "The blacksmith who never made an axe or a shoe has begun with an *nken*," a musical instrument reserved for the most accomplished craftsmen to make.
29. Rudin, *Germans in the Cameroons*, pp. 341–42.
30. *Schutzbrief*, Yaoundé, 29 August 1905, author's copy.
31. CNA 1526, p. 8.
32. Ibid.
33. Rudin, *Germans in the Cameroons*, pp. 192–94.
34. Ibid., pp. 194–95. Dominik, *Kamerun*, p. 231. T. Tsala, letter to author, 8 April 1969.
35. CNA 1526, p. 3.
36. Rudin, *Germans in the Cameroons*, pp. 199–201.
37. Ibid., pp. 202–3. Heepe, *Jaunde-Texte*, p. 241.
38. Atangana, "Signification des Mots Politiques," pp. 8–11.
39. T. Tsala, interview with author, Mvolye, 18 July 1968.
40. H. Skolaster, *Die Pallottiner in Kamerun, 25 Jahre Missionbeit* (Limburg, 1924), pp. 248–49.
41. C. Atangana, "Aken Sso (le Rite Sso) chez les Yaoundés-Banes," in *Anthropos*, 38–40 (1942–1945): pp. 149–57.
42. T. Tsala, interview with author, Mvolye, 18 July 1968.
43. Heepe, *Jaunde-Texte*, p. 137.
44. Dominik, *Vom Atlantik zum Tschadsee*, p. 38.
45. Heepe, *Jaunde-Texte*, pp. 87–89.
46. Ibid., pp. 107–111. Atangana, "Signification des Mots Politiques," pp. 3–5.
47. Ibid., p. 5.
48. T. Tsala, interview with author, Mvolye, 1 July 1968.
49. Pierre Elon, interview with author, Mvolye, 1 August 1968. In the mid 1960s, four members of the band were still alive, with tattered uniforms and bent German instruments. They made the rounds of Yaoundé's European restaurants on Sundays, playing for change, and were sometimes hired for airport farewells as well. When the author asked if they knew "Deutschland Über Alles," their aged leader whispered, "Yes, but we cannot play it while the French are here."

CHAPTER 4

The German Presence
Traders and Missionaries

During the German period, the influx of peddlers and goods from the coast significantly affected the patterns of Beti trade. The Beti were recent migrants to the lands they occupied in the 1880s and grew most of the crops necessary to sustain them; their crops were supplemented by hunting. There was some bartering of produce between women from different compounds, but no regular markets or currency existed. Small iron bars were circulated, but mainly for bridewealth payment. Locally made baskets, iron arrow tips, machetes, and hoes were exchanged by women for foodstuffs, but none of these items appears to have been traded to any extent between the Beti and other tribes.[1]

It is difficult to determine when the coastal trade began to reach the interior in any volume. Beti oral sources suggest that such trade was not extensive before the Germans arrived in the late 1880s.

Some of the coastal tribes had a long history of trading with the Europeans. The Duala, a small tribe living on the coast, had established contact with the Europeans since the late eighteenth century when they exchanged slaves with the Portuguese for guns, powder, salt, rum, and cloth. By the mid nineteenth century, the Duala had mostly abandoned farming and devoted themselves almost exclusively to trade, depending on imported tinned goods as a chief source of food. By 1820, several English firms were established on the coast, and the important German firm of Woermann in 1866 opened a factory in Douala.[2]

The greatest obstacle to the inland trade in this part of Cameroon was the intransigence of the Basa and their southern neighbors, the Ngoumba. The Basa never developed long distance trade, and both groups acquired goods from the Duala and traded them with Beti in the immediate neighborhood or allowed the coastal trade caravans to move inland once fees had been paid to the headmen. These Basa and Ngoumba headmen do not appear to have exerted political or military influence much beyond their own small territories but had the advantage of controlling a key location through which traders had to pass to gain access to

---

Notes for this chapter begin on page 72.

the interior. Among the Ngoumba, the headman Tonga was frequently mentioned by the Germans as a source of difficulty. He harassed Morgen's expedition and obliged the Beti to sell him their ivory and rubber, which he then traded with the Germans for a profit.[3]

The Caravans Move Inland

The Germans penetration of the interior radically altered the power of such intermediaries, chiefly by opening direct trails inland under armed German control, allowing free movement of Europeans and Africans between the coast and interior. In the late 1880s, the Kribi-Yaoundé trail through the rainforest took twenty-two days, but by 1990 the time was reduced to fifteen days, and the path was widened and improved. German traders now had direct access to the interior, and the Beti could move freely to the coast as well.

A major and unpredicted result of opening the new routes was that a proliferation of African traders leading small caravans increasingly made their way inland, often in competition with the Germans. While they lacked the range of merchandise available to the larger German sponsored caravans, many small traders visited points far off the main tracks and developed an elaborate credit system that often extended the payment period to six months or more.

German merchants also extended credit to some of these African caravan leaders. For example, a Duala caravan chief might be outfitted with trading goods on the condition that he return several months later with a quantity of ivory, palm oil, palm kernels, and rubber for the European trader who outfitted him. If it was necessary to give the African trader most of the goods on credit, he paid his European outfitter a proportionally larger amount of rubber or ivory than would another African caravan leader with some collateral.

African coastal traders skillfully played one European merchant off against another, even after the trader and his supplier had agreed to terms. Still, German government efforts to limit extending credit to African traders was strongly opposed by merchants like Woermann, who maintained that no government had the right to interfere with a private contract.[4] Trader-government differences were a feature of German colonial life, as they would be with the French a few decades later.

One German traveler, while moving to the coast from Yaoundé in 1895, passed sixteen caravans moving inland. He called the zone between Kribi and the Nachtigal Falls a free trade area and said the Basa's role as intermediaries had been supplanted; he implied the Duala were the chief beneficiaries of the increased trade. He noted that two African traders, leading their own thirty-porter caravans, had recently arrived at Yaoundé. These smaller African caravans made eight- to fourteen-day swings through the interior in quest of rubber and ivory, but they were costly endeavors for their African proprietors to mount. The larger German expeditions numbered up to 120 porters and stayed longer in the field.[5]

Hans Dominik, the Yaoundé station chief, complained in 1895 of the influx of ambulant African peddlers in the Yaoundé region, where he said they were siphoning the Beti trade away from the Germans. He believed the indigenous traders told the Beti to raise prices demanded by the Germans and complained that such peddlers had numerous disputes with the Beti over uncollected debts and for rubber promised but not delivered. Dominik decided to have all such peddlers register with the station as a way of regulating their activities. By 1908, there were four thousand peddlers in the colony, the largest percentage of them African.[6]

Dominik wanted to draw the northern Hausa traders toward Yaoundé and the Germans; in 1897, the first Hausa peddlers crossed Beti lands to the coast. The Beti remember the Hausa's coming, for they introduced a new and superior type of kola nut to the Beti. They say, however, the Hausa traders never came to the Beti regions in any numbers during German times, although many settled in Yaoundé during the French administration. Except as a source of ivory and slaves, the Hausa had little interest in the Beti and feared reports of Beti cannibalism.[7]

No figures are available on British and French trade with the Beti. It was probably small, as the main area of British trade interest lay considerably northwest of Beti lands, while the French were concentrated to the south and east in the Congo River watershed.

Ivory

During the first two decades of German colonial rule in Cameroon, the ivory trade dominated exports, but between 1905 and 1915 ivory exports dropped to almost half their former volume because most elephants in the Beti territory and elsewhere in southern Cameroon had been killed. From more than one million marks worth of exports in 1905, the Cameroonian ivory trade dropped to about half that figure by 1910.[8]

The inland ivory trade among the Beti and some neighboring tribes was a time-consuming, complicated process usually involving three or four different exchanges before the ivory reached the coast.[9] The sequence, as described by Zenker in 1895, was as follows: a coastal middleman, such as a Basa or Duala trader, spent several months among the Ewondo, encouraging them to procure ivory for him. The Ewondo headman's agents, probably his sons or brothers, then went to the Eton or another group living near the savanna to obtain an elephant tusk, for which they left a woman or child as temporary hostage until the transaction was completed. Then the Ewondo sold the ivory to the coastal middleman, who provided partial payment in European goods, often a rifle and powder. The middleman then returned to his own village with the ivory, indicating a date when the Ewondo should visit him to receive the completed payment. A few days before this date, the Ewondo, accompanied by kinsmen, arrived at the rendezvous point. The middleman cordially greeted him, after which a long haggle over final payment for the ivory followed. Once the exchange was completed, the Ewondo returned to his own compound and sent the necessary goods or money to the Eton who would release the woman or child left earlier as a guarantee. Zenker said the ivory could exchange hands another time among the coastal middlemen, thus completing a three- or four-phase transaction before it reached the European traders. He stated that the whole transaction often took several months to complete.[10]

Other exports were groundnuts and palm kernels. Children and old people gathered the latter, and the men made palm oil from them. An increasingly important export during the first decade of the twentieth century was wild rubber, tapped from local trees by the Beti, boiled, sold, and shipped to Europe.

In 1895, Dominik wrote that rifles, powder, iron implements, copper for body decoration, tobacco, rice, cloth, European clothes, umbrellas, petrol lamps, rum, gin, and salt were being imported into the interior. Salt was marketed in ten- to fifteen-pound bags, or smaller quantities of less than a pound, and was exchanged for slaves before the Germans forbid the slave trading. The Beti accused coastal traders of mixing sand with the salt, but the traders complained that Beti rubber, sold by its weight, often contained sand as well.[11]

Determining what the prices were during this period is difficult because trade was based on a barter system, which produced considerable variation in price, depending on the bargainer's skill. One report of prices in the mid 1850s was 11 marks per kilogram for ivory, 2.50 for rubber, 0.12 for palm nuts, and 0.22 marks a liter for palm oil. In the interior, prices were considerably less; for example, the cost of palm kernels inland was estimated to be one-third of what it was on the coast.[12]

Morgen gave an indication of prices for the Yaoundé region in 1889. These prices included:

- One chicken for either approximately three-quarters a meter of cloth, a small sack of beads, or an ordinary pocketknife
- One large sheep for a 7.5-meter long bolt of cloth
- One small sheep for approximately six meters of cloth
- One egg for two porcelain buttons
- Seven ears of corn for one porcelain button
- One stack of plantains for seven buttons
- One pineapple for four buttons

Porcelain buttons were used for paying porters. Six small buttons, worth about a pfennig at the time, represented a day's salary for a porter, which he exchanged for bananas, plantains, or yams. Morgen said such prices should not be considered astonishing because considerable distance separated Yaoundé from the coast, European goods were much in demand, and foodstuffs were abundant.[13]

Weights, Measures, and Currency

Several improvised measuring units were used for the coastal and inland trade, including the Kru, Beloko, Keg, Piggin, and bar. A Kru represented the amount of European merchandise that could be traded for a quantity of African goods that had been fixed at a value of one pound of sterling. A Kru divided into four kegs, eight piggins, or twenty iron bars.[14] The Kru had no set value of its own and both African and German traders, improvised its value as markets allowed. After 1894, the German government attempted to replace these improvised units of measurement with the metric system and payment in goods by payment in German marks.

German traders opposed the administration in this measure as they did in its efforts at firearms control, because they believed they would amass higher profits through continuing the barter system.[15]

In an effort to equalize currency values in 1905, the Germans set the worth of a pound of sterling at twenty marks and twenty French francs were valued at sixteen marks. The Austrian Maria Theresa thaler of 1870, long used as a coastal currency of choice, was forbidden by the Germans, who wanted their own currency to prevail, but the thaler could still be redeemed for 1.50 marks. For the Beti, the locally circulated iron bars used chiefly in bridewealth transactions were worth one pfennig each, and 100 such bars were worth one mark.[16]

In 1905, the administration began paying its workers in cash instead of goods. This was both part of the effort to establish a monetary standard in the colony and to cut the costs of providing food, since until then the administration assumed responsibility for feeding its workers. As a further effort to control currency, the Germans formally barred importing cowrie shells in 1911, but this measure did not affect the Beti, who did not use cowrie shells as currency.[17]

Although inland commerce came rapidly to the Beti regions, few Beti became traders. Beti headmen fostered the self-image of being "Noble" and preferred to collect tribute and emoluments from caravans crossing their lands. They collected income from the sale of palm oil and other products gathered by their followers, but heading out on the trail with a caravan of goods to be bought and sold was simply outside the self-image of a Beti man. Thus, the Beti did not adopt the new skills necessary to compete with the Duala and the Germans.

Of those few Beti who did engage in trade, their rivals, and they themselves, had many satiric stories suggesting that the Beti were not strongly suited to commerce. The stories often involve a Beti making his way to the coast and encountering a Duala or a Basa. In one version, the Basa allowed a Beti traveler lodging for a night, but gave him a bed with a leg nearly sawed off; when it fell, the Beti was charged for a new bed. In another account, a Beti visitor to the coast was given a piece of cheese, liked it, and was subsequently sold a block of yellow soap instead, which he found sharper in taste.[18]

The Beti as Plantation Workers

Another important economic result of the opening of the new trail inland was the exodus of a continuing number of Beti to the coast as porters and field and plantation workers. By 1894, Dominik reported that the Ewondo were represented in large numbers as workers on the coastal plantations: "The Yaoundé people are scattered throughout the colony, engaged as soldiers or personal servants of the Europeans." He said they went in large caravans to coastal rubber plantations where the local people did not yet understand working with rubber.[19]

Those who made the exodus to work on plantations or in the fields were not headmen but their younger brothers, sons, and clients who, lacking both wives and land, found the prospect of a steady source of food, shelter, and money for bridewealth appealing. Thus, while many Beti men went to the coast as porters and plantation workers, the elders, men who were often heads of polygamous households, remained at home, occupying themselves with their compounds. The manner through which Beti left their villages ranged from voluntary decisions to improve their lot on the coast to coercion at the end of a rope. Native soldiers or police conducted raids and headmen sent workers to the coast for a fee.[20] As the need for plantation workers outstripped the number of available men, gross coercion was used to take Africans to the coast, especially in the late 1880s and early twentieth century, during the Jesko Von Puttkamer regime (1895–1907). Puttkamer was determined to establish an inland railroad, increase trade with Cameroon's North, and expand the colony's southern plantation economy. Ruthless in his methods, especially in the forced recruitment on laborers, he was in frequent conflict with missionaries and local peoples and was finally dismissed from his post as governor.

The rate of illness and death among the new workers was high. The change in location meant a new and unfamiliar diet; it also meant work in the coastal malarial zone. The explorer Dr. Günter Carnap-Quernheimb, who headed the Yaoundé station between Dominik's assignments there, estimated that one-third to one-half of the workers returned at the end of their tour, the implication being that death took a large number of those who did not return.[21] Another estimate placed the death rate among plantation workers at 20 percent. A death rate between 7 and 8 percent was recorded in different Victoria plantations at various times during the first decade of the twentieth century.[22] According to Dominik, the Beti preferred work as porters to that of plantation laborers because they could earn more money and remain close to their wives and their own land, with its familiar climate and food. Moreover, carriers could more easily set the pace of their work than could more closely supervised fieldworkers.

In 1908, the Germans tried to regulate the growing number of abuses affecting carriers. A decree required all carriers to be grown men, and, despite objections from the German traders, carrier's loads were fixed at 66 pounds, plus an additional 11 pounds for personal needs. A day's marching distance was set at three to four hours' walking time, and caravans were required to keep one reserve carrier for every ten carriers with loads.[23]

Each caravan was supposed to bring sufficient food or have adequate means to purchase it, as there were frequent quarrels over food supplies between caravan members and villagers on their routes. Sometimes carriers, having spent their food allowances for other purposes, raided gardens or villages for food and women. Carriers and plantation workers usually had contracts of a specific period, six, twelve, or eighteen months, and received six, eight, or nine marks a month respectively. Usually, half of their pay was held until the contract was completed. Some workers were paid in marks; others preferred payment in European goods, including rum, guns, and gun powder.[24]

The number of caravans reaching the interior grew sharply each year. In 1908, more than one thousand carriers during a single day passed through Lolodorf, an important crossroads on the Kribi-Yaoundé road, through which caravans moved in several directions across the rainforest.[25] The effect of long-distance trade on Beti society was to make available a variety of European goods to the Beti in turn for ivory, groundnuts, palm kernels and oil, and wild rubber. It also brought the German mark to the interior, but the most important effect of long-distance trade was opening an easily accessible route to and from the coast, allowing the Beti to move out in great numbers as porters and plantation workers. It likewise permitted coastal traders, until then blocked by the difficult route and intransigence of middlemen, to frequent the Yaoundé region in great numbers and dominate trade in Beti lands.

In 1910, the Germans estimated twenty thousand to thirty thousand porters worked between the coast and the interior of Cameroon. However, they did not distinguish between the numbers for East and West Cameroon. By 1913, nearly eighty thousand carriers were employed on the Kribi-Yaoundé road alone. It was estimated at the same time that plantations employed nearly eighteen thousand workers.[26]

In addition, there were at least five thousand African day or contractual laborers working on a railroad that, by 1914, ran between Douala and Edea on the coast. The Germans planned to build an inland railroad to Yaoundé, but World War I intervened with the tracks not much past Edea on the coast. There is no breakdown of railroad workers by ethnic group, but considering the exodus by the Beti to the coast for other forms of work, it is likely that a large percentage of these workers was Beti.

Work on the railroad was less attractive than portage or plantation work. Mortality rates were high, and recruits were taken from their families, frequently were ill-fed and exposed to diseases like influenza. Railroad work camps moved frequently and stayed for long periods in unhealthy climates where malaria, dysentery and other tropical illnesses were widespread. Obtaining familiar food was a continual problem for workers who moved from one zone to another. The Germans complained of passive resistance to railroad recruitment by Africans, adding that men often disappeared in the forest until the recruiters left or sought work instead at the mission or at trading stations. But the German colonial presence was by no means monolithic; voices were divided between those who wanted progress at any cost and those who counted the human toll of colonization. Among the latter was Colonial Secretary Willhelm Solf, who wrote in 1913, "It is a sorry spectacle to see villages drained of all men folk, to watch women and children carry burdens, to find a whole people condemned to an itinerant way of life … family ties are severed because parents, spouses, and children are separated from each other. No more children are born because the women are separated from their husbands most of the year.[27]

The Arrival of the Missionaries

As the traders moved inland, so did the missionaries; both groups contributed to the transformation of traditional Beti society. One conclusion about the Beti encounter with Christianity during the German period is that the Beti quickly converted to Catholicism in large numbers and that their religious manifestations were orthodox. Beti became Roman Catholics as quickly as German missionaries came their way, and their acceptance of Catholicism seemed complete, void of the syncretism, religious bilingualism, and layering characteristics of other societies. The combination of Christian religion and a European presence was responsible for three major changes in the Beti society. German mission and government schools equipped Beti chiefs' sons and other young men with a new set of skills, values, and ambitions different from those available to their fathers. The *Sso* initiation rite was abolished, removing an important structural feature of Beti society and eventually destroying many of the symbolic explanations the Beti used for looking at themselves and their society. Polygamy was outlawed, and women were given a different role in society, although this transformation took decades to achieve.

German missionary work among the Beti, limited almost entirely to activities of the Roman Catholic Pallottiner order, began in 1890 and ended in January 1916, when the British entered Yaoundé, and the Germans were forced to leave Cameroon.

The first Beti to come in contact with Christianity were the children and young men Dominik sent to the Pallottiner School in Kribi. The Yaoundé students were attentive and enthusiastic to learn and before long represented half the schools' enrollment. By 1899, seventy-four boys and one girl had attended the school, including Karl Atangana, who within a decade would become the principal Beti employed in the German administration. Based on their children's contact with the mission, some Ewondo headmen asked the mission to establish schools in their regions, which coincided with the Pallottiners' desire to move inland.[28]

The first German missionary to enter Beti lands was Msgr. Henri Vieter, who with two other Pallotti fathers, arrived in Yaoundé on 13 February 1901. Msgr. Vieter, who had been apostolic prefect of Cameroon since it was declared a mission field in 1890, made the trip from Kribi to Yaoundé in sixteen days and rented two rooms from a Duala trader who was leaving for the coast.[29]

An Ewondo headman, Esomba Ngonti, gave the mission several acres of land on one of the highest hills in the area, a pleasant location half an hour from the German station. There were usually two or three priests and a brother at the station during most of the following fifteen years.[30]

The Pallottiner sisters, who arrived in 1903, taught the Beti women basic Catholic doctrine, household skills, the rudiments of healthcare and sanitation, and the values of monogamous marriage. These institutions were known locally as "sixa," pidgin English for "sister," and, despite the educational benefits they gave Beti women, they became an unremitting cause of friction with polygamous headmen.[31]

The Germans also created several Christian villages, such as Nkol Bisson and Mvog Ada, where converts lived together to avoid pagan influences. Eventually, as the number of Christians expanded, the number of such villages decreased.[32]

The Pallottiners' curriculum included an introduction to Catholic teaching, the rudiments of reading, writing, and mathematics and—in the afternoon—brickmaking, masonry, carpentry, and manual work at the mission station to pay for tuition.[33]

Catechisms in Ewondo, the Beti dialect spoken around Yaoundé, and German were published by the Pallottiners in 1910, and Ewondo was a required language for the German missionaries. As the missionaries moved to other parts of Beti lands, accompanied by Ewondo catechists and schoolteachers, the Ewondo dialect gained widespread use among the Beti.[34]

The Relationship between the Mission and Government

The missionaries' success was aided by the German administration's cooperative attitude, something that was generally not true of relations between French Roman Catholic missionaries and the French administration in later times. It was Dominik who had sent the first Beti students to the Kribi schools in the late 1890s, and on occasion he left women or children taken on punitive raids with the mission for upbringing. In the uncomplicated, vigorous style in which he expressed himself, Dominik approved of the "straightforward, practical, German Christianity" the mission taught, noting that the German sisters worked beside their students in the fields. He said the Ewondo were eager to learn, and many young men sought jobs as domestic servants for Europeans so they could later attend the mission school.[35]

Numerically, the mission's record was one of constant expansion. Church membership rose from a handful of converts who had come into contact with the Pallottiners at the coastal schools in Kribi in the late 1890s to over twenty thousand living Christians in 1916, most of them along the routes the Germans built or in enclaves near the mission station. The Beti accepted Christianity without resistance, and with more missionaries it probably would have made an even greater impact.

By the end of 1913, the cumulative number of Beti converts had reached 17,300 persons, of whom 5,590 had been added that year, and 6,580 catechumens were being prepared for church membership. Two schools at the Yaoundé station and thirty-two satellite schools were teaching 5,439 boys and 260 girls. Additionally, there were forty-one African lay teachers employed by the mission who assisted the six German priests, four brothers, and five sisters. By 1 January 1916 when the Pallottiners left Yaoundé, they had made 28,000 converts, of whom 21,000 were living; another 9,565 catechumens were preparing for church membership.[36]

Numerically, there was a gradual progression of Beti who became Christians. It is more difficult to ascertain the extent to which Beti society was restructured and the Beti worldview shaped by missionary contact. One important result of such contact was the abolishment of the *Sso* rite, the most important ritual in Beti society, by the Germans during the early twentieth century. This contributed greatly to changing the traditional Beti structure of society and outlook on the world. There are two accounts of the end of the *Sso* rite "in the time of Major Dominik," one given by missionaries, the other from Beti oral traditions; both are similar in their essential details but differ in their interpretations of what transpired. According to the German account, in H. Skolaster's book on the Pallottiner Mission, in 1901 a missionary attended a gathering of about three hundred African men near Yaoundé; one of his young monitors became involved in a dispute and lost a finger when struck by one of the pagan *Sso* candidates armed with a machete.[37]

The Beti account says the young man, who was uninitiated in the *Sso* rite, tried to enter the *Sso* candidates' compound, which all Beti knew was forbidden under pain of death to anyone but the initiated, and lost a finger when he was struck while being evicted by the candidates. The Beti said the interloper was a student in the mission school who, anxious to show that he eschewed paganism, disrupted one of the *Sso* ceremonies.[38]

To declare a rite illegal is different from actually abolishing it. What appears to have happened is that the *Sso* diminished over a decade or so as the administration-missionary presence spread. Yaoundé oral accounts say it was effectively abolished within the first few years after 1900. Among the Benë, there are isolated accounts of the *Sso* continuing until after 1910. In the opinion of P. Nekes, a Roman Catholic missionary writing about 1912, the *Sso* and similar rites were fast disappearing with the spread of mission schools. Children at mission schools were also given meat, which until then had been reserved for elders and *Sso* graduates.[39]

When in 1935 a French administrator interested in ethnography wanted to reconstruct the rite for a film, it was necessary for him to go to Eton country, where old men resurrected the rite for him. This was in part because the Christianized Beti around Yaoundé regarded the *Sso* rite as a souvenir of pagan days and opposed its being revived even for such an event.[40] There is no precise way of measuring the effect of the *Sso* rite's abolition, but there is reason to suspect that the consequences were extensive. The *Sso* was important at several levels. It marked the change among Beti males from being youths to becoming men; it was a way of creating alliances or ties of friendship among headmen, and as such was the most important means through which Beti headmen made contact with other headmen who were not necessarily kinsmen.

Religiously, *Sso* symbols provided most Beti explanations about the universe and human conduct in it. The hunter's quest for the antelope that never died and the other *Sso* images deeply permeated Beti culture. When the *Sso* was abolished, an important ingredient of Beti society and a set of Beti beliefs were outlawed. Probably the most striking effect of abolishing the *Sso* rite was the destruction of those symbols, explanations, and attitudes that the Beti had used throughout their history. Young men had been trained as warriors in a society where military action fast became an anachronism; they were schooled as hunters, but large animals were disappearing, and raising farm animals and vegetables was gradually surpassing hunting in importance for the Beti. Abolishing the *Sso* rite meant that young Beti men would have to find other ways to mark the passage from youth to manhood. One such way was to follow the Germans and gain acceptance in a school or employment from Europeans. Learning the *Sso* songs and dressing as a candidate was replaced by learning German songs and stories and wearing European dress.

Politically, the *Sso* rite was important because of the network of alliances it provided a headman and because it gave headmen the chance to demonstrate their largesse. There was no new way devised for headmen to create such alliances, but by the end of the German period such bonds became increasingly less important. Church ceremonies, such as Christmas, first communion, confirmation, and saints' days, became occasions for members to show hospitality and gain reputations for it, and expand their connections of obligation and favor.[41]

The *Melan*, a clan association whose function was to prevent sorcery, also disappeared during the German period for the same reasons that brought an end to the *Sso* rite. Members who were Christians turned their group's collection of family skulls over to catechists, who buried the skulls. The *Ngi*, a similar association, was also abolished, reportedly about 1910, when priests at the Minlaaba mission saw a site with piles of bones and reported it to the government, after which an investigation took place and the rite was outlawed.[42]

Polygamy

Polygamy was central to Beti social organization. Wives were an index of a headman's power and wealth. They were workers, child bearers, and instruments of alliance. Nothing could be more alien to such a social system than the idea that a man should have only one wife. Moreover, infertility and infant mortality rates were both high, and by decreasing his number of wives, a man would also reduce prospects of having heirs. The church taught that men could keep one wife and that excess wives should be freed and returned to their families. This raised complications because bride-price had been originally paid in most cases for the wives. Beti life was so ordered and compounds so structured that there was no place for single, unattached females. The missionaries also tried to stop the practice of exchange marriages from about 1909, saying such marriages were not compatible with church teaching.[43]

Except among converts, students, and those in the missionaries' employ, it is doubtful if the movement against polygamy had much success, for it remained a constant concern for missionaries and administrators among the Beti for several decades. The German administration instituted a tax on multiple wives. They also tried to control bride-price with decrees after 1908 and opposed the sale of young women. There is no indication that any of these decrees had much effect.[44]

Palavers over women were said to have been a staple in the native court system instituted by the Germans. In an attempt to regulate marriage practices, the government created a register for non-Christian marriages in 1914. The missionaries would already record the Christian marriages. Marriages could be legally dissolved for a fee of fifty marks.

Both the killing of widows and slaves at a headman's death and the practice of slavery were prohibited by decree and were the subject of vigorous opposition from church and state. These changes took place gradually, changing most noticeably in areas where the German presence was strongest, then spreading elsewhere. It is likely that widow and slave sacrifice at funerals ceased completely during the German colonial period, for later French administrative reports do not cite it as a problem. Domestic slavery continued into French times and was discussed in France's annual reports to the League of Nations. Its continuance was in part due to the lack of economic and educational possibilities for the legally freed slaves. By the late 1920s, it ceased to be a topic on which the French administration commented, which would indicate its demise.

The period of German control and missionary influence in Cameroon ended abruptly with World War I. The missionary impact was only beginning to reach its zenith when the war came. Numerically, the results of the missionaries' work had been important: more than 28,000 persons from the Beti regions had joined the church. Mission schools had educated a new elite, the clerks, translators, teachers, and soldiers who moved to positions of influence in the administration.

Summary

In retrospect, the most important changes affecting Beti society in the quarter century after the German arrival in 1887 were in response to German initiatives. Some Beti groups resisted change for as long as twenty years. Others soon accommodated to the Germans' ways, partly because they respected the visible signs of German power and partly because they hoped to use the newcomers as allies in disputes with other Beti and neighboring groups. More important were the substantial changes affecting all Beti groups, those who resisted and those who did not. These changes included the German hierarchy of chiefs and native administrators of varying rank and duties to replace or supersede the headmen of traditional society, the sudden inflow of long-distance trade into what had been a subsistence economy; the large-scale recruiting of laborers for public works and coastal plantations, and abolition of the important *Sso* initiation rite.

The cumulative effect of these changes was an almost total transformation of some aspects of Beti life, but this process of historical transformation was not like exposing photographic paper to light. The full impact of changes brought by colonization came most quickly and completely to the Beti who lived near the Yaoundé station or along the caravan trails that radiated out from it, in particular the main route leading to and from the coast of Kribi. Change came later, in diluted form, to those isolated groups in the interior who had little contact with either the Germans or their African agents. It was not a theme directly affecting all the Beti. It first affected headmen and elders, then gradually included the several hundred Beti who went to mission and government schools and those whom the Germans appointed as clerks, soldiers, translators, catechists, and chiefs.

Notes

1. Hubert Onana, interview with author, Ayéné, 5 August 1968. Théodore Tsala, interview with author, Mvolye, 10 March 1970.
2. H. Rudin, *Germans in the Cameroons: A Case Study in Modern Imperialism* (New Haven, 1938), pp. 37–38, 76–77, 229. "Der Handel der Duala," *Mittheilungen aus den Deutschen Schutzgebieten*, 20 (1907): pp. 85–90. Pierre Mebe, interview with author, Yaoundé, 7 April 1967. François Atangana, interview with author, Yaoundé, 2 May 1967.
3. H. Nekes, "Jaunde und seine Bewohner (Südkamerun)," *Kolonialen Rundschau*, 9 (1912): pp. 15–17, 1920. Rudin, *Germans in the Cameroons*, pp. 76–77. R. Fitzner, *Deutsches Kolonial-Handbuch*, pp. 82–83. For a study contrasting the spread of inland trade in another part of Cameroon, see E. Chilver, "Nineteenth Century Trade in the Bamenda Grassfields, Southern Cameroon," in *Africa und Übersee*, Band XLV/4, 1961, pp. 233–57.
4. Rudin, *Germans in the Cameroon*, pp. 225–27.
5. Ibid., p. 224. Fitzner, *Deutsches Kolonial-Handbuch*, pp. 82–83.
6. Cameroon National Archives (referred to hereafter as CNA), TA-39, "Rapport Dominik du 18.6.1895," p. 4. CNA TA-60, "La Situation sur la Station Yaoundé et la Région de la Sanaga," 1904–1906, p. 2.
7. H. Dominik, *Kamerun, Sechs Kriegs- und Friedensjahre in Deutschen Tropen* (Berlin, 1901), p. 230.

THE GERMAN PRESENCE   73

8. Rudin, *Germans in the Cameroons*, pp. 256–58.
9. François Atangana, interview with author, Yaoundé, 2 May 1967. S. Passarge, "Die Geschichte der Erforschung und Eroberung Kameruns," *Zeitschrift für Kolonialpolitik, Kolonialrecht und Kolonialwirtschaft* (1908): p. 557.
10. G. Zenker, "Jaunde," *Mittheilungen von Forschungsreisenden und Gelehrten aus den Deutschen Schutzgebieten*, no. 8 (1895): pp. 64–65.
11. CNA TA-39, "Rapport Dominik du 18.6 1895," p. 4. CNA TA-60, "La Situation sur la Station Yaoundé et de la Region de la Sanaga," 1904–1906, p. 2.
12. CNA TA-1, 1896, p. 6.
13. C. von Morgen, *Durch Kamerun von Süd nach Nord* (Leipzig, 1893), pp. 42–43. Fitzner, *Deutsches Kolonial-Handbuch*, I (Berlin, 1901), pp. 82–83. CNA TA-59, pp. 6–7.
14. Fitzner, *Deutsches Kolonial-Handbuch*, pp. 82–83. CNA TA-59, pp. 6–7. Rudin, *Germans in the Cameroons*, pp. 223–24.
15. Ibid., pp. 223–24.
16. CNA TA-2, p. 29. T. Tsala, "Les Noms des Jours," Yaoundé, 1968.
17. CNA TA-2, p. 29. Rudin, *Germans in the Cameroons*, p. 155. CNA TA-1, 1911/1912, p. 2.
18. Pierre Mebe, interview with author, Yaoundé, 7 June 1968.
19. H. Dominik, *Vom Atlantik zum Tschadsee, Kriegs- und Forschungsfahrten in Kamerun* (Berlin, 1908), pp. 35–36.
20. Rudin, *Germans in the Cameroons*, p. 326.
21. Quoted in Rudin, p. 328.
22. Ibid., p. 327.
23. Ibid., pp. 236–37, 308, 331–33. Dominik, *Kamerun*, p. 326.
24. Rudin, *Germans in the Cameroons*, pp. 330–33.
25. Ibid., p. 337. "Medizinal-Berichte über die Deutschen Schutzgebiete" (Berlin, 1909), p. 161.
26. Rudin, *Germans in the Cameroons*, pp. 316–17. R. Hermann-Weilheim, "Statistik der farbigen Bevölkerung von Deutsch-Afrika," *Koloniale Monatsblätter, Zeitschrift für Kolonialpolitik, Kolonialrecht und Kolonialwirtschaft* (June 1914): p. 252.
27. Solf is quoted in "Cameroon 1906–1914," *German Imperialism in Africa*, ed. H. Stoecker, trans. B. Zöllner (Atlantic Heights, N.J.: Humanities Press International, 1986), pp. 167–68. See also Rudin, *Germans in the Cameroons*, pp. 330–33. CNA TA-1 1911–1912, pp. 1–2, 9.
28. H. Skolaster, *Die Pallottiner in Kamerun, 25 Jahre Missionarbeit* (Limburg, 1924), p. 121. Heinrich Vieter, *Erinnerungen aus Kamerun 1890–1903*, Yaoundé, p. 85.
29. Skolaster, *Die Pallottiner in Kamerun*, p. 122. Vieter, *Erinnerungen aus Kamerun*, p. 97.
30. Skolaster, *Die Pallottiner in Kamerun*, p. 122, "L'Effort Camerounaise" (Yaoundé), 13 January 1967, p. 2.
31. Skolaster, *Die Pallottiner in Kamerun*, p. 126. T. Tsala, interview with author, Mvolye, 3 March 1968.
32. T. Tsala, interview with author, Mvolye, 3 March 1968.
33. Skolaster, *Die Pallottiner in Kamerun*, p. 231.
34. Skolaster, *Die Pallottiner in Kamerun*, p. 309. Nekes, "Jaunde und seine Bewohner (Südkamerun)," pp. 468–69.
35. Dominik, *Vom Atlantik zum Tschadsee* p. 37.
36. Skolaster, *Die Pallottiner in Kamerun*, pp. 236–37, 316.
37. Martin Mballa Foe and Cyprian Owona Oda, interview with author, Mbalmayo, 14 March 1968. Skolaster, *Die Pallottiner in Kamerun*, pp. 127–28.
38. Max Abe Foudda, interview with author, Nkolbewa, 23 December 1967.
39. Nekes, "Jaunde und seine Bewohner," p. 36.
40. A copy of the film was available through the Ministry of Information, Yaoundé, in the 1960s.
41. Laurent Ondoua Awomou, interview with author, Ebogo, 14 March 1968.
42. T. Tsala, interviews with author, Mvolye, 1 January 1968 and 6 June 1968.
43. Jean Fouda Ngono, interview with author, Ngomedzap, 16 March 1968.
44. Rudin, *Germans in the Cameroons*, pp. 299–303. Skolaster, *Die Pallottiner in Kamerun*, p. 121. T. Tsala, interview with author, Mvolye, 8 June 1967.

CHAPTER 5

The Beti and the French

The period of German control in Cameroon ended abruptly in 1916 with World War I, less than ten years after the first generation of German-educated Beti emerged, and less than a decade since the isolated Yaoundé post had changed from being a way station to a full administrative district.

The White Man's War

The land war in Cameroon began on 27 September 1914 when the Germans surrendered Douala to invading British forces without a fight, after blowing up the telegraph station and withdrawing to blocking positions in the interior. Yaoundé became the provisional capital of the colony for the next fifteen months, until the British and their allies reached it and the Germans again withdrew, this time to Spanish Guinea.[1]

The German strategy was one of gradual retreat toward the interior, ambushing and harassing the Allied columns advancing through the rainforest. The Germans had considerable terrain to hold with fewer troops and lighter arms than their opponents. At the same time, they knew the land, their African soldiers were loyal throughout the conflict, and the Germans generally controlled where the fighting took place, a definite advantage in such warfare.[2]

Still, the Germans never really had a chance. Their total force in late 1915 was estimated at four thousand soldiers, of whom the majority were probably Beti. The British-French contingent opposing them was more than double that size.[3] The Allies' plan was to move through Beti lands as quickly as possible and encircle Yaoundé. The main thrust came from a large British column approaching from the southeast. A French unit also moved east from Edea and Esseka, and additional French troops pushed northwest from the Congo. Other Allied troops descended from northern Cameroon.

It took the Allies almost nine months to advance within fifty miles of Yaoundé and the approximate southern limits of Beti lands. The German-led African troops held off the British-French advance for about a year, largely through ambushes and

---

Notes for this chapter begin on page 84.

raids followed by withdrawals into the rainforest. In June 1915, eight months after Douala had fallen, the British column had moved about 125 miles inland and was within fifty miles of Yaoundé, gaining about a mile a day. Before the month's end, they were driven back to the point from which they had originally embarked on 1 May, sustaining a 25 percent casualty rate; troops were also substantially weakened by dysentery and fever. If the British advance was checked, the French had no better luck in the east. They were still 140 miles east of Yaoundé in late June.[4]

Warfare was suspended during the rainy months beginning in July; then in late November, a final dry season offensive was launched on the capital. The advancing British column, pushing from the west, met heavy resistance from the Germans, but moved to within sight of Yaoundé by late December 1915.

Although they had built an elaborate system of trenches to defend the town, the Germans withdrew from Yaoundé without a fight, as they had from Douala. It would have been pointless for the Germans to risk a last-ditch encounter. Two decades of work would have been destroyed, and heavy casualties sustained, with no prospect of victory. The British entered Yaoundé unopposed on 1 January 1916, and during the next ten days the remaining Allied forces encircled the town from other points.[5]

The last significant military encounter in Beti land was a rear-guard action on the Nyong on 8 January 1916, when the retreating Germans returned all prisoners of war, as E. H. Gorges, the British commander, wrote, "amongst them being some British and French officers and civilians, native soldiers, and a few noncombatants who had been taken by the Germans at various stages of the campaign. All had received fair and humane treatment during their capture."[6] Mora, the last northern stronghold under German control, surrendered on 18 February 1916, ending the World War I theater of war in Cameroon.

Karl Atangana, seventy-two of the Beti chiefs, and several thousand Beti accompanied Governor General Karl Ebermaier (1912–1916) southward, eluding Allied efforts to halt their exodus. The Beti chiefs did not believe the Germans would really lose the colony and expected to return after a peace settlement was negotiated. Besides, Atangana and those around him encouraged potential rivals to come along with them as a precautionary measure, fearing other headmen might usurp their places. As replacements, they left kinsmen they trusted to surrender their positions on the chiefs' return. The Beti were reluctant to abandon the Germans, fearing what might happen to the Germans if they ventured into the rainforest alone. There was no question of Beti loyalty to the Germans wavering during the conflict, and many older informants recalled the Germans with respect a half-century later.[7]

Their loyalty to the Germans notwithstanding, the Beti found World War I a deeply unsettling experience. Their own feuds were short and involved small groups, with simpler arms and less devastating results than modern warfare. A Beti who knew the period said, "The First World War made a bad impression on the Beti. They spoke with horror of the white man's war. They had never seen anything like it. Their own wars involved only a few people over a short period of time and were consequently less destructive."[8]

World War I in Cameroon was a time marked by the breakdown of authority, both colonial and traditional. The Beti say there was an increase in stealing, with many individuals traveling the countryside in police costumes and extracting payment from villagers. Witchcraft accusations increased, and a new secret society, called the Leopard Society, appeared among the Beti. In the absence of traditional or colonial authority, members of the Leopard Society tried to influence the temporal and metaphysical order through sorcery and witchcraft and resorted to brigandage and intimidation as well. Members wore tails of palm branch, put calabashes on their heads, painted themselves with leopard spots, and carried wooden leopard's paws with nails for claws. With these they scratched the ground in front of a hut to tell someone inside, "You have a problem with the leopard."[9]

In February 1916, Governor Ebermaier and Colonel Zimmermann, who commanded the troops "and a large number of Germans and natives," completed their exodus to the south and turned themselves over to the Spanish. The Spanish received them favorably, and the Beti were given a parcel of land at Bekoko near San Carlos, where many remained throughout the war. The Germans moved to Fernando Po (an island off Africa's west coast in the Gulf of Guinea, now known as Bioko), and on 16 April, two Spanish ships transported nearly eight hundred Germans to Holland. Others went to Spain for internment. H. Skolaster estimated that twenty thousand Africans, including soldiers, went to Spanish Guinea with the Germans.[10]

Six Beti Chiefs in Spain, 1918–1920

After they had moved to Fernando Po, Charles Atangana and six other Beti chiefs accepted a German offer to visit Spain. Their trip had two purposes: to await the war's settlement, when it was hoped Germany would regain its colonies, and to recover over one million German marks that fifty Beti chiefs and notables had banked through the Basel Mission, a Swiss Protestant missionary society. The German government paid for their transportation to Madrid in 1918, lodged them at the Hotel Aurora, and provided spending money.[11]

The Beti chiefs spent most of the next two years in Madrid and one month in Barcelona. They visited the German Embassy in Madrid periodically and arranged repayment of the Beti accounts in Spanish pesetas, which they later changed to French francs. The political side of their mission was not successful for, as the Versailles talks continued, it became increasingly evident that the Germans would not regain their colonies. The Beti saw the Spanish King, Alfonso XIII, four times, and asked "Nkukuma Alfonso" to intercede with the French on their behalf. If he ever did, it was without success.

The Beti visitors were deeply impressed by Spain. Twice they were dinner guests of the royal family, and the king reportedly offered them a place in the administration of Spanish Guinea. The chiefs visited several high Spanish government officials, including the foreign minister, and carefully studied the Spanish government and parliament as a model of how Europeans governed their countries and discussed ways that commerce and industry, such as they saw in Spain, could be developed in Africa. "We talked and talked about what we saw," Max Abe Foudda, one of the chiefs who made the trip, recalled fifty years later, "and asked among ourselves how we could bring these things to our people." Photographs of the period, which Charles Atangana's family kept, picture the Beti delegation impeccably attired in European dress in a number of settings in Madrid.

They fared less well in Paris, for their fidelity to the Germans caused the French government to question their potential loyalty. The Beti answer was simple: the Germans had been Cameroon's colonizers, and the Beti had worked loyally alongside them, to the benefit of both parties; now they would do the same with the French. The Beti tell of a story in which Karl Atangana, while in Europe, was given a set of European flags and asked which country the Africans would prefer to have contact with. Atangana picked up all the flags and said, "We will be friends with all people." The actual incident cannot be documented; what is important is that the story spread among the Beti and is an example of their willingness to work with the French.[12]

Finally, on 8 June 1920, the French government allowed the Beti to return to Cameroon. Atangana was given several money orders from Germans who had fathered children while in Cameroon and who wanted to provide for their education. The Beti chiefs' last impression of Europe was when their ship docked for several hours at Los Palmas on the return journey. Max Abe Foudda saw a two-story Spanish hacienda, which impressed him. He sketched a plan of it and had a replica built when he returned to Nkolbewa, forty miles southwest of Yaoundé. It served as a model for other chiefs' houses in the rainforest as well. Meanwhile, other Beti chiefs and their followers had been slowly filtering back to Cameroon from Spanish territory, bringing with them new types of banana plants, pineapples and macabos they found on the coast.[13]

Cameroon Becomes a League of Nations Mandate

In March 1916, three months after the German exodus, the British and French had established their respective zones of influence in Cameroon, abandoning a short-lived effort to govern the territory jointly through a condominium. Then in 1922, Cameroon officially became a League of Nations mandate. As part of the Versailles settlement on former German possessions, France received a large section of what would subsequently be referred to as East Cameroon. Despite the fact that they had taken Douala, Yaoundé, and much of the coast and rainforest, the British withdrew from most of the conquered territory and simply added a portion of West Cameroon to their Nigerian territory. This land included the former German capital of Buea and the rich plantation lands in the vicinity of Mt. Cameroon.[14]

These initial years of French rule in Cameroon were an unsettled time for the Beti and other Africans. Several thousand Beti chiefs, clerks, soldiers, and families had departed from Cameroon, leaving the Beti without leaders experienced in dealing with Europeans. "Individual insubordination and disorder are the general rule among the tribes,"[15] a French administrator observed, and there were several examples of raids conducted or old feuds resumed by Beti and other African groups. The French hold on Cameroon at this time was fragile, local populations were not yet under their control, and conditions could have permitted the growth of resistance groups. Yet there were no revolts among the Beti.[16]

Cameroon's chaotic state in this transition period was outlined in an American missionary's letter, written in March 1916, from Metet, a mission station forty miles south of Yaoundé. Former soldiers roamed freely about the countryside, raiding compounds, seizing women, and looting goods. Self-appointed "policemen" and "messengers" with scraps of paper written in bad French or sometimes German took livestock and possessions from villagers.[17]

In the absence of effective European control, many African chiefs used "police-boys," guards the administration allowed them to keep, as messenger-soldiers. A commander in Yaoundé in 1919 said that "the country is practically under the control of police-boys." Anyone who could put together some semblance of a military costume could pass himself off as an agent of the administration, pillaging and taking goods as he pleased.[18]

The French policy toward local administration was vague and experimental during the colonial power's first few years in Cameroon. France was faced with both a serious lack of personnel and a leadership vacuum among the Beti. Subdivisions were in charge of soldiers who, "if they had been brave soldiers, could not but make mediocre administrators." The eastern region of Cameroon in the immediate postwar years was controlled by a company with strength reduced to five or six Europeans. The Germans had divided the same region into three districts with more than fifty European personnel.

The governor general in 1919 said he saw no solution to the problem until the situation in Europe became clearer and more administrators for the mandate territory became available. Meanwhile, he exhorted French military and civilian administrators to base their policy on colonial administrator Colonel Joseph-Simon Gallieni's *tâche d'huile* (oil spot) or *toile d'araignée* (spider web) concepts.[19] It was only by the broadest poetic license, however, that the efforts of the former French soldiers at native administration might be considered expanding an oil spot or building a spider's web.

An Administration in Place

Four years after the war had ended, the French administration began to take shape. The administrative organization the French devised for Cameroon in the early 1920s was a government headed by a governor general responsible for political, economic, and financial control of the mandate territory. A new system of courts was established. A public works department of the government was responsible for construction of roads and a railway. A customs service, treasury, and land survey office were established.

One of the first administrative actions the French took was to establish a legal code for Cameroon patterned on that used in France's other African territories. French justice made a distinction between civil and criminal cases, but the League of Nations' report stated that persuading African magistrates to make a similar distinction was difficult. Disputes over bridewealth, theft, and poisoning were all treated in the same manner.[20] In civil cases, the matter was first brought before a local assessor. The parties were convoked with their witnesses, and if one party failed to appear, the other could ask that local police bring him to the tribunal, thus avoiding the possibility of judgment by default. If the two parties could not reach agreement with the assessor, the matter went before a three-member African appeals court, the *tribunal des races*. Force could only be used in carrying out decisions of the tribunal, and disputes were generally settled through protracted negotiations: "before the indigenous assessor there exists only an amicable arrangement."[21]

In 1924, there were 14,750 cases handled by African courts in Cameroon. Of these cases, 5,101 were treated in the Yaoundé district, seven of which actually went before the *tribunal des races*. The remaining 5,094 cases were arranged between the parties with the help of the assessor. Most of the disputes dealt with women's rights, including numerous cases about bridewealth and the disposition of widows, who were no longer considered chattels to be inherited with a dead chief's goods. In fact, widows now could inherit a portion of their husband's possessions and had the right of judicial appeal both in questions of marriage and inheritance.

Tax Collection

One of the principal French concerns during their first decade of control over Cameroon was raising sufficient revenues to run the government of the new mandate territory. From 1916 to 1922, France attempted an improvised system of tax collection, the basis of which was a ten-franc head tax on adult males. The results were disappointing. The Germans had raised nearly 6,000,000 marks through a head tax in a single year before their departure; the French totals in 1917 came to two million francs, although the administration had hoped to raise more than four times that sum.[22]

Taxes were collected through local chiefs, and according to one French administrator fraud was widespread. The tax collection system was easy to manipulate. Chiefs omitted their own kinsmen from the tax rolls, overcharged others, and pocketed the excess amounts. The chiefs altered their tax quotas by reporting some of the women in compounds as sisters or visitors and by sending some of the less useful wives back to their families and attempting to gain reimbursement of the bridewealth paid for them. Often such wives were returned by their families and became the subject of lengthy palavers between the two lineages.[23]

The head tax was then extended from men to include women with less than two children. However, it proved almost impossible to collect because the Beti were not cooperative in giving information about the composition of their compounds. This tax was abandoned for a straight per capita levy on all women.[24]

In 1923 the head tax was increased from ten to twelve francs for adult men in the Yaoundé district and from five to eight francs for each woman. The administration hoped to increase the district's revenues from 392,300 to 1,823,000 francs through these measures. The new levies were expected to increase the one-million-franc budget of the previous year by sevenfold.[25]

The French continued the practice established in German times of giving chiefs a portion of the tax revenues they collected. This was an 8 to 10 percent rebate for chiefs on revenues collected during the first three months, and progressively smaller percentages for subsequent quarters (6 percent in the second quarter, 4 percent in the third, and 3 percent in the last quarter). Villagers who did not like their chiefs would withhold payment until the fourth quarter when the chief received the smaller percentage of the take. Some chiefs who had the money paid all of their taxes during the first quarter from their own pocket, thus gaining the larger rebate.[26] In addition to collecting taxes for the French, the chiefs provided workers for the railroad, built and maintained roads in their districts, supplied food to workers (one baton of manioc for four workers), and settled minor disputes.

Chiefs were subjected to judicial proceedings, but none could be exiled or imprisoned in their own locale. They could also be removed from office by the administration.[27] To lead the African side of the administration, shortly after their arrival in 1916 the French appointed Joseph Atemengue as chief of the Ewondo and Benë, an appointment that lasted until 1922, when they recalled Charles (who by now had dropped "Karl") Atangana. Originally, the French were suspicious of Atangana, whom they called "a creature of the Germans."[28] A French report said "the presence of Atangana on Fernando Po, very near in other words, and the surveillance his family exercises" on Atemengue contributed to the latter's difficulties in establishing himself in his new chief's role.[29]

An annual evaluation on each chief was written by the French administration. French accounts of the other Beti chiefs they found or appointed in this period are not very enthusiastic. There were two sides to the administrator's judgment of chiefs; their "sincerity," which meant their loyalty to France, and their "energy," which meant their enthusiasm for tax collecting. A French report from approximately 1918 stated, "The most characteristic trait of the mentality of these chiefs is generally an admiration for the German administration that they do not seek to hide. Almost all their speeches begin generally with the words 'In German Time.'"[30]

The Beti chiefs were carefully controlled, willing agents who complied completely with the French administration. The French kept tax rates high, inaugurated a system of trade permits, which limited the number of incoming merchants, and in theory required passes of anyone who crossed their lands. Chiefs opposed tax exemptions for convalescents from sleeping sickness and wanted to continue the much-opposed *corvée* conscripted work gangs as the only sensible way to promote new public works, such as the building of roads. The system invited corruption; chiefs skimmed a percentage of revenues for themselves, kept close family members off the work rolls, and used conscripts to work their own fields.[31]

In 1925, Max Abbe Foudda provided a large number of workers for the Mbalmayo-Otele railway extension, and 250 workers for the Sangmelima-M'Balmayo road, plus 50 tons of fresh food for the workers. He also sent fifteen loads of potatoes to Yaoundé and cultivated a 30 hectare cocoa plantation. His harsh demands on local populations grew, and in 1934 Père Pierre Pichon of the Minlaaba mission denounced Foudda to the administration, who subsequently removed him from office.[32] When asked about his removal, Foudda shrugged his shoulders and said something to the effect of "I did what I had to do," indicating that he, like other chiefs, were subject to the steady demands of the administration.[33]

The Return of Charles Atangana

Charles Atangana and the chiefs who had accompanied him to Spain arrived by ship in Douala in December 1920. They were met by the representative of the French government who took them to government headquarters for questioning about why they had left Cameroon, why they were now returning, and what was their real attitude toward the Germans. No legal charges were filed against them, and five of the chiefs were sent to the mountain city of Dschang not far from West Cameroon, where they worked with road building crews from December 1920 to December 1921. Max Abe Foudda, who had accompanied Atangana to Madrid, supervised the one thousand workers building the Dschang-Nkongsamba road; Atangana was engaged in similar projects.

One of Atangana's first acts after returning to Cameroon was to arrange the marriage of his German-mission-educated daughter, Katerina, to Joseph Atemengue, his replacement as the nominal leading African in the French administration. Such marriages were commonly arranged between headmen in traditional Beti society to the advantage of both families, but this one was not successful. Katerina soon left her much older spouse and returned to her father, in whose house she lived until his death in 1943.

In December 1921, the French recalled Atangana to Yaoundé as *chef supérieur* of the Ewondo and Benë. By then they had no reason to suspect his motives in cooperating with them. They needed someone to organize the road, railroad, and public building programs, as well as to supervise a tax collecting system that would bring in revenues. Joseph Atemengue, who had replaced Atangana, had no special skills as an organizer and was not a forceful personality. He was moved to the prestigious post of chief judge of the local African court, where he served to the satisfaction of both the French and Africans.

When Atangana returned to power in 1921, he tried to install a sort of cabinet government such as he and the other Beti chiefs had seen in Spain. The system was called *Nsi Meyong* after the location near Mvolye where the group convened. Several Beti clans sent representatives to live there and to act as liaisons between Atangana and the French and their own people. Some of the Beti were given special duties, such as overseeing tax collection and advising on where schools should be placed. The cabinet system did not work, in part because Atangana was reluctant to delegate authority and in part because the other Beti did not have much experience in administering in the European manner. The experiment was scrapped in 1925.[34]

By the mid 1920s, 278 Beti chiefs were recognized by the administration. The organization failed at its primary objective, collecting tax revenues, and Atangana was obliged to pay delinquent taxes out of his own pocket; they were recovered with considerable difficulty. Atangana said revenue raising was not easy because "the number of taxable people, and the power and influence of certain chiefs diminished during the war." Moreover, he no longer enjoyed undivided support.

Some Beti openly contested Atangana's authority, complaining that "for all the things that we have sent to the Europeans, such as chickens and eggs, through Atangana, we have received nothing."[35] In 1924 several Benë chiefs climaxed a four-year attempt at securing their own *chef supérieur*. They tried to arouse the Benë against Atangana through secret meetings and sorcery; when their efforts were discovered, however, they were sent by the French to a northern prison for six months and were given an *interdiction de séjour,* a prohibition against travel, of between five and ten years. The Benë also organized a strike against the payment of taxes and urged noncooperation in the furnishing of food for laborers on public works. The fissure left ugliness and general unrest among many of the Benë against Atangana.[36]

Atangana's Difficulties

In 1925 the French reduced the number of chiefs from 278 to 40 and divided the Beti region into seven districts, each with its *chef de groupement*. Some chiefs kept both their hereditary and administrative roles, but Atangana no longer exercised direct control over the Beti groups around Yaoundé. However, in 1928 when disputes arose among some of the groups and local chiefs proved incapable of handling them, he was again given this responsibility, which he had held before the war.[37]

By 1928, Atangana was *chef supérieur* of the Ewondo-Benë group, which included approximately 130,000 people, and was chief of his village of Mvolye and of the eight regional and seventy-two village chiefs.[38] He had weathered one major revolt among the Benë who wanted their own *chef supérieur*, and was faced with a growing number of Beti groups who saw no reason why they should not have their own paramount chiefs. At the same time, French demands for more taxes and laborers for public works increased, making his position increasingly difficult.

Throughout the 1920s, the French were aware that the system of chiefs they had devised was working to neither their advantage not that of the Africans. The revenues were not coming in at desired levels for the administration and not many of the chiefs had the willing support of their followers. With hope of altering this situation, the French in 1933 undertook a major reorganization of the *chefferie*; the resulting structure did not change appreciably until after World War II. A new three-tiered hierarchy of chiefs was established, including *chefs supérieurs ou de région*, *chefs de groupement*, and *chefs de village*. Later, two categories of chiefs analogous to the latter two were added—*chef de canton* and *chef de quatier*.[39]

The chiefs were selected, as much as possible, from the groups they would command, although other appointed chiefs instead of lineage heads were consulted in their nomination, and appointment came from the French government, not from the Beti. However, the 1933 reorganization of the *chefferie* was successful in creating a more efficient way to control local populations, especially for tax collection purposes, but the *chefferie* always remained an external institution forced on the Beti. It had no roots in Beti society; chiefs, for example, had different duties than headmen of traditional society, were elected in a different manner, and owed their position to the French, not to the elders or ancestors. Many were reactionary in outlook; they often opposed the spread of schools, supported a system of passes that would control traffic through their lands, and advocated government-sponsored work gangs for public works projects. Despite its panoply of military-type uniforms, walking stick, and tax rebates, the *chefferie* was an unstable institution. It depended on French support, and without French support it would collapse.

In 1938, Atangana wrote to the French administration to propose further modifications in the *chefferie*, something the French were already considering; the changes went into effect the following year. Atangana's tone in the letter was in marked contrast with the confidence and energy displayed in his comments in the *Jaunde-Texte* or in his written discussion of the *chefferie* a decade earlier. These were the complaints of an aging man in ill-health. The letter contains a long discussion of the difficulties of recruiting laborers among the Beti. Atangana wrote that "the indigenous people do not have any idea of endurance" and that they became "easily discouraged." The Beti "work with ill will for the administration or for private enterprise, where they hide to save themselves when the administration has given the chiefs an order in the public interest, or for their own good."[40]

The Beti resisted the government work gangs because they had borne the brunt of recruitment for work on the inland railroad under the Germans and later the French, and the memory of extensive deaths and illnesses, hard work, and food shortages for the workers were only a decade old. Atangana said workers were still required for maintaining the railroad and the several roads leading to Yaoundé, but the pool of Beti laborers upon which chiefs could draw was diminished by the demands of plantations and forestry projects, and by the growing number of jobs in towns like Yaoundé.

Several years earlier, Atangana's public utterances stressed his closeness to the Europeans and his confident hold over the Africans. Now he wrote that the "notables, having diminished influence, have become inert because of the impotence of the number of their recalcitrant followers." It was difficult for a chief to control more than five thousand people, he wrote, and he further recommended a reorganization of the *chefferie* in the Yaoundé region into sixteen groups under three chiefs. Two of the three chiefs received an annual sum of twelve thousand francs from the French, and the third received ten thousand francs. Atangana suggested that other chiefs should receive monthly indemnities to encourage them in their work.[41]

By the mid 1930s, Atangana ceased to have the most important African role in Beti-French politics. The French annual report for 1939 does not even mention him among the chiefs being discussed. It speaks instead of other chiefs: "We have in large measure confidence in the excellent chiefs Martin Abéga and André Amougou for the administration of their *chefferies*."[42]

Atangana's Declining Power

Despite his understanding of colonial rule, and despite twenty-two years of working with the French, Atangana never regained the power he had once wielded in his time spent working for the Germans. For the French, the African chiefs served only as administrators with limited powers, principally to collect taxes, recruit workers for the railroad and public works, and disseminate French orders. It was not an assignment that would advance Atangana's popularity, except with his lieutenants who shared in the tax rebates. He actively collaborated with the Catholic missions throughout his career and worked for public health projects, such as the building of dispensaries and campaigns to wipe out sleeping sickness and other epidemic diseases. Like the other Beti chiefs, he did little to encourage the spread of schools, which he believed would, and ultimately did, educate a generation of Beti who wanted to eliminate the role of the chiefs.

Although the position was whittled away by dissident Beti groups demanding local leaders of their own, Atangana always retained his place in the center of Beti politics. When a new *chef supérieur* was appointed, it was he who announced it, telling the new chief that he, Atangana, and the French administration had decided on the appointment. When visiting chiefs came to Yaoundé, most stayed at his large villa, and he extended generous hospitality to visitors, while keeping track of their business. As principal chief at the capital, he had considerable influence, and most of the clerks, interpreters, and soldiers in Yaoundé were from Beti groups under his nominal control. He traveled widely throughout his region of Cameroon, visiting and staying with other chiefs, and attending chiefs' funerals and other important Beti ceremonies. Atangana acquired a motorcar in the mid 1920s, a prestige symbol that ambled along mud roads; he and other Beti chiefs also purchased trucks, which they used for private commerce, such as shipping food to Yaoundé.[43]

By temperament, Atangana was not a revolutionary. He had seen the Germans put down revolts among the coastal Duala, culminating in the hanging of the local chief, Duala Manga Bell; he had participated in many German "pacification" missions, then saw the French take over Cameroon. His greatest skills were as a negotiator, arbitrator, and reconciler. But the French, operating from a position of strength, did not need his skills.

Atangana never joined the independence movement. Such a prospect was not even a political dream for the Beti until after World War II; but subtly, almost imperceptibly, Beti society was undergoing a transformation. These changes did little to affect the stagnant *chefferie*, which remained essentially the same from the 1920s to the 1940s. However, during the same period an increasing number of Beti began participating in public affairs. The spread of cocoa farming provided steady incomes to men who had none before, and the presence of mission schools helped create a class of Beti who seriously questioned the power of the headmen and chiefs and the value system through which this power was buttressed.

Notes

1. E. Gorges, *The Great War in West Africa* (London, n.d.), pp. 148–52, 254–56.
2. F. Moberly, *History of the Great War Based on Official Documents: Military Operations, Togoland and the Cameroons, 1914–1916* (London, 1931), p. 421.
3. E. Gorges, *The Great War in West Africa*, pp. 268–69.
4. Ibid., pp. 237–39.

5. Ibid., pp. 231, 263.
6. Ibid., pp. 268–69.
7. T. Tsala, letter to author, 8 April 1968.
8. Ibid.
9. T. Tsala, interviews with author, Mvolye, 2 February 1968 and 6 May 1968.
10. H. Skolaster, *Die Pallottiner in Kamerun, 25 Jahre Missionarbeit* (Limburg, 1924), p. 293.
11. Max Abe Foudda, interview with author, Nkolbewa, 23 December 1967.
12. Ibid. Photographs in possession of Max Abe Foudda, Nkolbewa.
13. Max Abe Foudda, interview with author, Nkolbewa, 23 December 1967.
14. V. LeVine, *The Cameroons From Mandate to Independence* (Los Angeles, 1964), pp. 32–35.
15. Cameroon National Archives (referred to hereafter as CNA), 11.828 (1918), "Exposé de la Politique Générale, attitude des chefs, esprit des populations."
16. CNA 11.828 (1918).
17. CNA 6518, "G. Schwab to Yaoundé Commandant," 29 March 1916.
18. CNA 11.828 (1918), "Chef de la Circonscription de Yaoundé," June 1919.
19. CNA 11.828 (1918), CNA 10.010, "Exposé Général de la Situation dans les Territoires Occupés de l'Ancien Cameroun," pp. 6–12, 46–47 (undated, circa 1920). For a listing of French regulations on the *chefferie*, see the index "Chefferies Coutumières" in H. Chêne, *Répertoire Générale des Textes Législatifs et Reglementaires applicables aux Cameoun*, Douala, 1954, p. 26.
20. *Rapport Annuel du Gouvernement Français sur l'administration sous mandat des Territoires du Cameroun, Pour l'année 1923* (Paris, 1924), p. 80.
21. Ibid., p. 80.
22. CNA 6217 (1917), "Le Gouvernement des Colonies à Chef de la Circonscription de Yaoundé, Douala," 6 January 1917.
23. CNA 11.828 (1918).
24. Ibid.
25. CNA 10.010.
26. Max Abbe Foudda, interview with author, Nkolbewa, 23 December 1967.
27. Ibid.
28. CNA 11.828 (1918).
29. Max Abe Foudda, interview with author, Nkolbewa, 23 December 1967.
30. CNA 11.828 (1918).
31. J. Guyer, "Head Tax, Social Structure and Rural Income in Cameroon, 1922–1937," *Cahiers d'Études Africaines*, XX, vol. 3 (1980): p. 322.
32. J. Guyer, "The Administration and the Depression in South-Central Cameroon," *African Economic History*, 10 (1981): pp. 70–74.
33. Max Abbe Foudda, interview with author, Nkolbewa, 23 December 1967.
34. Ibid. Max Abe Foudda, "Histoire des Betis (Ewondo)," Yaoundé, 1968, p. 6.
35. J. Guyer, "Food Economy and French Colonial Rule," *Journal of African History*, vol. XIX, no. 4 (1978): pp. 577–97. Théodore Tsala, interview with author, Mvolye, 2 February 1968.
36. *Rapport Annuel adressé par le Gouvernement Français au Conseil de la Société des Nations Conformement à l'article 22 au Pacte sur l'administration sous Mandat des Territories du Cameroun Pour l'année 1936* (Paris, 1937), pp. 42–44.
37. CNA 6296, Rapport Annuel, Subdivision Akonolinga, 1939.
38. Ibid.
39. CNA 11.819. "Charles Atangana to Chef de la Région de Nyong et Sanaga, Mvolye," 23 August 1938.
40. CNA 6213.
41. Ibid.
42. Ibid.
43. J. Guyer, "The Food Economy and French Colonial Rule in Central Cameroon," *Journal of African History*," vol. XIX, no. 4 (1978): p. 589.

Charles Atangana, center, with cane, *Oberhäuptling* of the Beti under the Germans and *chef supérieur* under the French, with other Beti chiefs, Yaoundé, 1929. With Atangana are several *chefs de groupement*, or regional chiefs, and behind them are a number of *chefs de village*, or village chiefs. Under the French administration, the primary role of these appointed chiefs was to collect taxes and recruit workers for road gangs, the Douala-Yaoundé railroad, and as soldiers in World War II. Such chiefs had little popularity with their subjects. Ministry of Information photo.

One of the Beti chiefs' houses of the French period. Several Beti chiefs visited Spain at the end of World War I. When returning to Cameroon, one of them, Max Abe Foudda, sketched the plans of a Spanish hacienda at Los Palmos, Majorca, where their ship stopped for several hours. Several of the chiefs had similar buildings constructed when they returned to the Cameroonian rainforest. The buildings were used primarily for entertaining visiting European officials. Chiefs preferred to live in smaller, nearby traditional dwellings. Photo by author.

Atangana's band. When he was named a chief by the Germans in 1914, Karl Atangana sent a group of Beti musicians to the coast to learn German military and promenade music. The band, called Fanfare des Ewondos in French times, symbolized his prestige. Atangana sent them to play at weddings, funerals, and public gatherings. Long after his death 1943, what remained of the ensemble circulated through hotels on weekends or played for airport departures. Ministry of Information photo.

Top: Yaoundé, Cameroon, administrative and commercial zone in 1951. Bottom: Beti women's huts, ca. 1950, near Yaoundé. Each wife of a headman had her own hut. Buildings were usually constructed in a straight line. In more prosperous compounds, mud bricks were replaced by cement walls and thatched roofs by tin ones. Ministry of Information photos.

The Abbé Théodore Tsala, a Beti scholar and one of the first ordained Roman Catholic priests (1935). Educated in German and French mission schools, he published works on Beti folklore, history, and language. Photo by author.

Hubert Onana, a Beti headman or *mie-dzala,* and a cocoa planter at Ayéné. He knew Charles Atangana and many of the Beti chiefs of the German and French periods. Onana wore a red stocking cap as a symbol of chiefly authority, replacing a hat of red parrot feathers of an earlier era. Photo by author.

Daniel Ze, clerk at the Cameroonian National Archives, Yaoundé, and former secretary to a Beti chief, Max Abe Foudda (with homburg), a *chef supérieur* of the Beti, and Frederick Quinn, author. Photo taken at Foudda's compound, Nkolbewa, south of Yaoundé, 23 December 1967.

CHAPTER 6

Times of Expansion
The Inland Railroad, Cocoa Production, the Catholic Church

The Inland Railroad

One of the most important economic developments affecting the Beti was the completion of the railroad from the coast to Yaoundé. The railroad had been built by the Germans from Douala to a short distance beyond Edea when the war intervened. The French war spoils included complete German plans for construction of the railroad for the next sixty kilometers beyond its 1914 terminus point, as well as most of the equipment needed for the work.[1] This additional seventy-five miles of railroad was completed by French army engineers between 1922 and 1927. Their greatest difficulties came with a twenty-five mile stretch between Njock and Maka on the first segment of construction east of Edea. It took three years to move the railroad that short distance through hilly country with deep ravines, thick growth, and a devastating malarial climate. After that segment, laying the rest of the track to Yaoundé was relatively easy, as the roadbed crossed the central plateau. Despite its devastating human cost, the railroad brought many advantages to the Beti region. By 1927, the trip to the coast, which a decade before might have taken twenty days by foot, was reduced to sixteen hours by train; goods and people moved quickly and cheaply in both directions.

The Beti understandably resisted work on the railroad; many sought work on West Cameroonian plantations instead. Pay for railroad workers was low, the rate of death and illness high, and recruitment was a constant problem during the five years it took to extend the railroad to Yaoundé. In 1922, the ratio of conscripts to volunteers was approximately eight to one; four years later it dropped to approximately four to one. In 1923, there were 3,502 conscripts and only 977 volunteers among African railroad workers. At least one thousand of the laborers were Beti. By 1925, the number of railroad workers had risen to 5,652, of whom 4,535 were conscripts and 1,117 were volunteers.[2]

Work on the railroad was hard. The work day stretched from 6 AM to 11 AM and then from 2 PM to 6 PM, with no work on Saturday afternoons and Sundays.

Notes for this chapter begin on page 99.

Volunteers were paid 0.75 francs a day, conscripts 0.50 francs per day. African supervisors received from one to three francs a day.[3] Contracts in principle were for six months at a time, but many workers complained about being kept on after their contracts expired. Chiefs supplied both men and food, but workers complained constantly of food shortages. Billard, in his study of the railroad's construction, said that both housing and food for the workers were inadequate. He called the diet "insufficient for hard labor"; he wrote, "During the rainy season, mortality is always higher than during the 1910–1914 period."[4]

Another problem with the railroad's construction was that the period of its extension inland coincided with the spread of a typanosomiasis epidemic in Cameroon. Dr. Eugene Jamot, internationally known for his sleeping sickness eradication programs, was ordered out of the Yaoundé district by French officials for protesting the health conditions of the railroad laborers.[5]

High Rates of Death and Illness

Mortality and illness rates among the railroad workers were devastatingly high. The administration statistics were prepared for required annual reports to the League of Nations, for Cameroon was a mandate territory, not a colony, although that did not influence French administrative practices. The 1923 report claims that thirty-four persons died in December 1923, while 267 others received medical treatment and one hundred were released from work for poor health. In May 1924, thirty-three persons are said to have died; another 379 were said to have been treated and 135 released "for tiredness or physical ineptitude." But such statistics do not cover the months of heaviest rainfall, when the rate of deaths and illnesses climbed higher.[6]

Averaging the December 1923 and May 1924 statistics across a twelve-month period, the administration's figures indicate that among the 4,000 to 5,000 railroad workers, approximately 400, or 10 percent of the work force, died. Another 1,500 were released for medical reasons, and 3,600 received various forms of medical treatment. Such grim statistical information would not support the idyllic conclusion contained in the 1924 report by the French to the League of Nations, which described the scrupulous attention accorded to medical facilities, workers' diets, and living conditions, concluding that "[o]ne is agreeably pleased by the view of these workers, whose work follows the rhythms of traditional chants, ready to smile at the least encouragement."[7]

Music can provide a form of resistance for a conquered people, especially so when other forms of armed opposition would be futile. One of the Beti protest songs, frequently sung when Europeans visited their worksites, was about a bad-tempered small dog, which stole the workers' food and bit them. Its verses were answered by a refrain from the workers, "Hé, get away from that dog." Since the words were in Ewondo, the Europeans would have no idea of its biting content.

Hé get away from that dog.
That white dog is a mean one.
That dog is very mean,

He has taken my manioc,
He has taken my meat.
He has bitten me on the leg,
He has bitten me on the buttocks.
My brother, let me hear you!
Refrain and chorus: Hé, get away from that dog.

Another of the workers' chants complained of the "albinos" who had been allowed to come inland from Douala. It also singled out one of the Beti chiefs who supervised the work gangs:

Ahanda, will you get a white woman for this?
Ahanda, who has told you the whites are your friends?
Ahanda, will you marry a white man's daughter?
What have I done, Ahanda,
That you detest me so?[8]

At the same time as they were constructing the railroad, the French government improved the existing roads in the Yaoundé area and added some new ones between the capital and distant points. Each district was required to furnish a quota of laborers but in 1922, the French observed that many Africans were fleeing to other regions or to the bush and forest to avoid work on road gangs, as they had the railroad. The scarcity of workers soon reached crisis proportions.[9] In a three-month period in 1922, the Yaoundé region furnished 19,200 workers, who spent six days at a time working on nearby roads, and 441 laborers for the railroad.[10]

The administration realized that some chiefs were manipulating the conscription system to keep their own families off the work rolls, while calling on nonrelated lineages under their control for higher quotas. To counter this practice, the administration began assigning quotas by village instead of by region, assuming this would produce a more equitable spread of workers than before.[11]

The Chiefs as Work Gang Recruiters

It was primarily the Beti chiefs, appointed by the government, who supplied the workers; they received bonuses for each worker supplied. Max Abe Foudda, a *chef supérieur* of an Ewondo group south of Yaoundé, said that in 1923, he helped build the road from Yaoundé to Otele, several miles south toward the coast. He supplied 500 workers who spent six months on the project. In the following year he supervised workers on a stretch of the Yaoundé-Lollodorf road, which took four months and required 150 workers. In 1925, he furnished 600 workers who, in the course of a year, built the Mbalmayo-Sangmaleina road.

In addition to salaries and tax rebates provided by the administration, chiefs received fees for recruiting laborers and half the unspent money that remained when a road-building project was completed. The remaining half was returned to the territory's budget. Thus, according to his own calculations, Max Abe Foudda was paid 180,000 francs in 1926, when the road for which he had provided workers was completed, and 220,000 francs in 1928, when the Mbalmayo-Ebolowa road was completed.[12]

By the late 1920s, the coastal-inland railroad was fully operational, and a system of roads radiated from Yaoundé in several directions; other roads were being built, as well. Large trucks were used for the first time to transport goods to the interior. The result was the number of porters dropped from several thousand to a few hundred by the end of the decade. As transportation by railroad and road expanded, caravans that had once provided a profitable source of employment for Beti men diminished to almost nothing. In 1917, an administrator of the Yaoundé district listed portage as the district's main economic resource.[13] At that time one of the first acts of the new French administration was a decree regulating the working conditions of porters. It resembled earlier German regulations. Loads could not exceed 25 kilograms, plus 5 kilograms of personal belongings; for every ten porters there was to be one reserve carrier. Salaries were fixed at a franc a day with load and 0.25 francs a day without load.[14]

Moreover, the carriers' routes changed from the long trek to and from the coast to shorter hauls, usually from the bush to access roads or short trips with individual peddlers to hard-to-reach locations. Thus, by 1930, what had provided a significant source of revenue for the Beti since the opening of the coastal route around 1900 ceased to have importance.[15]

Agricultural Change: Cocoa as a Cash Crop

The Yaoundé region during the 1920s and 1930s produced rubber and palm kernels for export, as well as ivory in increasingly diminishing supply as the population of elephants dwindled due to hunting. Meanwhile, new crops were being introduced, including cocoa, rice (which was hard to grow in a rainforest) to feed the railroad workers, and European food crops to feed the growing European community in the expanding administrative capital. By 1933, the breakdown of the population was estimated to be just over 6,000 Cameroonians, 260 foreigners, plus up to a 1,000 additional requisitioned laborers, 300 to 400 prisoners, and 200 hospital patients or workers.[16]

During the 1920s, there was a gradually increasing market for cocoa, which became the Beti's principal crop. Generally, cocoa was grown by family units averaging from three to five persons, working a holding of perhaps 2.5 to 5 acres, which would have been a representative local plantation. In one survey, 60 percent of the plantations were between 2.5 and 5 acres, and 20 percent were 10 acres or larger; usually the latter would be the property of important chiefs or family heads. Paid, non-family member workers were rare among the Beti until after World War II.

Of the 4,500 tons of cocoa exported from Cameroon in 1924, some 4,000 tons came from local African production, and the remainder from French plantations. In 1931 the French estimated that 4,940 acres of land in the Yaoundé district were used to grow cocoa. Cocoa production spread widely among the Beti following a French government effort to extend its production beginning in 1924/1925. From then until the beginning of World War II in 1939, crops almost doubled every four years; when the Great Depression wiped out most European farms in the Beti region, almost all cocoa production in that part of Cameroon shifted to African farmers. In 1938, East Cameroonian cocoa production amounted to 30,000 tons. By 1950, it had risen to 49,000 tons, and in 1960, to almost 60,000 tons. While production figures are not broken down on a regional basis, much of the cocoa growing would have been in the Beti lands.

Cocoa production was an attractive alternative for small farmers during the Great Depression; it was, for example, more profitable than palm kernels. In the early 1930s, the number of small cocoa plantations around Yaoundé grew. Many were not successful; some of the first generation of cocoa planters lacked the skills to successfully grow and tend the crops. Soon cocoa growing caught on, and those at the lowest levels of the economic scale saw it as a way to become income earners and establish independent, monogamous Christian family units. This shift resulted in a correlating decline in the number of polygamous marriages.[17] Guyer has observed that cocoa cultivation became the work of Beti men for three reasons. First, it provided a way to make tax payments; second, it allowed men to make permanent claims on cultivatable land; and, third, it coincided with traditional Beti male farming practices of using long-handled hoes and digging sticks or machetes.[18]

Africans around Yaoundé produced increasing quantities of vegetables for marketing in urban centers at this time. A report written in the Yaoundé district in 1925 said the Beti were augmenting production of traditional foodstuffs such as bananas, macabos, and yams because they could find a good price for them in towns and at places where construction was taking place. Some Beti were also developing plantations of rice or groundnuts. Markets remained limited to towns, and the Beti never developed regional bush markets of any importance.[19] The Beti also continued to gather palm kernels and produce palm oil.

Although commercial agriculture was thus becoming widespread in the Beti lands, the French observed that the Beti tended "more and more to have abandoned collective projects for small, very dispersed individual plantations." Headmen preferred to run their own farms rather than to form larger combinations, and individuals who had once been dependent on headmen did likewise once they obtained their own land, seeds, and workers.[20]

This time, the French recognized that conditions in Cameroon were not favorable to developing a European planter class. There were a few European plantations in the Yaoundé region, but the French believed the future of such culture would rest in indigenous hands.[21] Still, while a European planter class did not emerge, during the 1920s and 1930s, Levantine merchants came to Cameroon in considerable numbers, as one Beti put it, "following the French like pygmies after cattle." They were primarily small traders establishing themselves in general stores or as cocoa speculators in outlying administrative centers.[22]

Some clues about the effects of the Great Depression on the Beti economy are available in scattered administrative reports. In one locale, there was a sharp drop in the number of court cases. This would indicate a falling off of activity in general. In another place, there were "protests and temporary exoduses without motivation,"[23] caused by the Great Depression and an increase in local taxes.

Probably the depression's effects were not too severe on the Beti because the traditional Beti subsistence economy provided basic food and shelter. The Great Depression caused several French cocoa plantations to close, thus leaving almost all production to Africans. The economic upheaval would have been most severe on the wage earners and those engaged in trade, but this was a small percentage of the Beti, and for most Beti, the depression in all likelihood marked a slowing down of the process of economic modernization. After 1931, production of cocoa and food stuffs increased and economic expansion resumed.[24]

Economic Profiles of Individual Headmen

The economic position of a range of individual rainforest headmen in the mid 1920s was described in a French report for the League of Nations, which represents a useful index for measuring the economic status of a sampling of central Cameroonian agriculturists of the period. Although the headmen were Bulu, a group related to the Beti, it is unlikely that their situation differed much from that of their nearby Ewondo and Benë neighbors, and the profiles are probably as typical as could be drawn of rainforest chiefs for this period.[25]

Edjo Mvondo, the most important chief in the Ebolowa region, ruled his own compound, which consisted of fifty persons, as well as 145 other compounds. He received an annual income of approximately 9,000 francs, 5,000 of which came from the government as salary, 1,500 for serving as a magistrate on the local court, and about 2,500 from his plantation, where thirty-five women and forty children lived. Mvondo lived in a wooden house elevated above the ground in the manner of European colonial construction, but his women lived in traditional woven-grass huts. Of his annual income, 3,000 francs went to his workers, auxiliaries, and relatives, and 3,500 bought clothing and accessories for his women. With the remaining sum, Mvondo paid his taxes and bought European-made products, such as ammunition for hunting, and toiletries and household items, such as tools and salt. Food and lodging, the main items in the budget of European workers, were not expenses for rainforest headmen.

Another relatively well-to-do African of that period was Zilly Bengon, who was employed by the administration as a road supervisor. Bengon, who had one wife, also grew cocoa and groundnuts; his annual income of 2,440 francs came from his salary and plantations. More than one-third of that sum was used to buy clothes for him and his wife. The rest went for salaries, tools, and salt for his plantation workers.

Somewhat less affluent was Bita Bingwa, an aged village chief. All but three of his wives had left him. He had 30 children, 2,000 cocoa trees, 200 hundred palm trees, and 3 goats. In 1922, his income was 555 francs, 150 of which came from bridewealth collected for a daughter, and the rest from the sale of cocoa, groundnuts, rice, and maize. His expenses for the year totaled 145 francs, which included funds spent on taxes as well as on clothing for himself and his family. Like many rainforest headmen, he worked enough to take care of his needs but did not cultivate his lands to anything approaching their full potential. The French estimated that Bingwa's cocoa could have brought 4,000 francs in revenue if it were properly tended; it produced only 200 hundred francs, which Bingwa saved to purchase a hunting gun. Apart from that, his needs were "gathered from the forest and the ground."

Lower on the economic scale was another older chief, Essendoum, who had two wives and two children. He owned a mere eighty cocoa trees (but no palm trees). His possessions consisted of three machetes and a local hoe, which were sufficient to tend his gardens. In recent times he had sold fourteen francs worth of groundnuts and was a poor man by local standards. His prospects were somewhat better for 1924 because he inherited two loads of palm kernels and one of cocoa, which he could sell, and received some clothes as bridewealth for a daughter.

The French administration regarded these examples as typical of conditions facing rainforest chiefs in the mid 1920s. Most of the requisites of life were provided locally. However, new demands were changing the traditional rainforest way of life, such as the requirements of money for taxes, the introduction of cash crops and the increasing availability of European goods, which included demands for clothing and farm and house implements that could only be purchased with cash.

Thus, during the quarter century between World Wars I and II, several important economic developments affected Beti society. They included the spread of long-distance transportation, through both the inland railroad and roads to all parts of the interior, and the gradual growth of cocoa as a cash crop, bringing income to several thousand farmers who otherwise would have continued to depend on a subsistence economy and the largesse of headmen.

A Cameroonian Pentecost

At the same time as the Beti economy was being transformed through cocoa production and the spread of roads and the railroad, increasing numbers of Beti were exposed to Western education and ideas through mission schools. After the Pallottiner fathers were deported from Cameroon in 1916, the Roman Catholic Church was left temporarily under the supervision of French military chaplains. This consisted of several members of the Congregation of the Holy Spirit, a missionary order with wide African experience, who were demobilized officially to serve as schoolteachers. Other priests from the same order followed from France; it was this missionary order that directed the further spread of Christianity among the Beti for the next forty years.

From 1916 to 1919, there were only twelve priests in Cameroon, although when the Germans left, they had 34 fathers, 37 brothers, 31 nuns, and 223 African catechists. There had been approximately 2,100 Christians in the Yaoundé area, and an almost equally large number of catechumens. By 1927, the number of Catholic Christians in the Yaoundé district had grown to an estimated 118,000 persons.[26]

Sixteen years later, in 1942, the number of Catholic Christians had almost tripled. There were 340,000 baptized persons, 150,000 catechumens, as well as 38 missions in the Yaoundé district. Thus, the widespread evangelization of the Beti, which began under the Germans, continued under the French with an increasingly large number of converts. A Beti priest referred to the interwar period as a "*Pentcôte Camerounais*" (Cameroonian Pentecost), and a French abbé remarked, with regard to African interest in religion, "The Blacks in Cameroon go to confession as in France one goes to the movies."[27]

An Alsatian Bishop

In 1922, religious administration of the Cameroon Diocese passed to Msgr. Francois-Xavier Vogt, a man of remarkable energy and inventiveness by any standards. At the time of his appointment, he was fifty-two years old and had served for fourteen years in East Africa. Named Apostolic Vicar in May 1923, he spent the next twenty years directing the spread of Catholicism among the Beti and other rainforest and savanna peoples.[28]

Msgr. Vogt's trip inland to Yaoundé in some ways paralleled that of Msgr. Vieter two decades earlier. However, part of the distance this time was traveled by railroad, and all along the way there were catechists' huts where he could stay. Charles Atangana greeted the Alsatian bishop, with whom he could speak German, and put his carriage at his disposal. Christians lined the road, and a group of Beti chiefs served as an honor guard. The Bishop, preceded by a large throng, entered the church on his arrival in Yaoundé, and the organist struck up a selection learned from the military occupation, "Quand Madelon Vient Nous Servir à Boire" (When Madelon serves us drink).[29]

The type of Catholicism displayed by the Holy Ghost Fathers was a product of the times and was also influenced by the formation the priests had received. Many of the missionaries were former soldiers, and a number came from Brittany and Alsace. In some ways the Holy Ghost Fathers resembled the French Foreign Legion of that period. Vigorous, self-reliant, uncompromising combatants, they were not easily susceptible to "going native" or being overly influenced by their surroundings. Their religion was presented largely in legalistic terms and depended heavily on the law and on rules, regulations, rewards, and punishments. Theirs was first of all a religion of the word and of obligations.

Msgr. Vogt had no desire to discard the religious practices introduced by the Pallottiners, except to diminish what he regarded as the Germans' emphasis on mystical spirituality and replace it with a more clear-cut pray-and-obey format. Beyond that, he stressed the continuity of faith and practice between the two groups of missionaries, an approach different from that taken by French administrators of the same period toward the Germans who had preceded them. The Bishop revived several of the parish associations for men and women started by the Pallottiners and added others. He also encouraged Africans to decorate their huts with "One or two pious images, a crucifix, a blessed palm branch."[30] Although songs and prayers in Ewondo were employed in the church, the Bishop cautioned against the introduction of Beti dances and made no effort to incorporate African beliefs and symbols into Christian rites. Coexistence with or sympathy for traditional religious beliefs was not on the horizon.

Msgr. Vogt developed three priorities in his work. The first was exposing the Beti, especially young children, to Christianity; then came teaching young men and women who were preparing for marriage how to be Christians and how to practice monogamy. Finally, by the early 1930s, he had began to form an African clergy.[31]

In 1925, Vogt wrote a *Petit Syllabaire Ewondo-Français*, which went through six editions and had a total printing of 10,000 copies in ten years. With Joseph Ayisi, chief catechist at Yaoundé, Bishop Vogt developed a catechism in Ewondo. It was widely circulated in the rainforest and savanna and translated into other African languages as well.

Lay African Catechists

The brunt of the mission's teaching effort was borne by lay catechists. They were the principal African auxiliaries of the French clergy; by the late 1920s, there were between thirty and forty French priests and over one thousand African catechists. The catechists' role was analogous to that of the interpreters and clerks for the administration, and their power was comparable. Their main duty was instructing the masses of Beti wanting to become Catholics in the catechism and preparing them for baptism and marriage; moreover, if there was a Christian village, they served as headmen, whether or not they would have been accorded such a position in traditional Beti society.[32] While there were some exemplary persons among the catechists, many were *catéchists de fortune*, opportunists lacking in education and using their influence to gain payment of money, a few chickens, or some fieldwork from the catechumens before the latter were given church membership.

The administration objected to the catechists interfering in matters over which they had no jurisdiction, and disputes between catechists and chiefs were numerous. In an effort to resolve such disputes, in 1927 the administration decreed that catechists should refrain from interfering with the village administration and should limit their teaching to doctrinal matters. They were not supposed to hold classes during regular working hours. On the other hand, Sunday was accepted as a day of rest, and chiefs and the administration were supposed to treat it as such. Chiefs and African police were not allowed to interfere with the spread of religious education.[33]

The Catholic missionaries opposed the southern spread of Islam into the savanna and rainforest. They built a string of mission posts beyond the outer periphery of Beti lands in places like Doumé, Lomié, Bertoua, Batouri, Somo, and Bafia to "block the road to the Mohammedans."[34] But the Beti were never influenced to any extent by Islam, although many Hausa settled along trade routes to and from the capital and formed a small Hausa quarter in Yaoundé. Years later, when men from many tribes adopted the colorful, comfortable Sudanic robes, missionaries discouraged their wearing them to church because of their Islamic connotation.

Another danger to their position, in the eyes of the Catholics, was the gradual spread of Protestant missions moving north from the coast where they had been established since the nineteenth century. The 1920s were not an ecumenical era, and Msgr. Vogt ranked the Protestants as a threat second only to the Muslims. Still, he wrote, "Protestants are Christians just the same."[35]

One of the principal conflicts between the church and Africans concerned marriage customs. The Christian position was unequivocal: one man, one wife. The issue was more complicated for the Beti, for whom women represented an index of wealth. Children also provided a source of wealth; daughters were both workers and sources of bridewealth, and sons were workers and heirs to the headman's possessions. A Beti headman wanted many wives for these reasons, and for another: disease often left him with 50 to 70 percent of his wives unable to bear children, and among children, infant mortality was comparably high.[36] Some Beti found ways around the church's strictures. One French administrator said that sometimes the baptized chief would keep one wife, but transfer seventy or eighty others to a brother or cousin who became their guardian, but in reality nothing had changed in the basic relationship.[37] Others, with large numbers of wives working their lands, delayed converting until their deathbeds.

Two institutions fostered by the French missionaries were Christian villages and *sixas*, or training schools for young girls. Christian villages, which had been founded by the Germans, were continued by the French after World War II. By then, Christianity was so widespread among the Beti that such villages were no longer necessary. Originally, the villages were Christian enclaves in a non-Christian region. Catechists, instead of headmen, directed them, and members came from many lineages. Their numbers included converts who did not want to return to a pagan environment, as well as men who had left their own compounds because of disputes and women who wanted to avoid polygamous marriages. The villages were opposed by the chiefs, who saw their authority contested by them, especially on the marriage question, and by the administration, which contended that many persons fled to the villages to escape assignments to the *corvée* work gangs.

The Beti used the word *sixas,* pidgin for "sisters," to describe the *maison des fiancées* run by the nuns to prepare young Beti women for marriage. This activity was started by the Pallottiners and expanded considerably by the Holy Ghost community. Young Beti women spent several weeks or months in *sixas* receiving instruction in raising Christian families as well as in basic skills such as sewing, child care, and running a household.[38] In payment for the mission course, women were required to perform many hours of manual work for the missionaries. The *sixas* were centers of prolonged controversy for they struck at a central issue in traditional Beti society: the role of women. Beti headmen believed that women were an index of wealth, and the more women a headman possessed, the wealthier he was. He cemented relationships with other headmen by giving or receiving brides, and the considerable bridewealth sums he might receive from giving a daughter were important sources of revenue. Part of the acrimonious dispute between the missions and the administrations, which surfaced in the late 1920s, centered on the *sixas*. It was triggered by the death of one young woman and the injury of several others in a landslide near the Yaoundé *sixa*. The administration raised its frequently stated charge that the *sixas* were operated by forced labor. Msgr. Vogt answered in February 1930 that the women were being given an education for marriage and were expected to work for their keep, but this was not the same as forced labor.

He countered with an argument calling the administration's attention to several instances when it had requisitioned both men and women as porters and road workers, and said the administration had "a hundred times more reason to pursue...all the chiefs, scribes, secretaries, police guards, and employed workers of all kinds, including extension agents and, above all, medical personnel."[39]

In May 1934, the French administration also took a position on the important and complicated question of women's rights by promulgating a circular on African marriages. It forbade the marriage of girls who had not reached puberty, and said women younger than fourteen years and men younger than sixteen years could not contract marriage. Both must consent to the marriage. Widows were urged to remain in the families of their former husbands, but could be liberated, in turn, for which their families must return the bridewealth paid for them. The decree skirted the touchy question of bride-price in African marriages.[40]

In 1931, Msgr. Vogt, by then sixty-two years old, had named Père René Graffin as bishop coadjutor. Père Graffin, who had spent five years in Africa, was thirty-two years old at the time. He assumed controlled of the seminary and the formation of the African priests. Msgr. Graffin was hardworking and an accomplished organizer; he was paternalistic in his attitude toward Africans, but was not a racist. When one of his French clergymen refused to serve as acolyte at a mass being said by an African priest, he served himself. He was, however, possessed of a difficult and abrasive personality and had little tolerance for those who disagreed with him, white or black.

Toward an African Priesthood

On 8 December 1935, four Beti men were ordained priests. Before his death in 1943, Msgr. Vogt ordained a total of forty-three Africans, thus culminating a long-term effort to establish an African priesthood that had begun with the Germans.

The Pallottiners had started a school for catechists at Buea in 1907 that they hoped to turn into a seminary but that was closed with the onset of World War I. In 1923, Msgr. Vogt concluded he would never have enough French priests to complete the missionary work in Cameroon and decided to start a seminary for the formation of African clergy. It was difficult work, in part because of opposition from his French clergy, and in part because of the lack of trained seminary teachers and facilities. Of the prospective candidates, he said, "They will never be Europeans, that is asking for the impossible. On the other hand, they have qualities that we do not have."[41]

In 1923, the Minor Seminary opened at Mvolye with the Bishop as the principal teacher. By 1925, it had attracted twenty-five students; three years later, when it was moved to Akono, there were ninety-four students divided into five classes. Within the next year, twenty-eight students joined the Major Seminary. One of the first students to enter the seminary was the son of Charles Atangana, *chef supérieur* of the Ewondo and Benë. But despite his father's longstanding interest in the church, the son left the seminary after a short period. The students first spent a year or two with the priest in their mission, where they learned the rudiments of Latin. Next came the Minor Seminary course, which lasted for five years. In the first two years of training, the academic concentration was on Latin. This was to test seminarians' perseverance and also to weed out those who might enter the seminary simply to improve their education as a way of gaining employment in the administration or commerce. Seminarians were also taught French, mathematics, history, and geography.[42] About one-third of those who entered seminary dropped out after Minor Seminary. At the Major Seminary, students learned philosophy and theology, and spent two years teaching or assisting a priest in a church mission. Msgr. Vogt was clear in his instructions that the Africans should not be treated as "Second class clergy, reduced in rank to simple auxiliaries. The indigenous priests should one day become our equals."[43]

The African seminarians objected to the manner in which Msgr. Graffin ran the seminary and to the *Règles de Vie Sacredotale* by which it was administered. The seminarians would have carried their objections to Rome except that their complaints would have rebounded on the now aged Bishop Vogt. African clergy, according to the regulations, could not preside over a service, meeting, or community activity unless there were no Europeans present. Supervision was strict in all facets of life. Seminarians were allowed to buy "serious books" with the superior's permission. Their reading was otherwise limited to the "diverse religious journals and the newspaper 'La Croix,' 'Pélerin,' etc., that one receives at the mission."[44] Abbé Tsala thus described this period, "The colonial literature portrayed the black as a large child, a perpetual minor, to be kept under a protectorship. The contents of our rule took this in account."[45]

All letters were sent and received through the superior of the mission, who read them, except letters of spiritual direction. Relations between the African clergy and Europeans were to remain brief and "limited to what politeness demands."

While at the mission, the African clergy ate the same food as did the French fathers, but when alone or on journeys they were to eat African food. The consumption of tobacco in all its forms was forbidden, and the priests were admonished to employ moderation in the drinking of palm wine, especially outside of meals. Moreover, "Jamais un prêtre indigène ne devra assister à ces longues conversations ou veillées entrecoupées de calèbasse de vin de palme dont sont coutumiers les indigènes di Vicariat" (An indigenous priest should never assist at those long conversations or evenings with containers of palm wine, which are the customs of the inhabitants of the vicarate).[46] Their dress was simple, a white or black cassock, and to their posts they brought a small parcel of clothing, a canteen, two regular pairs of shoes, and a pair of "Sunday shoes, which they received at the Sous-Diaconat."

More than a decade of preparation by the seminarians finally culminated on 8 December 1935 with the consecration as priests of eight Africans, four at Edea, and four at Yaoundé by Msgr. Vogt in the presence of the governor general and a large crowd of Cameroonians, some of whom had walked more than one hundred miles for the event. Among the four ordained at Yaoundé were Tobie Atangana and Théodore Tsala. Tobie Atangana was the leading student at the seminary and a collector of African folklore, which was left as several incomplete manuscripts at his premature death in 1944. He was the first of the African priests to be named head of his own mission.[47]

Abbé Théodore Tsala, who was about thirty-three years old at the time, was among those ordained as priests in 1935. His father, an Eton, was a healer, and his brother worked as "boy" and later a clerk for the German administration. Tsala went to German and French mission schools, and he had lived with a woman and fathered a child before he was ordained. During most of the next two decades, he taught at various church schools or served as vicar or curé in several parishes. After retiring, he published an Ewondo-French dictionary and several articles on Beti customs and wrote a text on Beti grammar. He also published a book of Beti proverbs and prepared a collection of fables and a dictionary of useful plants.

Catholicism, as taught by French missionaries of the interwar period, helped create a political awareness among the rising Beti leaders, although this was far from the missionaries' intention. The church taught a doctrine that emphasized discipline and hierarchy but still provided the basis for a fundamental questioning of those political and ecclesiastical hierarchies that had been superimposed on Cameroon. The missionaries trained a nucleus of Beti clergy who, in religious if not political authority, were the equals of their French counterparts; they dined at the same tables with them and shared the same spiritual mission.

While the number of converts increased numerically among the Beti throughout the French period, it is less easy to determine exactly how the rules, symbolism, and practices of the church were understood by the Beti and translated into their own culture. For example, there is a popular, long narrative poem sung by the *mvet* singers about *Nem-Bobo*, a spider that disputes the Christian God. On the surface, the poem appears to have elements of a Christian morality play. The spider, the subject of numerous rainforest proverbs and poems, insults God and is punished for his failure to repent by being left hanging in the air throughout eternity. But on second reading, a different interpretation of the poem is suggested. The spider (the Beti) contests the God (the colonizers) and loses to the superior power. Still, the spider wins a victory of sorts. He keeps God waiting twelve hours, is not the least bit repentant, is chastised for his insouciance, and manages to cause a postponement of the Celestial Banquet. In the poem's closing lines,

> La fête que dieu avait organisée au ciel,
> Cette fête n'eut pas lieu
> À cause du procès d'Araignée Toilière
> Qui était en contestation avec le Seigneur Dieu.[48]

> The celebration that God organized in heaven,
> that fete was not held
> because of what the spider did
> which was to dispute with the Lord God.

The theme is reinforced elsewhere in the poem: the banquet of bread and wine could not be held at its appointed time because of the confrontation of God and the spider. "The spider endures," the singer closes and asks for a drink of wine, not that offered in the liturgical imagery taught by the missionaries, but the more familiar palm wine of the rainforest.

Thus, for the Beti, the period of the French mandate in Cameroon resulted in an intensification of changes already begun under the Germans. Politically, a three-tiered hierarchy of chiefs became a permanent addition to the Beti society. Economically, a network of roads spread through the rainforest and savanna, the inland railroad was completed, and the widespread commercial exploitation of forestry, cocoa, and rubber production brought work to an increasing number of Beti. Religiously, the interwar years were the period of the Cameroonian Pentecost, the rapid expansion of Christianity among the Beti.

In many ways, this quarter century brought clear gains to the Beti: schools were opened throughout the region, and several thousand Beti learned to read and write and obtained government positions as clerks or teachers. Economically, though the Beti lands were exploited by large commercial firms, many Beti men emerged as planters of considerable wealth by local standards; large numbers of Beti became skilled masons, mechanics, and carpenters. Yet in a profound sense, this period left the Beti between two worlds. It cannot be said that the traditional Beti culture and social system was completely changed during this time, for in places it remained almost unaffected. Nevertheless, in some important ways, Beti society experienced an almost total transformation, especially in the creation of a new chiefly class, whose duties differed from those of Beti headmen but whose place in the French administration was of decidedly secondary importance. The French did not accept the chiefs in full confidence, and there was a growing gulf between chiefs and the populations they governed. A visit from a chief usually meant tax collections or recruitment for work gangs, and neither prospect improved a chief's position with local people. Although there were at least three reorganizations of the *chefferie* during the next quarter century, none of them halted the mainly administrative evolution of that institution.

Thus, the gap between the French and the chiefs did not close; but the distance between the chiefs and their subjects widened. None of these factors would have been evident, however, to a visitor to a prefecture in the interior of Cameroon in 1940. The handful of administrative buildings, seemingly cast from a mold that was used from Morocco to Indochina, the *commandant,* the dutiful African clerks, the folios of official correspondence, and the somnolent atmosphere of the nearby villages presented a scene that could be expected to endure forever, or so it seemed in 1940.

Notes

1. P. Billard, *La Circulation dans le Sud-Cameroun* (Lyon, 1961), p. 61.
2. *Rapport Annuel du Gouvernement Français sur l'Administration sous mandat des territoires du Cameroun pour l'année 1923* (Paris, 1924), pp. 75–76.
3. Billard, *La Circulation dans le Sud-Cameroun*, p. 62.
4. Ibid.
5. Ibid.
6. *Rapport Annuel*, pp. 78–79.
7. Ibid., p. 79.
8. These Beti songs were collected during the summer of 1967 by Pierre Betene, a Beti researcher, who translated them into French from Ewondo, after which the author translated them into English and shortened them for inclusion here.

9. Cameroon National Archives (referred to hereafter as CNA), 6295.
10. Ibid.
11. Ibid.
12. Max Abe Foudda, interview with author, Nkolbewa, 23 December 1967.
13. CNA 6213.
14. Ibid.
15. CNA 65199.
16. J. Guyer, "Feeding Yaounde, Capital of Cameroon," *Feeding African Cities, Studies in Regional Social History,* Jane I. Guyer, ed. (Manchester, UK, 1987), p. 120.
17. Ibid., p. 45.
18. J. Guyer, "Female Farming and the Evolution of Food Production Patterns amongst the Beti of South-Central Cameroon," *Africa,* vol. 50, no. 4 (1950): p. 349.
19. CNA 6519.
20. Ibid.
21. Ibid.
22. J. Champaud, "L'économie cacaoyère du Cameroun,'" p. 108.
23. CNA 6519.
24. Champaud, p.108.
25. *Rapport Annuel,* pp. 75–76.
26. R. Dussercle, Du Kilima-Ndjaro au Cameroun, Monseigneur F. X. Vogt (1870–1943) (Paris, n.d., ca. 1950), p. 80.
27. Ibid., p. 82.
28. Ibid., p. 76.
29. Ibid., p. 86.
30. Ibid., p. 102. T. Tsala, interview with author, Mvolye, 14 June 1968.
31. Dussercle, op. cit., p. 108.
32. Ibid., pp. 119–29.
33. CNA 6519.
34. Dussercle, op. cit., p. 94.
35. Dussercle, op. cit., p. 96.
36. Dussercle, op. cit., pp. 135ff.
37. Ibid., p. 138.
38. Ibid., p. 142.
39. Ibid., p. 146.
40. Ibid., p. 148.
41. T. Tsala, "Regles de Vie Sacredotale," Mvolye, pp. 2–6.
42. T. Tsala, "L'abbé Tobie Atangana, l'un des huit premiers pretres camerounais," Mvolye, p. 2.
43. "Regles de Vie Sacredotale," p. 8.
44. Ibid., pp. 5–6.
45. Tsala, "L'abbé Tobie Atangana," p. 5.
46. "Regles de Vie Sacredotale," p. 6.
47. Tsala, "L'abbé Tobie Atangana," p. 5.
48. G. and F. Towo-Atangana, *Nden, l'araignée-toilière (conte Beti)* (Yaoundé, 1966), p. 26.

CHAPTER 7

The Beti from World War II to Independence

Four main events shaped Beti history from the 1940s through 1960. World War II took place, bringing with it a slackening of French control of its African territories, and a class of educated *évoluées* (evolved) emerged. The *évoluées* had aspirations beyond what traditional society might have permitted them, and they threatened the established chiefs at every level. The chiefs, whom the French called "old, tired, and discouraged," continued to lose their hold on the populations under their control. Finally, the independence movement developed, giving Cameroon new political prospects, including African governance, and new political structures, through territorial assemblies, political parties, and eventually African control of the executive branch of government.

These events began with World War II. This war actually had less direct impact on the Beti than had World War I, but by this point, conditions in Cameroon were ripe for widespread political change. There was no fighting in Cameroon, and no mass exodus, although several thousand Beti joined the French Army and returned later as *anciens combattants* with government pensions and the status of traveled men.[1] The main events of the war in this part of Africa, the drama as to whether or not the mandated territory would side with General Henri Pétain or General Charles de Gaulle, was not one decided by Africans.[2]

There was a slight recrudescence of pro-German sentiment among some of the older Beti chiefs during the war, but this was not politically significant. A few chiefs remembered the German days with nostalgia and assumed the Germans would reward them if the latter returned. In fact, eventually the Germans gave modest sums to the relatively few survivors. Some aging teachers of the German period dug deep into their trunks for copies of textbooks preserved since German days and passed them on to younger Beti with the injunction to "learn German, it will soon be worth your while![3] But these were isolated instances, and there never was any indication of popular support for the Germans among the Beti.

One significant effect of the war was the permanent loosening of the French hold on Cameroon. French political control over Cameroon had until had remained unquestioned, and a generation of young Africans had been taught that Paris was

---

Notes for this chapter begin on page 114.

the pinnacle of civilization, and now it had fallen to the Nazis. But France would never again control Cameroon in the way it had before the war. What happened was a shift in attitudes; France was no longer seen as invincible, nor was its mandate seen as eternal. There was no revolt of the Beti, nor did the Beti engage in strikes or demonstrations of political activity.[4] The territory's budget was increased to aid the war effort, and additional taxes among Africans were levied to buy war supplies. Villages received posters with a large picture of an airplane and a caption reading "Here is the plane for which you gave the money."

The French carefully monitored what they called the *esprit des populations*, as well as the activities of travelers. They also followed events in surrounding countries with an eye toward their possible impact on Cameroon. When the French discovered cloth printed with the Nazi swastika being sold in African markets in Angola, they alerted administrative posts in Cameroon in case there was any attempt to distribute it in French territory.[5] The atmosphere was charged with Gallic suspicion; when American medical missionaries brought several boxes of equipment to their rainforest hospital by canoe, a French bush administrator, wondering if this was a plot to smuggle a Geiger counter into Cameroon, reported the incident accordingly.[6]

New Social Groups

The Évoluées

By the 1940s, the power of the Beti chiefs was seriously threatened by the emergence of the *évoluées*, who were free of the control of a chief, were relatively educated, and held jobs, however menial. This gave the *évoluées* a modicum of independence in relation to their traditional lineage. Their numbers grew to include government clerks, students, public health workers, and others employed by the colonial administration. Such people maintained that chiefs blocked the spread of education in the country and, through control of women and demands for high bride-price, kept young Beti from taking wives. As this new group gained access to the French courts and administrators, many made life difficult for the chiefs.

Many such people came as strangers to expanding urban centers to work in shops, for the administration, or in European homes as servants. They lacked both cohesion and goals, except for opposing the chiefs and creating better lives for themselves. Such people came to urban centers in increasing numbers, in search of work; they sought lodging with kinsmen, however distant, or with people from their villages. Many were poorly paid, unhappy with low salaries, the high cost of living, and the paucity of European manufactured goods for them to buy. For many, racial rivalries grew more acute, instead of disappearing, in the cities.[7] For diversion some gathered on Sunday afternoons for gossip or dancing, and when they could afford it, for afternoons spent drinking beer or palm wine with members of their own ethnic group. Many saved portions of their small salaries for European clothes, shoes, sunglasses, and briefcases, and later for bicycles and motor scooters.

Manual workers could often spend eight or ten days with an employer and, after collecting their wages, return to their villages for a week or two before returning or seeking new work. Contracts were unpopular with Beti workers, not because of salary terms, but because of their desire for independence. A French official in 1951 noted that the African masses appeared to be "derouted: they followed during several years a very rapid evolution in all domains."[8]

Returning Soldiers

Another important social group in the immediate postwar period was the *anciens combattants* who had been stationed throughout Africa, Europe, and the Orient. They provided villagers with news about conditions in other parts of the world, and their prestige rivaled that of the chiefs, most of whom had spent the war years in the rainforest. The chiefs unanimously reproached the *anciens combattants* for creating disorder in the villages, for inciting people against their authority, and for refusing to work.[9] But the former soldiers never became a political bloc, and a French report in 1951 observed that "the former soldiers appear rarely except for receptions, official ceremonies, and to seek tax exemptions."[10]

Changes in Village Life

The Spread of Cocoa Production

Economically, the dominant fact of the 1950s for the Beti was the increase in cocoa production, which meant more money was available to them. A 1954 survey of the family budgets of nearly five hundred Beti farmers suggested that 70 percent of their income was derived from the sale of cocoa. The second source of income was bridewealth, which accounted for on average about 10 percent of a household's income.[11] One side result of the increased cocoa production was that taxes were easier to collect, since more cash was in circulation. Beti farmers were individualistic in outlook and prosperous enough not to be prone to strikes and *jacquerie* (peasant revolts), and the political message of extremist groups like the UPC (Union des Populations Camerounais) had little appeal for the Beti.[12]

As urban centers expanded, the demand for foodstuffs increased; Beti women grew maize, groundnuts, manioc, plantins, and eventually European vegetables to sell in the cities. In January 1947, more than 25 tons of food spoiled in the Yaoundé market in a consumer's boycott against increased prices.[13] By the 1950s, most of the major roads around Yaoundé were completed, and, as motor vehicle ownership became more widespread, Africans could travel quickly and easily through the district. This also made it easier to transport foodstuffs to town and commercial goods to rural markets.[14] By the 1950s, an average-sized household in a Beti cocoa-producing region could include five people, two of whom would be productive adults.[15] The Beti lands were fertile, and fruits and vegetables were abundant during the post–World War II period; hunting was in sharp decline; and settlement patterns were stabilized. Since the 1920s, the French had used force to move the Beti from the forest to small villages, in which anywhere from 200 to 1,000 people would live; the villages were situated adjacent to roads, facilitating the hiring of laborers and collecting of taxes. Guyer has observed, "The quasi-impossibility of moving settlements or creating a new one for several decades, has contributed to changing land-use patterns, as well as containing the old political cycle whereby new leaders hived off. Houses were now individualized, and one never sees the *abaa* of the past, the men's meetinghouse with its fire at night for collective gatherings. The present houses, with their tin roofs and no fire except in the women's kitchens, are thought of as 'cold houses.'"[16]

Shirley Deane, an Australian English teacher who worked in Cameroon during the 1970s and 1980s, spent weekends over three years with the women of Etam, an Eton village 20 kilometers from Yaoundé. There she noted the changing role of women as farmers. As the capital grew, demand for food increased. Peanuts, yams, macabos, and manioc, once grown by women for home consumption, became cash crops, and every Saturday before dawn women began walking to make the Yaoundé Saturday market. Thus, they became income earners, along with the men, who grew the main cash crops, coffee, and cocoa.[17] "At the same time, the needs of a village, however humble, have become more sophisticated," Deane wrote. "More and better pots and saucepans, two lamps instead of one, and most expensive of all, education. For every villager I met in Etam was determined to send his children to school, and give them chances they never had, despite the expense—not only fees and books and pencils, but clothes respectable enough to go to school in."[18]

David Gardinier has estimated that the number of salaried working-class employees in Cameroon rose as high as 130,000; those employed by the government rose to 26,000 people by the late 1950s. To these groups were added a small peasant farmer class and a *petite bourgeoisie* engaged in agriculture and commerce.[19] These changes in the Cameroonian economy also reflected social changes.

The Spread of Schools

A lycée was opened in Yaoundé after World War II, and several hundred Beti attended it annually. The Roman Catholic missionary schools also continued to function, as did the major and minor seminaries, turning out both clerics and persons who became employed by the government. In the postwar period, several hundred Beti and other Cameroonian students were also sent to schools in France. Here they met other Africans and witnessed the turbulent postwar French political atmosphere. Their studies included the works of Voltaire and Montesquieu, and it was not long before the arguments of such French thinkers were applied to an African context; their appeals for liberty and rationality were found inimical with colonial control. From classic French satirists like Molière, the young Africans learned that nothing in the political or religious kingdom was above scrutiny and humor. Two Beti writers, Mongo Beti (also known as Alexandre Biyidi, 1930–2001), and Ferdinand Oyono (1929) contributed substantially to portraying the African-European encounter of their day. Père Drumont, the beleaguered French bush priest in Mongo Beti's 1956 book entitled *Le Pauve Christ de Bomba*, and Zacharia, his scheming cook, set out on an ill-fated tour of the interior. Zacharia demanded women, goats, and palm wine from Christian villagers while the priest was instructing Africans in how to be faithful Christians. Meanwhile, Denis the favored local catechist, infected several members of the *sixa*, the mission center for preparing young women for Christian marriage, with venereal disease. The book, a best seller decades later, allowed a generation of literate Beti readers to look at missionaries and administrators and their African followers at their most vulnerable points.

Ferdinand Oyono, in *Le vieux nègre et la médaille* (1956) and *Une vie de boy* (1960), also portrayed bush missionaries and administrators as they were seen by villagers, in the first novel from the viewpoint of Meka, an aged villager who was given a medal but then was dismissed by the French official who awarded it to him at a subsequent reception. Meka spoke at the reception, telling the "great chief" no African has ever been invited to dine with a white man, but he would like to invite the "great chief" to share a meal of young goat offered by his people in celebration of the medal he has been awarded by France. The great chief responded through an interpreter, "He eats your goat with you in thought and is sorry that he cannot come and eat it with you because he is going away. But he invites you to come and eat with him some other time. And this promise is the beginning of a new era, something like that."[20]

The second book depicts the viewpoint of a serving boy living among Europeans. Little of the personal lives or the shortcomings of the rural representatives of church and state was left unexamined by these two Beti writers. Their work exposed the inner workings of the French presence for all the world to see.

The career trajectories of Beti and Oyono went in different directions. Beti, after graduating in 1951 from the Lycée Leclerc in Yaoundé, studied classics at the Sorbonne and became part of the *Présence Africaine* movement of African and francophone intellectuals. He stayed in France until 1991, teaching classical literature in several provincial schools while producing a stream of satirical political novels, such as *Ville cruelle* (1954), *Mission terminée* (1957), and *Le Roi miraculé* (1958). His biting prose style drew blood among government audiences, and most of his works were forbidden in Cameroon. In *Main basse sur le Cameroun, autopsie d'une décolonisation* (1972), he turned his attention to the dark side of French colonial political and economic exploitation. The book included a searing attack on the politics of Ahamadou Ahidjou, and its sale was forbidden in France. This attack was led by another Beti author, Ferdinand Oyono, at the time Cameroon's ambassador to France. A 1976 French court order allowed distribution of the book, and Beti followed it with another, *Remember Ruben* (1974), a fictional tribute to the UPC independence leader, Ruben Um Nyobé, a leftist trade unionist who was killed in 1958 by the French Army in the Cameroonian rainforest. Returning to Cameroon in 1991, after thirty-two years of exile, Beti became a human rights and free speech activist. His *Lettre ouverte aux Camerounais, ou, la deuxième mort de Ruben Um Nyobé* was a frontal attack on the politics and corruption of Ahidjou's successor, Paul Biya. Beti was the victim of police brutality in 1996 and died of kidney failure in Douala on 6 October 2001.

By contrast, Ferdinand Oyono was a more conventional establishment figure. After studies in Yaoundé and Paris, he attended law school at the University of Paris and the prestigious École Nationale d'Administration. Next he became a career diplomat, serving initially in the French foreign service, then as a Cameroonian diplomat in Algeria, Liberia, the European Community, the United States, London, Paris, and at the United Nations (1975–1983). His literary production came entirely during his student days in Paris in the 1950s. *Le vieux nègre et la médaille, Une vie de boy,* and *Chemin d'Europe* (1960) became mainstays in anthologies of African writings of the late colonial era. Oyono returned to Cameroon in 1985 and in 1986 became minister of housing and urban affairs, and in eventually minister of state in charge of cultural affairs.

Thus, the Beti in the 1950s were increasingly gaining a modicum of economic independence from their own rulers, and, through education, they had achieved a critical spirit that allowed them both to laugh at and seriously question the claims of traditional rulers and the French who governed them.

As Yaoundé's population grew, other ethnic groups established a strong presence, leaving the Beti with diminished influence in their homeland. By 1957, the population of Yaoundé grew to over 54,000 (this figure would double within a decade). But only 55 percent of the population was Beti, mostly Ewondo and Eton, in whose region the capital city was set. The other large ethnic group was the Bamiléké, who represented 15 percent of the city's population and who just outnumbered the Beti in the important commercial sector, by 1,001 to 939. The Bamiléké, who originated in the grasslands near the West Cameroon border, increasingly came to Yaoundé and other Cameroonian cities as traders in the postwar period. Their numbers, their commitment to helping one another through mutual aid societies, and their talent for commerce quickly made the Bamiléké the dominant economic group in Yaoundé.

The Beti, as before, had the largest numbers in the administration (with over 3,700 government employees). Of the 12,000 Africans in the capital who could read and write French, 7,000 were Beti. This is a pattern that would continue; literate Beti would provide many of the office worker-clerical positions in government offices.

Change in the Church

The number of Roman Catholics among the Beti continued to grow in the postwar period. At the same time, the gradual Africanization of the Catholic clergy produced a generation of clerics whose nationalistic outlooks supported the movement toward Cameroonian independence.

In 1947, there were about 115,000 Roman Catholics and 5,200 Protestants in and around Yaoundé. There were twenty Cameroonian priests and thirty French priests. An additional 150 Roman Catholic schools were scattered throughout the region, with a total of approximately 9,000 students. By 1960, the number of Catholics among the Beti in the Yaoundé and Mbalmayo dioceses was 400,000.[21]

Influenced in part by the *Présence Africaine* movement of writers, artists, and intellectuals of the late 1950s, some of the African clergy, like the Beti Jesuit priest, Englebert Mveng, sought to incorporate African music, art, and beliefs into Roman Catholic worship. Bishop René Graffin was opposed to such changes, and when Dr. Louis Aujoulat, a lay missionary and politician, advocated naming an African bishop, a long-smoldering dispute between him and the French bishop erupted. The African clergy had been hoping for an African bishop for more than a decade, but the issue had never been raised in public.[22]

Yielding to pressure, Bishop Graffin consecrated an African auxiliary, Paul Etoga, an Ewondo, in 1955. Bishop Etoga was later transferred to the newly created diocese of Mbalmayo, and in 1961, Abbé Jean Zoa (1924–1998) was named auxiliary bishop of Yaoundé, with right of succession when Graffin retired.[23] Bishop Zoa, thirty-three years old at the time, was a Beti from the Mangisa ethnic group at Saa. He had attended mission schools near his home and the seminaries at Akono and Mvolye, and in 1949, went to Rome where he earned a doctoral degree in theology in 1952. After returning to Cameroon, he spent two years at Ombessa, on the northern side of the Sanaga River and then in the crowded urban parish of Mokolo in Yaoundé. In 1958, he was named director of diocesan works, founded a review called *Nova et Vetera*, and, through the parishes, organized night courses for adults and young people. Bishop Zoa also published a tract *Pour un Nationalisme Chrétien au Cameroun*, in which he tried to juxtapose the positions of emerging Cameroonian nationalism with Christianity. He argued that Catholicism, Protestantism, and Islam were all religions imported into Cameroon and that adherents of all three should cooperate, live in peace, and contribute to building the Cameroonian nation.

The church continued to oppose polygamy in the postwar period, but it is difficult to escape the conclusion that economic, not religious, pressures caused its decline among the Beti. An administrative survey from 1952 showed that, out of 100 chiefs, seventy were Roman Catholic, twenty-three animist, four Protestant, and three Muslim. Only thirty-one of the chiefs were monogamous; those identifying themselves as polygamous listed anywhere from 25 to 35 wives (some respondents claimed to have 40, 60, and 80 wives).[24] Shirley Deane, an Australian teacher of English who lived among the rural Beti, described the postwar decline of polygamy and the response of some Roman Catholic clergy to it. Persons married in the church were assumed to be Christian. But if a Christian husband took a second wife, the couple could attend church but not receive communion, although the first wife could. "So times are changing," Deane wrote, "and in fact the practice of polygamy is less common than it used to be. This is partly an economic necessity, as large chunks of the rural population move to towns and the developing industries. Such wives have no fields to cultivate, so need no help with them. And it's hard enough to feed one wife and her children on a salary without fields, let alone two or three."[25]

The Bridewealth Question

The church also opposed the payment of bridewealth, as it had before, but often to little avail. In 1947 in Akonolinga, one of the less affluent parts of the Beti lands, bride-price, which included quantities of sheep and salt, ran anywhere from 3,000 to 10,000 francs among rural families. In 1950 in Yaoundé, it could run as high as 50,000 francs and 30 goats, and one Beti employee of the police reportedly paid 60,000 francs in bridewealth for his wife.[26]

In 1953, the French tried to set maximum rice figures by regions. One Beti abbé said that without enforcement, the proposal would not work because there would always be "les dots de marché noir" (black-market bridewealth). Sometimes payments came in three stages, the agreed-upon sum to let the marriage take place, a second round of gifts or obligations made at the marriage ceremony, and, finally, long-term obligations made to the bride's family. A brother might desire a pair of shoes, an uncle might see this as an opportunity to obtain a new suit, others as a way of obtaining European goods.

In 1953, it might have taken ten years for an African earning between two and three thousand francs a month to raise the seventy thousand francs of money and goods needed to complete his payment. In traditional Beti society, a major purpose of marriage was to create links between lineages, but high bridewealth obligations extended over long periods of time risked creating friction instead.

The Declining Power of Chiefs

The Beti chief's power diminished markedly during the postwar period, and the chiefs never regained the importance they once had. Their role was reduced to little more than messengers when the *corvée* was abolished and the direct collection of taxes administered through the government. Looking back across the span of Beti history, it is difficult to see how it could have been otherwise. The chief's power was neither firmly anchored in traditional society nor in the French administration. When it ceased being useful to the administration, the *chefferie* was left to wither on the vine.

By 1946, the administration acknowledged "an open opposition against the authority of the chiefs." The following year, an administrator in Yaoundé said "the indigenous leaders are overwhelmed" and "a general unrest and indescribable confusion" affected the *chefferie*.[27] "Young or old, the chiefs have lost their authority and new ideas of a political and economic nature have upset the old hierarchy."[28] As evidence of the chief's declining influence, an administrator said that he and a chief made a trip together to obtain workers for a forestry concession and emerged with only twenty-six laborers. A decade earlier such an effort would have turned up several hundred workers.[29]

Rivalries among the chiefs were also widespread at a time when the administration and educated Cameroonians increasingly regarded the chiefs as an anachronism and a hindrance to progress. The main, but not the only, such rivalry was a personality conflict between Martin Abega, successor to Charles Atangana, and Andre Amougou, *chef supérieur* of the Bane.[30] Martin Abega was named *chef supérieur* by the French after Atangana's death in 1943. He was forty-nine years old at the time and kept the post until his death fifteen years later. A Roman Catholic with ten sons and six wives, he was recognized by the French as a hardworking and competent administrator. The French gave him frequent letters of commendation, including one for having successfully decorated the town of Yaoundé on General de Gaulle's passage through it in 1941.[31] By local standards Abega was wealthy. He owned nearly forty thousand cocoa plants and cost the French government nearly ten million francs in 1951 in basic salary, tax rebates, bonuses, and financial assistance in constructing a large residence and tribunal. The French felt that Abega's utility to them did not justify such substantial sums.[32] Abega is recorded as having made two public utterances during the last years of his *chefferie*. In 1949, when a United Nations fact-finding group visited

Yaoundé, he gave a long panegyric praising the French for their contributions to Cameroon in education, public health, and agriculture. A few years later he castigated a rival chief for having called a meeting of the Association Amicale des Chefs Traditionelle du Cameroun, of which he was president, without consulting him.[33] As the *chef supérieur* died, they were not replaced, and their territories were divided into smaller chiefdoms, each directly responsible to the administrator of the subdivision.[34]

Several forces contributed to the further decline of the *chefferie*. There were stirrings of what would become widespread political activity in Cameroon, and it was their former subjects who took advantage of the opportunities presented. There were five important elections in the period 1945–1950, and each marked a progressive loss in the chief's ability to influence events. For example, in 1952, Bane territory was divided into four electoral zones; residents of each one voted for different lists of candidates, none of whom were supported by the chiefs.[35] In the 1952 elections for municipal counselors, the chiefs lost heavily, then had to deal with their former subjects as equals. The chief were described as "old, tired and discouraged" and the counselors "more young, more active, more adept to new times." Moreover, as the urban centers grew, chiefs of specific ethnic groups and chiefs of African groups who had moved to town from elsewhere were replaced by neighborhood chiefs (*chef de quartier*).[36]

The troubled status of the Beti chiefs was set forth in a set of annual report cards the French administration had established on each by 1952. For that year a hundred reports on chiefs are available for the Nyong and Sanaga regions, covering thirteen *chefs supérieurs*. The rest were *chefs de groupement* and a few lower chiefs. Slightly less than half the chiefs received favorable comments in the narrative section, and the chiefs most in favor were noted for their loyalty to France and the administration, their ability to collect taxes, and the absence of serious disputes in their districts. No chiefs were criticized for their political views; presumably such chiefs would have been removed before the reports were prepared. Objections were generally that chiefs lacked ambition or were solely occupied with personal gain. There was a string of descriptions, such as *têtu* (headstrong) and *parresseux* (parasitic), and not a few were remarked on as being a *figure du passé* (a figure of the past). One was accused of confusing his administrative calls with *parties de chasse* (hunting parties). Four of the chiefs had stood in local elections; only one was elected.

A third of the chiefs were past fifty years in age; only twenty-six of the one hundred chiefs were younger than their early forties. In terms of religion, seventy were Roman Catholic, twenty-three animist, three Muslim (from near Nanga-Eboko and the northeastern frontier of the Beti region), and four were Protestant. More than half the chiefs were decorated by the French government from the Légion d'Honneur with medals for crop growing; twenty-one were listed as having some fluency in French.[37]

The Beti chiefs made little contribution to the development of Cameroonian nationalism or the independence movement, nor did they appear to be aware of the implications of such movements. They fought the *évoluées* and did little to encourage the spread of schools and local institutions, such as cooperatives, town councils, or political parties, which they interpreted as threats to their power. By indoctrinating their sons in the ambiance of the chiefly life, they left their potential successors without the educational skills or vision necessary to function effectively in the new Cameroon. As they died, the Beti chiefs were not replaced.

Postwar Politics

In 1945, the United Nations was founded, and it assumed responsibility for the former League of Nations mandate territories such as Togoland and Cameroon. The fact that these territories had the statutory right to eventual independence became increasingly important to their inhabitants. Many Cameroonians had been aware that their status was different from that of a colony, but the difference did not seem important until after World War II. It is tempting to assume that events in countries such as Gold Coast or India, Indochina or elsewhere, contributed to the development of the independence movement among Cameroonians. For the Beti, at least, the evidence of such outside events contributing toward independence sentiment is negligible. There were no African newspapers until after World War II, and radio broadcasts were closely controlled by the government. More important to the independence movement than external influences was the return of a steady stream of Cameroonians, first from military service, then as students in France, in the later 1940s and early 1950s.

In 1946, the labor code was revoked by France. This meant that the administration could no longer summarily requisition Africans to work on road gangs or for government projects. In that same year, mixed communes were created, providing a French-African council of limited powers in certain municipalities. The newly elected African councilors frequently feuded with the chiefs, and the administration tried to solve the problem by calling the roles of counselor and chief complementary. Chiefs were supposed to represent traditional authority, and councilors only exercised authority when councils were in session, but this distinction satisfied neither side.[38]

In October 1946, deputies from Africa were elected to the French National Assembly for the first time; the following year, a territorial assembly was created for Cameroon. The voting franchise was also progressively broadened. Voting lists were drawn from notables, medal winners, veterans, *fonctionnaires*, clergy, planters, persons who had been salaried workers or members of cooperatives or unions for at least two years, as well as those who had laborer's papers, hunting permits, or driver's licenses. Later the franchise was extended to anyone who could read French or Arabic.

At one time there were eighty-four political parties in Cameroon. Three of the parties are important to this narrative, the Union des Populations Camerounaise (UPC) because of its use of violence and because it brought the issue of independence to the forefront; the Bloc Démocratique Camerounaise (BDC) because it was the party that attracted the Beti; and the Union Camerounaise because, with its leader Ahamadou Ahidjou, it ultimately won the dominant place in Cameroonian politics.

The Failure of the UPC among the Beti

From about 1950 to 1955, the Union des Populations Camerounaise helped make the issue of independence an immediate question for Cameroon. The UPC raised the issue through violence and terrorism and through skillfully creating an international forum for Cameroonian independence through the United Nations and in France. Its financial and political sponsor in France was the Communist party.

The UPC's most important achievement was forcing Africans and Frenchmen to talk about independence. In Cameroon the party was well-organized but always had a small following, chiefly among the Basa and Bamilékée peoples. It never was strong among the Beti.[39]

The UPC called a general strike in April 1951, but it failed. The Beti, who were enjoying a high price for cocoa, their principal crop, and were not inclined to strike. Also in 1951, the UPC was outlawed by the French council of ministers and expelled from the Rassemblement Démocratique Africain. After that, the UPC went underground, functioning as a clandestine organization. On the broader front of Cameroonian politics, its electoral showings were always poor and its parliamentary influence nil. Ahidjou and the Union Camerounaise stole the UPC's thunder by not only advocating independence but by negotiating a timetable for Cameroonian independence.

The party favored by the Beti was the Bloc Démocratique Camerounais, which had ties with the Parti d'Independance d'Outre-Mer, a center-left party of the French Fourth Republic. The BDC's leader was a locally well-respected French physician, Dr. Louis-Paul Aujoulet, who had come to Cameroon as a lay medical missionary in 1935. Aujoulet was elected one of the three deputies from Cameroon to the French National Assembly in 1947. He won again in 1951 but on an African ticket, as his politics in support of African social and economic betterment had lost him followers among French residents in Cameroon.[40] The Beti supported Aujoulet because of his long history working as a medical doctor. A French administrator of the period wrote that the Beti voted for Aujoulet because they believed that "if Aujoulet is elected we will have medicine."[41] Aujoulet was president of the Cameroonian Territorial Assembly from 1951 to 1954 when Paul Soppo-Priso, a Duala businessman, defeated him. Soppo-Priso had the support of André-Marie Mbida, the most important Beti political figure in Aujoulet's party.

André-Marie Mbida, Prime Minister

In 1956, André-Marie Mbida (1917–1978), Aujoulet's main African supporter, felt strong enough to run against his old mentor. Mbida defeated Aujoulet with 64,397 of the votes (to Aujoulet's 18,915). It was an acrimonious campaign. Mbida broke with the BDC, labeling them the "Bloc des Démagogues du Cameroun" and the "Bourgeoise des Démagogues Camerounaise." The era in which a European could expect to have an elected political following among Africans was over by 1956, and Aujoulet withdrew from Cameroonian electoral politics. After Mbida's victory in 1956, the old BDC party dissolved, and Mbida fused its remnants with his followers from the Démocrats du Cameroun Party to form the Groupement des Démocrats du Cameroun Party, which held a thin majority in the assembly.

Mbida, who was about fifty years old at the time, was a product of Roman Catholic Schools. He had attended seminary for eight years, but was dismissed in July 1943, shortly before his scheduled ordination, after a dispute with the seminary's Swiss director. Mbida's seminary education helped shape his political outlook. He studied Greek and Roman history and was impressed, as were other young Africans, by Hannibal's defeat of the Romans. "That struck me the most," he once recalled. Vercingetorix's defeat of the Romans and Alexander's victory over the Greeks also impressed the young seminarians. By contrast, the French Revolution, although also taught in the seminary history courses, apparently did not impress Mbida to any degree.[42] He became a government teacher at Balsing, near Dschang, in the Bamiléké region from 1943 to 1945, but left teaching after a disagreement with the French director of schools for the region. From 1945 to 1953, he was an *Avocat-Defenseur* in Ebolowa and Sangmalina, where he defended Africans against the French administration, especially in cases of alleged violations of the labor code. His entry into politics came in 1952, when Aujoulet invited Mbida, as an Eton leader, to join an electoral list composed of himself, the Chief Martin Abega, and an Ewondo candidate. They were elected to the territorial council.

On late Sunday afternoon, 10 May 1957, High Commissioner Pierre Messmer summoned Mbida, then a deputy and leader of the twenty-deputy Groupe des Démocrats Camerounaise (GDC), and asked him to become Cameroon's first prime minister. Mbida was picked by the French because his party had a thin majority of the deputies and because he did not advocate independence but based his political program on close ties with France.[43] As prime minister, he appointed a cabinet including seven members of his GDC party. Ahidjou became vice prime minister, and five members of his party were included in the cabinet.

Mbida served as prime minister for nine troubled months. The future course of relations with France were uncertain. At the same time, the new government had to deal with UPC terrorism and growing sentiment for independence and reunification of the two Cameroons. On 21 February 1960 the Cameroon Republic was formed of former French Cameroon, and on 1 October 1961 former British Southern Cameroon was joined to what became the Federal Republic of Cameroon, an uneasy union of a large former French and a smaller former British state. Moreover, Mbida's majority in the cabinet and assembly was always tenuous, and his rigid, blustery manner contributed actively to his steady loss of power. In September 1957, four months after the prime minister came to power, the UPC announced it was willing to lay down arms if given amnesty, new elections, immediate independence, and dissolution of the assembly. Some support existed among members of the assembly for one of the proposals, granting amnesty to UPC members, but the prime minister rejected the offer. Mbida's answer was to go to the home village of the UPC leader, Um Reuben, and threaten reprisals against all who did not come out of the forest and return home within ten days. He stood there at the village limits, waving his fists and bellowing into the rainforest, but his tactic did not work. Next, he went to Paris and demanded more troops to patrol the UPC region. Although he got the troops, the strident manner in which he made his presentation to the French earned him few friends, and his reputation for intransigence grew.

In several ways Mbida failed to gauge popular political sentiment during his nine-month premiership. As late as 1957, he talked vaguely of independence at some further date, possibly ten years hence, but by then popular sentiment favored immediate independence. Ahidjou's Union Camerounaise campaigned on an "independence by 1960" platform. The Union Camerounaise also adopted the popular issue of reunification with West Cameroon, a topic not included in Mbida's agenda. On 18 February 1958, cabinet members belonging to the Union Camerounaise resigned, provoking a political crisis from which Ahidjou emerged as prime minister. He went briefly into voluntary exile in Conakry, Guinea, and after his return in 1960, was again elected to the assembly, jailed for an alleged anti-Ahidjou conspiracy, then released in 1965.

Mbida was prime minister of Cameroon at a difficult time, but he did not succeed in dealing with any of the major problems facing him. A major reason for his failure was his personality. He was a solitary operator in a situation that required political cooperation and balance; he was also a rigid moralist who loudly and publicly dismissed anyone who objected to his plans. He did little to bring Cameroonian parties and peoples together. In fact, he managed to alienate many of his Beti supporters. In the mid 1950s, Benoit Bindzi, who would later become foreign minister of Cameroon, was a customs officer and active member of Mbida's party. They disagreed on an issue, and when Mbida became prime minister, he sent Bindzi to the customs brigade at Fort Foureau, the northernmost town in Cameroon on the Chad border. Some Ewondo said that Mbida, as an Eton, used his office to settle old scores that had accumulated over several generations of Ewondo looking down on the Eton.[44]

What ultimately became more significant to the Beti than the Mbida premiership was the fact that Africanization of government jobs meant that many Beti, who were products of mission and French schools, moved to important positions in the Cameroonian bureaucracy. Cameroon's foreign minister had generally been a Beti, as had many of the major posts in the Foreign Office and many of the other government ministries.

On 12 June 1958, the Cameroonian assembly voted for complete internal autonomy, independence, and an end of the trusteeship. On 2 October 1958, the assembly opted for independence on 1 January 1960. On 5 May 1960, Ahidjou was elected Cameroon's first president, a position he held until his resignation for health reasons on 4 November 1982.

Since 8 November 1982, Paul Biya has been Cameroon's president. Biya rose from being a civil servant to becoming Cameroon's president in twenty years. A Bulu, a southern rainforest group related to the Beti, Biya was born on 13 February 1933 in the village of Mvomeoka, the son of a Roman Catholic catechist. After attending mission schools and the Lycée General Leclerc in Yaoundé, he received a scholarship in 1960 to study Latin, Greek, and philosophy at the University of Paris, where he stayed twelve years. Following his return to Cameroon in 1962, Biya became a trusted aide of President Ahamadou Ahidjou. Biya was the loyal, educated Christian southerner who complemented the northern Muslim politician, Ahidjou, and his loyalists. Biya became minister of state and secretary general to the president from 1968 to 1975, then prime minister in 1975. His rise in the Union National Camerounais (UNC), backed by his patron, the president, was equally meteoric. Then on 6 November 1982, Ahidjou, affected by adverse medical reports, resigned the presidency. Biya, as prime minister, stepped in. Soon the loyal northerners of the Ahidjou era were replaced in the even longer Biya era by loyal southerners, many of them Beti. In 1983, faced with unrest and a coup attempt, Biya forced the removal of Ahidjou from his party position, although by then the former president was in exile, alternating residence between Dakar and France. Meanwhile, Biya consolidated his tight control of the government and the country's sole political party, which became the Rassemblement Démocratique du Peuple Camerounais (RPDC) in 1984. In the presidential elections of 1988, 1992, and 1997, Biya stood as the only candidate, and claimed nearly 100 percent of the vote, not without considerable internal and international protest.

Notes

1. E. Mveng, *Histoire du Cameroun* (Paris, 1963), p. 404.
2. V. LeVine, *The Cameroons: From Mandate to Independence* (Los Angeles, 1964), p. 131.
3. Mveng, *Histoire du Cameroun*, p. 26. Benoit Bindzi, interview with author, Yaoundé, 20 May 1968.
4. Mveng, *Histoire du Cameroun*, p. 403.
5. Cameroon National Archives (referred to hereafter as CNA), 6478.
6. Ibid.
7. CNA 6210.
8. Ibid.
9. Ibid.
10. Ibid.
11. CNA 6214.
12. Quoted in J. Champaud, "L'Économie cacaoyère du Cameroun." In Cahiers O.R.S.T.O.M., *Sciences Humaines* (Paris), vol. III, no. 3. (Paris, 1966): pp. 105–24. Champaud, pp. 116–17).
13. CNA 6183.
14. CNA 6210.
15. J. Guyer, "The Provident Societies in the Rural Economy of Yaoundé, 1945–1960." Boston University African Studies Center, Working Papers, Series No. 37 (Boston, 1980), p. 350.
16. J. Guyer, "Family and Farm in Southern Cameroon," Boston University African Research Studies, Working Papers, Series No. 15 (Boston, 1984), p. 12.
17. S. Deane, *Talking Drums, from a Village in Cameroon* (London, 1985), p. 72.
18. Ibid., p. 11.
19. David E. Gardinier, *Cameroun, United Nations Challenge to French Policy* (London, 1963), p. 31.
20. F. Oyono, *The Old Man and the Medal*, trans. John Reed, Jr. (London, 1969), p. 107.
21. D. Gardinier, *Cameroun, United Nations Challenge to French Policy* (London, 1963), p. 31.
22. CNA 6210-6.
23. Bishop Jean Zoa, letter to author, 4 December 1967.
24. CNA 6183.
25. S. Deane, *Talking Drums, from a Village in Cameroon* (London, 1985), p. 69.
26. CNA 6183.
27. CNA 6210.

28. Ibid.
29. CNA 6214.
30. CNA 6210.
31. Ibid.
32. CNA 62105.
33. CNA 6292.
34. CNA 6210-8.
35. CNA 6214.
36. CNA 6219.
37. CNA 6210.
38. Mveng, p. 408. Benoit Bindzi, interview with author, Yaoundé, 20 June 1968. Jean-Faustin Bétéyene, interview with author, Yaoundé, 18 July 1968.
39. CNA 6217.
40. Mveng, p. 443. CNA 6292.
41. CNA 6292.
42. André-Marié Mbida, interview with author, Yaoundé, 20 July 1968.
43. *L'effort Camerounaise* (Yaoundé weekly newspaper) 19 May 1957, p. 1, 26 May 1957, p. 1.
44. Benoit Bindzi, interview with author, Yaoundé, 20 June 1968.

Conclusion

A way of contrasting the changes in Beti society from the 1880s to the 1960s is to consider what an aerial photograph of the Beti lands would reveal for the two periods. In the 1880s, such a photograph would show rainforest, unrelieved except for a web of footpaths between some of the thousands of individual headman's compounds. Space was cut for gardens around the compounds, and these gardens provided for the immediate needs of those who lived near them, but not much more. Wild animals, including elephants, were visible in parts of the rainforest and in the savanna to the north.

Such a photograph would say something about Beti society and its interests in the 1880s. There was no capitol nor sizeable population centers; a compound was an isolated, independent unit, governed by its individual headmen. Life in the rainforest at this time was leisurely; communication with the coast was rare until German times. Headmen spent much of their time hunting or conversing with other headmen in the courtyard or in the *abaa*, the large headman's reception hut.

There would be substantial changes in a picture taken of the same region in the 1960s. The rainforest had receded, and all through it were passages indicating cocoa plantations and gardens to supply the growing urban centers, or forestry concessions, run by French companies, who systematically denuded the rainforest of its large trees. There were trails through the rainforest, but also roads extending like radials in all directions from Cameroon's capital, Yaoundé, by now a sprawling city of 60,000 inhabitants from many ethnic groups.

The railroad to the coast, which took nearly twenty years to build, functioned now as if it had been a permanent fixture of the landscape, and an airport was built outside Yaoundé, connecting the capital with other large Cameroonian cities and Cameroon with other countries in Africa, France, and the wider world.

An aerial view of the Beti lands in the mid twentieth century would show some of the large houses and plantations that had once belonged to chiefs like Charles Atangana and Max Abe Foudda. These houses were not kept up as the *chefferie* declined in importance, and many large plantations by this time had been divided into smaller units among kinsmen.

If the physical appearance of the Beti land underwent substantial changes in the course of a century, the political, economic, and cultural changes experienced by the Beti were no less profound. The broad lines are fairly easy to trace. Traditional political organization was characterized by several thousand independent

---

Notes for this section are located on page 118.

headmen, and the Beti economy was largely self-sustaining, depending on hunting and growing. Culturally, the *Sso* rite provided the mythos from which most Beti explanations about the world and its deeper questions were drawn. In the German period, the Beti experienced several important structural changes. An order of appointed chiefs, which was backed by the administration was responsible for collecting taxes and finding laborers for public works, replaced many of the headmen of traditional society. Long-distance trade brought an influx of coastal traders to the interior, but the Beti never became traders as a group in the way that, for instance, the Bamiléké did. While many Beti men went to the coast as porters or plantation workers, the Beti as a whole missed out on becoming a class of commercial entrepreneurs and businessmen, leaving those roles to others, while exacting tribute for those who crossed their lands.

During the German period, the *Sso* rite was outlawed and gradually replaced by Roman Catholic Christianity, and the Beti became converts in great numbers. An increasing number of Beti became government workers, clerks, policemen, and medical attendants, creating the foundations of what would be an expanding Beti presence in government employment. During the French period that followed, the chiefs, while apparently strongly in control on the surface, represented a crumbling institution. They were gradually superceded by a new wave of persons who were educated in French schools and found jobs as clerks and office managers in the French administration. Government employment would be the ticket for upward mobility for most Beti who desired to improve their lot. As the government expanded, educated Beti found positions in its highest echelons, including cabinet posts. Cameroon's first prime minister was a Beti, and in 1982 Cameroon's second president came from the Bulu, a Beti-related Bantu group. Economically, the spread of roads, the building of a railroad, and widespread cocoa production brought a cash economy and gradually rising income to the Beti. Roman Catholicism continued to attract the Beti, and the numbers of converts rose steadily. However, the church was less successful in combating polygamy and in eliminating bride-price.

The dynamics of social change among the Beti was stated somewhat differently by Jane Guyer, who worked with rural women farmers around Yaoundé in the mid 1970s: "[T]he economic and political structure had been revolutionized,... fundamental relationships overruled by law, indigenous ritual outlawed and religion superceded by Catholicism, house styles have been changed, settlement patterns administratively fixed, the game more or less hunted out, and the forest turned into a patchwork of cocoa farms."[1]

In the postwar period, the growing adoption of French law and economic practices favored the spread of smaller peasant family structures engaged in small unit cocoa production around Yaoundé. Men of any status, not necessarily headmen, could now become cocoa farmers. Women could earn money growing vegetables for sale in the growing capital. This did not produce a panacea for the problems faced by Beti women, but women's gains in the modern period were better than in traditional and colonial times. Guyer observed, "Women were not accumulating independent wealth and status, but the basis was being laid, in monogamous marriage and a feminized food production pattern, for a greater share in the rural product."[2]

The process of historical change in a society such as the Beti is not like the changes that take place on photographic paper when it is exposed to light. Not all individuals and institutions changed with the same speed or in the same way. Some individual headmen, at least during the German period, actively resisted the European intrusions, sometimes militarily. Others, like many students and workers in the German and French administrations, quickly became acclimated to European ways and adopted them as their own. Still other tribesmen, far from the urban centers and away from the main roads, experienced little change in their outlook or way of doing things until late in this period. Even then, the main changes they would experience would be the demand for taxes or time spent on government work projects.

In the final analysis, the story of the Beti belongs to the larger history of the Africa, Asia, and Latin America societies whose stories form part of the world-wide historical transformation of modern times. Some of these societies have most, but not all, of the ingredients, that would allow them to emerge as viable political units in modern times. The Beti represent such a society. They had a common language, culture, and homeland that was more than adequate for their needs. But they also had a traditional political structure that worked against their finding a cohesive place in the modern world, as did the Mouridiya and Tijaniya Brotherhoods of Senegal or Hausa and Youraba in Nigeria (albeit in different circumstances). Beti headmen were generally content with their lot, forming advantageous marriage alliances, but holding an attitude that, if you were a compound chief, you had reached the pinnacle of success. Where cooperation was needed, the Beti stressed individual action; when a sense of Cameroonian nationalism emerged, and political alliances were being formed among Cameroonian leaders, not many Beti moved initially beyond their traditional sense of ethnic self-identity. Theirs was a static way of looking at the world, possessed of cultural richness, but not political or structural adaptability. To be sure, in the post-1960 period, especially after 1982 when Paul Biya assumed the presidency, many Beti, through education and activism in politics, gained lucrative positions in government. But they did this as individuals and not as a group. And the Beti, as an ethnic unit, failed to develop those modern organs of government that would allow them to function as a discreet unit in a modern state.

Notes

1. J. Guyer, *Family and Farm in Southern Cameroon*, Boston University African Research Studies No. 15 (Boston, 1984), p. 2.
2. Ibid., p. 58.

Appendix A
Traditional Beti Literature

These Beti songs were collected during the summer of 1967 by Pierre Betene, a researcher and seminary student, who translated them from Ewondo into French. Then I translated them into English and shortened them, eliminating most of the refrains and repetitions.

Among the Beti, songs were often sung in the evening by women, who were both soloists and chorus members. There were also professional praise-singers (*mvet*) who recounted the exploits of various chiefs and recalled events in Beti history and mythology.

Instrumental accompaniment was by drum, flute, xylophone or *mvet*, a cordophone instrument, a long piece of hollow bamboo to which three strings were attached and which resonated through three hollow gourds.

Several of the songs were published in "Eight Beti Songs" in *African Arts* (Los Angeles), vol. IV, no. 4 (summer 1971) and "A Beti Song Cycle," in *Griot: A Journal of African and AfroAmerican Culture* (Berea, KY) (fall 1998) and are reprinted with permission.

MINSANGALI, OPEN THE DOOR FOR ME

"Minsangali, lovely lady, open the door for me."
"Who is there that I should open the door?"
"It is I, the Panther, the most gallant in the forest."
"Panther, go quickly back from where you came
It is Minsili-Ebana-Zene who is my fiancé.
I do not think of anyone but him for whom my hair is well-dressed."
"Aie, Aie! Look at me, rejected by a woman!"

N.B. The panther as a trickster is a familiar rainforest image.

THE PYGMIES HAVE KILLED MBARGA NSUDU

(Sung by the chimpanzees in the rainforest who have a cynical joke about the fact that the Pygmies have killed a certain Mbarga Nsudu.)

The Pygmies have killed Mbarga Nsudu,
And with our spears we bat his head about,

And make a mosquito net of his small intestine;
His nose will serve us as a whistle,
His eyes are mirrors for us,
And his teeth our combs;
The Pygmies have killed Mbarga Nsudu.

N.B. The Pygmies were the original inhabitants of the part of central Cameroon into which the Beti eventually migrated, and were renowned for their ability to move through the rainforest undetected. Chimpanzees and gorillas figure in many Beti songs and proverbs, usually as symbols of strength or age.

HUNTING SONG

(The hunt was an important Beti activity, and there were numerous Beti hunting songs, such as the following.)

Let the children who know how to make hunting nets
Come quickly, come quickly,
So that we can race through the bush,
So that we can kill the small antelope with gray horns.

The hunt has existed since the beginning of time.
The peppery juice
Slides pleasantly down the throat each night.

Bring the meat, I'll bring the other foods,
And we will divide them with full equality.

You stay there, hungry for meat;
Do you not see how the others go to the forest,
To the hunt, hein!

SONG OF THE WOODCUTTER

I inherited the strength of my father,
The legendary strength of my father,
Esi Ndono, who was he?
Esi Ndono, what am I doing?
Me, the son of Esi Ndono.
Esi Ndono, where am I going?
Esi Ndono, who was he?
Esi Ndono, I am captured by work.
Work is like warfare;
My war is against that giant,
And for one of us the war will be fatal.
Ah, yes, I am captured by work, but
I have inherited the strength of my father,
The legendary strength of my father.

WAR SONG

Wife of Nkodo Embolo, wife of Zoa Anaba, whose maternal uncle is Ondoa Akumu,
Come, help us.
The enemy gathers in large numbers and small,
War will break out.
Come, help us.
My children, bring guns and all your arms and come.
Will our brother Owona Ada be left to die
Like a pig?

N.B. Traditional Beti warfare was largely feuding with other Beti groups. Bands of combatants could range from twenty to a hundred participants, usually composed of kinsmen or neighbors. The use of European rifles, or those made by coastal tribes, was fairly widespread by the late nineteenth century.

ATANGANA NTSAMA, THE WAR IS OVER

Atangana Ntsama, the war is over...,
He! Atangana Ntsama, the war is over!
The cannon are broken,
Go tell it to the son of Ndono Edoa,
To the great man who is the son of Ndono Edoa.
Run quickly, why do you languish there?
All you Ewondo, come and run quickly,
Come and run quickly, brothers;
Go tell it to Mindili Ebulu, son of Ndono Edoa.
How is it that you would like me to leave so many goods behind?

He! They will surprise you in your greed!

Such richness. I should take some!
You others, move off, what are you doing there?

Friend, there were as many goods as in a market;
Friend, we have marched through all of that without taking anything!

N.B. This is a song the Beti women sang at the end of World War I.

Charles Atangana (Atangana Ntsama in the song) was a Beti headman whom the Germans named *Oberhäuptling*, or chief of all the Beti, shortly before the war broke out. He is also referred to as Mindili Ebulu, or as the man whose house is so large that it had roof divided into nine sections instead of the two sections of an ordinary dwelling. (*Mindili* = roof sections in Ewondo; *Ebulu* = nine, a number with powers above other numbers.)

On 1 January 1916, Atangana and seventy-two other chiefs, several thousand Beti, and the Germans began a two-month exodus to Equatorial Guinea. This song announces that the war is over. It also concerns an incident on the march. Some of the women talk about seizing the departing German's goods, which they compare to those in a market, but others inveigh on the women to leave the goods and march south without them.

NO WAR SINCE THE WHITE MAN CAME

(A young Beti warrior complains that he cannot fulfill his natural desire for combat, and that his enemies can easily kill him. The chorus answers that since the white man has come, for better or for worse, the intruders have sought to keep peace among the tribes.)

"No war since the white man came."
My mother, no one can do this to me;
Atana Odi will kill me,
Enyege Abene will kill me,
That is not something I desire;
My mother, how can I sleep tonight?
Thesson Mfege will kill me,
My mother, what can I do?
Refrain: "No war since the white man came."

N.B. One of the first interests of the Germans, after they arrived in the interior of Cameroon in the late 1880s, was to put an end to Beti warfare.

HOW DID YOU GET IN YOUR HEAD?

How did you get in your head...?
You, Ovugvugu, that you are a lord?
The sparrow has been killed,
The sparrow's throat had been cut
Because of what the wren did.
How did you get it in your head that you were a chief?
You, Ovugvugu, how did you get it in your head?
The sparrow has been killed and the other bird killed....

N.B. "Ovugvugu" is what the Beti called the first German to come to that part of central Cameroon, circa 1887. Perhaps, "Ovugvugu" is how the Beti heard his name. "Sparrow" and "Wren" were his unfortunate companions in this ironic song about the first encounter between the Beti and their colonizers.

DRUM MESSAGE SIGNALING THE ARRIVAL OF RECRUITERS FOR THE WORK GANGS

A horse (man) crosses the country.
He will stop all the men. All.
When you walk on the road,
Do so with measured and cautious step;
No one should forget the bush.
Heroes of the wars, do you not know the
Caves, hein?
Move quickly.

SONG ABOUT THE WORK GANGS

The tom-tom beats at Yaoundé,
The tom-tom which will ruin this country.
The tom-tom of the work gangs.
What does it say?
It says clear out,
Leave your possessions for the Chief.
Get out!
The tom-tom beats at Yaoundé.
Tell my mother and father,
And tell my mother to save me some food.
Hé! My brother, will I survive the work gang?

RAILROAD WORKERS' SONG GREETING THE WHITE MAN

Hé, get away from that dog.
That small dog is a mean one.
That dog is very mean,
He has taken my manioc.
He has taken my meat.
He has bitten me on the leg,
He has bitten me on the buttocks.
My brothers, let me hear you!
[Refrain and chorus:] Hé, get away from that dog.

RAILROAD WORKERS' SONG

There are hills to level,
Rocks to break,
Earth to move.
If I work they beat me on the back,
If I don't work, they beat me.
Who has brought these "Albinos" from Douala?
Who showed them how to find Yaoundé,
And who has made Ahanda, son of Mfefe, so cruel?
Ahanda, will you get a white woman for this?
Ahanda, who told you the whites are your friends?
Ahanda, will you marry a white man's daughter?
What have I done, Ahanda,
That you detest me so?

N.B. Ahanda was an Etudi chief in charge of work gangs on the Yaoundé-Kribi road.

DEATH

Death, having taken my father, also took my mother
And I went out on the roads, crying:
"Is it I that has brought death?"
Death, having taken my mother, also took my brother,
Death, having taken my brother, also took my husband's father,
Death, having taken my husband's father, also took my father's father
And I went out on the roads, crying:
"Is it I that has brought death to earth?"

N.B. The Beti considered misfortunes such as crop failures, sickness and death resulting because the ancestors were displeased with the conduct of their living successors. Diviners determined the cause of the misfortune, and a council of those concerned, men and women, met and offered a sacrifice to propitiate the ancestors.

PANTHER'S DEATH

Ze, Ze, Ze my husband!
Who will take care of our children?
Ze, my husband!
I am crying, my husband,
For the plight of our children.

When I went fishing, Ze stayed with the children,
When I went for water, Ze was with the children,
When I gathered wood, Ze was with the children.
And now, Ze, Ze, Ze my husband,
Who will take care of our children?

ESANI

(Funeral Dance)

Fuda never went into things of little importance,
Fuda never took sides in warfare
Without arms and heads falling.
Fuda, the son of Mumo Mbala, son of Owona Esomba,
Fuda never went into things lightly.
Fuda was a great warrior.

MY MOTHER, DO NOT CRY FOR ME

(The child sings this song to his mother shortly before his death.)

Do not bury me in a dunghill,
For there people pour anything,
Leave anything,
Throw anything.

Do not bury me in the courtyard,
For there anyone can walk,
And anyone can sit.

Do not bury me under the footpath,
Where anyone can pass.

Do not bury me in the forest,
Where there is too much noise,
Where people can cut anything,
Where they hack trees down.

Bury me among the raffia grass
For there the frogs will cry,
The frogs will cry a lot...
My mother, do not cry!

N.B. Death was no stranger to the rainforest. The average life expectancy was under forty years, and infant mortality was high. Consequently, many Beti songs deal with death, and some of them show a great dignity and stoicism. The child's plea against an inconsequential burial is not far-fetched because funeral rites among the Beti were usually limited to elders.

Appendix B
Aspects of Traditional Beti Society, by Abbé Theodore Tsala

The Beti linguist Abbé Theodore Tsala was a prolific author who, in addition to his published works, left several manuscripts on aspects of Beti life and history. Three such texts are included here: (1) *Le gouvernement des Beti* (1 June 1968), some comments on the structure of traditional society; (2) *La mort de Zibi Ngomo et les sacrifices humains* (26 March 1968), a description of sacrificial killings at the death of an important herdman ca. 1900; and (3) *L'opinion d'un prêtre camerounais sur la dot* (September 1953), a wide-ranging commentary on the bridewealth question from the viewpoint of a parish priest from the village of Atega. These documents represent an important Cameroonian scholar's appraisal of aspects of traditional Beti society.

Le gouvernement des Beti

Les Beti avaient un gouvernement démocratique. Le peuple exprimait sa volonté dans des assemblées. Tous les citoyens avaient, avec adaptations aux circonstances, les mêmes droits et les mêmes devoirs. Ils étaient bien disciplinés. Toute collectivité, si minime soit-elle, avait son chef. Celui de la première cellule de la société s'appelait *mie-dzala*, ou façon-neur de village.

Le mot *dzal, (dzala)* que nous traduisons improprement ici, par "village" signifie domicile isolé, même réduit à une seule chambre habitée par un seul homme. L'habitant est un *mie-dzala*, un façonneur du village. Tous ceux qui viennent après sont sous lui. Il exerce sur eux une autorité paternelle mitigée. On ne peut se soustraire de sa tutelle qu'en abandonnant le lieu. Sous certains rapports il restera dépendant de son mie-dzala d'origine.

Le *mie-dzala* qui présidait l'assemblée clanique ou tribale prenait le titre de *mie-nnama*. Il était élu par le Conseil lequel n'arrêtait son choix que sur on bon patriote remarquable par le gouvernement de sa famille, son impartialité, son courage, en un mot, par les qualités d'un bon chef. Le *mie-nnama* en charge pouvait aussi, d'accord avec le conseil, désigner son successeur. Il en faisait son adjoint.

Quoiqu'en dise Karl Atangana dans le *Jaunde-Texte,* ce titre n'était pas héritaire au point de toujours passer de père en fils ou à celui qu'en tenait lieu. Il ne donnait pas non plus le droit de réclamer un impôt quel-conque. L'impôt n'existait pas. Il n'a même pas de nom en langue beti. Le mot *Toya* par lequel on le désigne est un néologisme, la déformation de l'allemand "Steuer". D'ailleurs l'impôt est fait pour subvenir aux frais de 'Etat et l'Etat Beti n'en faisait pas. Toute charge publique demandait une main-d'œuvre publique.

Le Conseil

Il y en avait à cercle retreint et á cercle élargi. Les premiers jouaient le rôle de tribunal de conciliation, les seconds traitaient des affaires importantes et prenaient des décisions. Ils jugeaient sans appel lorsque les intérêts de la tribu étaient en cause, tous les *mie-dzala*, sous la présidence de *mie-nnama* devaient se présenter au conseil sinon en personne du moins par représentation. Dans ses genres de réunions l'orateur, appelé aussi juge, dans ce sens que c'est lui qui proclame les sentences du clan, a droit à une certaine rétribution appelée *akon ntol*, laquelle est à la charge des plaignants.

Quand on désire la présence d'un orateur déterminé dans une séance où tous avaient le droit de prendre la parole et qu'on craigne son absence, on lui apporte à domicile, quelques jours d'avance, un cadeau appelé *ebodosi* ou frais de déplacement pour le décider à venir coûte que coûte.

Dans certains cas, la petite réunion des anciens prenaient des sanctions qu'homologuait le clan.

Sanctions

1) Restitution de l'objet réclamé avec, s'il y a lieu, réparation des dommages émergés;
2) Organisation d'un rite fétichiste. Certains comme le *so* coûtaient très chers.
3) Amende honorable au pays (*ekpaa-nnam*) au supérieur offensé (*metu-nena*). Un jeune homme de *kon* (aujourd'hui faubourg de Yaoundé) mange en cachette la viande de pangolin, réservée aux vieux. Découvert il fut condamné à payer cinq cabris. Dans la société des Beti, il n'était pas avantageux d'entrer en jugement avec son supérieur, car on était toujours obligé de lui payer quelque chose soit pour lui faire amende honorable s'il a raison soit pour le relever de sa chute, s'il a tort.
4) Bastonnade, garottage, mise aux ceps, réduction en captivité;
5) Exclusion du clan ou *Ekud-bikob*.
6) Condamnation à mort. Cette peine n'était guère appliquée qu'aux étrangers.On ne cite qu'un cas d'une condamnation à mort d'un autochtonc, par la noyade.

Les Tribuneaux Extraordinaires

On n'y recourait qu'en désespoir de cause surtout lorsque le défendeur est dans une autre tribu d'accès difficile. On les divisait en trois espèces, à savoir:

I – *Mimbog ou saisie*
Le créancier ou tout autre personne agissant en son nom s'emparait d'un objet appartenant à son débiteur ou à quelqu'un de sa collectivité jusqu'à l'acquittement de la dette réclamée. A cette époque l'individu était considéré comme un simple

élément de la personne morale, de la collectivité. Il suffisait quand on ne pouvait pas atteindre l'intéressé de s'attaquer à n'importe quel membre de son clan. Quand on arrêtait une personne on lui mettait une canque (mbog) au pied. La famille de la personne arrêtée allait faire pression sur le débiteur pour exiger le paiement de la dette.

II – *L'ayanga ou asan ayanga*
Les deux mots viennent respectivement de *san*, découper, *yanga*, attendre, et ont pour premier sens, il attend, il découpe-il attend.

Lorsqu'un débiteur menaçait de ne pas payer sa dette, le créancier pouvait se rendre chez un personnage puissant, et, sans rien dire, découpait ses plants ou tuait ses animaux. A la demande d'explication, il répondait: "Je suis furieux contre un tel qui me doit ceci, cela et ne veut pas me payer. L'homme puissant se hissait sur le tam-tam-parleur et faisait résonner ces mots: *"Me në a tsigi, tsigi, a sana, sana."* Je suis tout coupé, coupé, tout découpé, découpé. Ses gens arrivent armés jusqu'aux dents. Il leur fait constater les déprédation et à rembourser la dette. S'il ne le pouvait pas on le ramenait captif.

III – *Evuson*
L'evuson (de *vui*: retirer la terre et *son*: tombe) est une adjuration au nom d'un ou des morts. Un créancier bafoué allait dire à un homme fort: *"Ma vu wa son vë... "* je t'adjure au nom de ... de ma faire récupérer telle ou telle dette. L'adjuré se rendait avec ses gens chez le débiteur pour exiger le paiement de la dette et les frais de ses déplacements.

Dans *l'asan-ayanga* et dans *l'evuson* s'il s'avère après enquête que le plaignant a tort tous les frais sont à sa charge. Il reste possible d'autres sanctions.

Vers la fin du 19e siècle, un individu vint trouver *Ngema, mie-nnama* de *Mvog-Manzë*, à *Minlaba*, l'actuel arrondissement de *Mbalmayo*, et lui dit: *"Ma vuwe son ve ebol esoa.* Je t'adjure au nom de la pourriture de ton père, d'aller me prendre une dette à un débiteur récalcitrant." Ngema dit au plaignant: "Tu es venu m'appeler chez moi, tu dois m'y reconduire". Arrivés au village le Chef lui dit: "Comment as-tu osé insulter à la pourriture de mon père alors qu'on ne te devait rien? Aujourd'hui même tu vas lui dire qu'il a laissé sur terre un fils qui tient à lui faire honneur. Sur ce, il le pendit sans autre forme de procès".

L'Organisation Judiciare

1) *Particularités sur le pouvoir*.
L'organisation judiciaire des *Beti* est différente de celle des Français comme l'est aussi sa structure sociale. Certains termes beti, dans cet ordre d'idées, n'ont pas d'équivalents en français. Force m'est d'en faire ample usage dans cet exposé. Je tâcherai, cependant, de les expliquer en recourant, au besoin, à leur étymologie pour en mieux faire ressortir le sens.

Le tribunal n'avait ni police, ni greffier, ni édifice déterminé, ni assesseur désigné. Le tribunal se réunissait là, où le voulait le demandeur. Les intéressés étaient convoqués au son de *nkul* ou tam-tam parleur. Le jugement était gratuit. Seul le juge pouvait recevoir une certaine indemnité dite *akon ntol* ou lance de l'aîné ou lance de jugement, le *ntol* signifiant l'un et l'autre. Tous les hommes qui assistaient à un tribunal avaient voix consultative. Quand un personnage influent, pour une raison ou pour autre, ne voulait pas venir à la réunion, l'un des plus intéressés allait lui offrir une indemnité de déplacement dite *ebodosi*, c'est-à-dire instrument qui fait lever du sol. La valeur de cet *ebodosi* était proportionnelle à la dignité du personnage et à la distance à parcourir.

On faisait peu de distinction entre le civil et le criminel. Par contre, le naturel et le surnaturel, disons mieux le préternaturel étaient tellement enchevêtrés qu'on les voyait partout ensemble. Le Beti croyait mordicus au *mgbel* (rapprocher d'*amgbë*: chrysalide). Le mgbel est l'enchantement, la guerre des sorciers, la guerre des hommes transformés en d'autres êtres. C'est une force d'un autre plan. Pour en déceler les effets, il fallait recourir à une puissance de même plan. Cette puissance s'appelait *ngam*, la mygale, la reine des araignées censée habitée par un esprit bienfaisant, omniscient. Les féticheurs trouvaient sa réponse par des moyens ingénieux. Celui qu'incrimine le *ngam* était présumé coupable tant qu'il n'avait pas prouvé son innocence par le recours aux ordalies dont la plus important était *l'elon*, poison d'épreuve. Pour plus ample information, voir les mots *ngam* et *elon* à leur chapitre respectif.

2) Détenteurs du pouvoir.
Les détenteurs du pouvoir dans un clan des Beti sont:

1°) – Le *miedzala*. *Mie* ou *me*: façonner, modeler. *Me mvie*: modeler une marmite d'argile. *Dzala*, de *dzal*: village, hameau. C'est le modeleur de village, le *pater familias* des Romains. C'est le premier responsable de village. Le mot *dzal* n'a pas de correspondant en français. Nous le traduisons par village, faute de mieux. Il indique habitation isolée composée d'un groupe de cases ou non. Elle peut même être réduite à une case d'une seule chambre. Un *dzal* n'avait qu'un *miedzala*. Les autres occupants, mariés ou non, étaient les *bongo be dzal*, les enfants du village, les mineurs en un mot. C'est pourquoi tout homme qui se respectait aimait à se tailler une demeure à l'écart où il était *miedzala*.

2°) – Le *miennama*. De *mie* (voir plus haut) et de *nnam*: pays, territoire, localité. C'est le modeleur de son clan ou de sa tribu, de son pays. Il veille sur la conservation et l'accroissement de sa collectivité.

3°) – Le *ntsig ntol*. *Tsig* = couper, trancher. *Ntol* = (de *tol*: ramasser en masse. Dans le partage de l'héritage, l'aîné prenait la part de lion) aîné et par extension, le palabre. Le *stig ntol* est le trancheur des palabres. Le *ntsig ntol* devait être un grand orateur, instruit sur la jurisprudence du pays et ayant la vérité pour meilleure amie, *magis amica veritas*. Il se confondait souvent avec le *miennama*. Chez les Bakoko, on l'appelait *mut mbog*. Pour mériter ce titre il fallait citer, dans une assemblée d'experts, en plusieurs séries de neuf des cas de jugements bien rendus.

4°) – *Ngengâ mod* (de *ngâ*: être surélevé et *mod*: homme) c'est un surhomme, un héros. D'autres font dériver ce mot *de ngan ngan mod* c'est-à-dire homme plein de recettes magiques.

5°) – *Mbege-mfeg*: porteur du sac, sous-entendu: à fétiches. C'est le chef des initiations aux associations fétichistes.

6°) – Les *mengi-mengi*. Littéralement gorilles-gorilles. Allusion à la croyance du pays selon laquelle de grands personnages morts se transformaient, à volonté, en gorilles. Les *mengi-mengi* étaient "les vieux de pays, plus près de la tombe que du berceau," le trait d'union entre les forces vives du pays et les ancêtres disparus. Ils formaient le sénat du clan. Ils avaient une voie prépondérante.

7°) – *Etogan nnam*. Le conseil de clan. Il jugeait sans appel le *miedzala* et le *miennama* avaient un pouvoir plutôt disciplinaire. Celui de ce dernier était mitigé mais renforçable par celui des *mengi-mengi*. Le *mbege-mfeg* réglait les litiges entre les membres de son association.

Une séance du conseil.

La veille de la réunion du Conseil, le demandeur ou son représentant, monte sur le tam-tam parleur pour convoquer les gens pour la réunion. Cf. *Nkul adzo*.

Le lendemain, de bonheur, tout le monde se réunit à l'endroit indiqué car c'est un devoir de tout bon citoyen d'être présent au retire pour délibérer. Il se compose essentiellement du juge, de un ou deux représentants de chaque partie et de quelques hommes non directement intéresses dans l'affaire. Au retour, le juge reprend l'exposé des faits, stigmatise le mal et donne sa décision.

Le conseil se tient toujours en plein air. Le juge parle debout, tenant d'une main, une lance *akon ntol* (tout autre orateur n'a droit qu'aux lances) et de l'autre un chasse-mouches *akpaag nnam* ou l'un de ces deux objets seulement. Il est progue en gestes. Il rayonne dans toute la cour sous les positions variées correspondantes aux impressions qu'il sent ou qu'il veut provoquer chez les autres. Si l'un des assistants trouve un argument qui corrobore sa thèse, il se lève et lui demande la parole par ces mots: *Ma tsing wa baa a minken*: je mets du *baa* sur vos hampes, la *baa*: poudre rouge d'acajou est l'emblème de la victoire.

A un très bon orateur, on fait des cadeaux avec de lances au hampes brisés pour signifier que son éloquence désarme les plus décidés. On lui crie: *o nga vaa mimbim a son:* Tu enleveras les cadavres des tombes. Tu feras déterrer les cadavres sans que personne riposte; parce que gagné par ton éloquence.

De temps à autre l'orateur réveille l'attention de l'auditoire par des expressions comme celles-ci: *Yebegana ma a!-Heee*. Approuves-moi! – Cela même. *Bi ne kin a!* Nous sommes d'accord, hein? – Parfaitement.

Le différend est examiné dans tous les sens. S'il en subsiste quelque ombre, on le renvoi à une session ultérieure. On disait alors d'une affaire embrouillée: *Binkë bia kobo a meba mebaa*: Nous en parlerons en de multiples séances.

Les sanctions

Il y avait deux sortes de sanctions: les sanctions disciplinaires et les sanctions judiciaires. Il n'y avait cependant pas une cloison étanche entre les deux. Les premières qui étaient surtout corporelles étaient réservées à *miedzala* et *miennama*.

Ce sont: *ebom:* la bastonnade. Ablation des oreilles (pour esclaves); *ngadag*: garottage; *mibog*: mise aux ceps.

Le pouvoir judiciaire avait:

eyian: restitution. C'est la loi de talion sur les objets. A l'objet enlevé on met un autre de même valeur ou quelque autre chose équivalente.

Ntan: dédommagement. On restitue au propriétaire l'objet enlevé et on le dédommage en même temps pour les ennuis que son ablation lui a occasionnés.

Proverbe: *Eyian e së ntan*: restituer n'est pas dédommager. On peut demander la restituer de son objet sans cesser pour autant d'être ami.

Ekpee akan: Condamnation à l'organisation d'un rite fétichiste.

Certaines comme celle de *so;* réclamation de plusieurs dizaines de cabris sans préjudice d'objets divers.

Ekud bikob: privation de droit de citoyen.

Metunena: l'amende honorable. Un jeune homme de *Kon* est allé manger à l'étranger la viande de pangolin que seuls les mengi-mengi de son clan avait seuls le droit de manger. A son retour il fut condamné à payer à ces derniers une amende de cinq cabris.

La peine capitale était très réservée.

Selon la croyance du pays, celui qui versait le sang d'un parent ou d'un proche parent encourait ipso facto le *tsoo*, maladie de poitrine et d'autres encore. Or, dans un clan, à l'exclusion des esclaves et des femmes mariées, tout le monde est parent. Si un étranger au clan y commettait quelque chose qui méritait la mort, sa condamnation était assurée. A l'enterrement d'un grand personnage, ou tuait des femmes et des esclaves pour qu'il n'aille pas seul. On parle cependant, parmi les riverains de la Sanaga, de quelques condamnations à mort par noyade ou par pendaison.

L'ekud-bikob.

L'expression *ekud-bikob* signifie littéralement percussion des peaux. Lorsqu'un homme se montre rebelle à la décision de clan ou à celle du juge, il reçoit la visite de *mengi-mengi*. Ils le somment à obéir. S'il résiste encore ils lui dissent: En désobéissant au juge ou au clan, tu nous as ignores. Nous t'ignorons aussi. Nous secouons contre toi ta poussière qui s'est attachée sur nos peaux (on portait alors des peaux). Sur ce, ils se lèvent secouent leurs peaux et disparaissent. Dès lors, aucun homme du clan ne va plus chez le rebelle et ne le reçoit. Est-il attaqué, personne ne va à son secours. *Wem night zu raten ist, dem ist nicht zu helfen*, dissent les Allemands. Qui n'entend pas conseil, ne mérite pas l'aide. Dans un pays où l'individu ne vit pas de sa vie seule mais aussi de celle du clan, en être séparé était, en quelque sorte une mort lente. Aussi le proscrit ne restait-il pas longtemps sous cette peine. Il allait vite trouver l'un des *mengi-mengi* pour lui faire part de ses bonnes dispositions à se conformer à la sentence qui l'avait frappe. Il lui apportait, pour gagner sa bienveillance, un coq un régime de bananas dit *elad-ekon*, bananes d'union. Dans les cas plus graves un cabri remplaçait le coq. Tous les mengi-mengi, mis au courant du retour du fils prodigue, se réunissent, le font venir et lui imposent l'amende qu'ils jugent nécessaire. Le pénitent doit l'accepter en fils soumis, car une petite moue de sa part peut gâter toute l'affaire.

Relever de malédiction

Pour relever d'une malédiction un fils maudit, on le place au milieu de la cour. Son père ou tout autre homme en tenant lieu se lève, tenant un *akpaag* (chasse-mouches) à la main. Il fait le récit de la cause de la malédiction encourue, il expose ensuite les signes d'un sincère repentir qui plaident en faveur du coupable. Il déclare qu'il voit l'homme assez bien disposé pour mériter le pardon. Il demande à tous les assistants s'ils partageaient ses vues. Tous répondent par un "oui unanime". Il racle alors une écorce d'arbre. Il divise la raclure en trios parties. Il met la première sur la main droite qu'il appliqué ensuite sur le front du pénitent et la tire jusqu'à la nuque. Il délaie la deuxième dans l'eau qu'il fait boire au coupable. Il prend la troisième et la divise en autant de parts qu'il y a des *mengi-mengi* dans l'ensemble de l'assemblée. Il met la sienne dans la bouche, la mâche et la crache sur le front du pénitent. Tous les autres en font autant. Tous, mettant la main sur lui pour l'aider à se lever prononcent ensemble la formule d'absolution:

> *E mongo wan a toa nyo, A a ngleg belë*
> *Ki fe etom ye bia a! – Heee.*
> *Bi man ya lad ye nye a! – Heee.*
> *Amana ya bia tuni a! – Heee.*
> *Mod a vegë nye mbé dzam, Emen a dugan ye nye a! – Heee.*
> *E nye biatie a si nyo a! – A maas.*
> Notre enfant que voici,
> N'a plus de palabre avec nous, hein? – Parfaitement.
> Il nous a fait amende honorable, hein? – Parfaitement.
> Nous nous sommes réconciliés avec lui, hein? – Parfaitement.
> Que celui qui lui prépare un piège,
> Soit prit dans son propre piège, hein? – Parfaitement.
> Le voici que nous levons du sol. – Avec une facilité merveilleuse.

La mort de Zibi Ngomo et les sacrifices humains.

Vers l'an 1900 meurt à Nkon-Abog, village des Mvog-Fuda, un notable du nom de Zibi Ngomo. Le lendemain, affluent dans son village des hommes venus en visite de condoléances. Les *ban kal*, c'est-à-dire les hommes nés d'une fille des Mvog-Fuda, eux n'arrivent pas. Ils restent en chemin près du village et s'attendent. Vers le déclin du jour ils s'amènent en une procession funèbre. Quelques-uns tiennent en main une grosse corde terminée par un noeud coulant: l'ekoe. Ils les jettent devant les assistants et se retirent dans un coin du village. Ils ne veulent pas participer au deuil tant qu'ils ne sont pas satisfaits. Le chef des funérailles, escorté des siens, se lèves et va vers eux. "Neveux, voici votre part", leur dit-il, en désignant l'homme qu'il pousse devant lui: un esclave du défunt. Un rictus féroce sillonne les visages assombris. Ils entourent aussitôt l'esclave et se mettent à danse l'*esani* dont les tam-tam résonnent de plus-on plus fort. A un moment donné le doyen d'âge intime à l'esclave l'ordre de se retirer. Dès qu'il tourne le dos, il lui assène de son coutelas un coup mortel. Les autres l'imitent. L'esclave s'écroule. Les coups continuent à pleuvoir sur lui. Chaque neveu tient à lui porter le sien. Ils ramassent ensuite le cadavre déchiqueté et les lambeaux de chair et vont les enfouillir dans une fosse en brousse.

Owona Ngo Ndum, chef du clan, s'avance dans la cour pour parler. Le silence se rétablit complet. Il harangue la foule sur les vertus de disparu et sur les méchancetés des sorciers malveillants qui ont arraché à l'affection des siens un homme si cher. Zibi n'est pas l'homme à descendre seul au séjour des morts. Pour cette femme il était tout. *Ebobom ki, eton ki*. La chute de la palme entraîne celle du régime. Il y a aussi d'autres femmes qui lui ont donné beaucoup de tracas. Elles ne rêvaient que sa mort. Sans aucun doute, elles y ont coopéré. Les laissera-t-on regarder Zibi descendre dans la tombe? Il ne faut pas tolérer un pareil affront. Après sa harangue les notables se retirent avec lui pour délibérer. Leur retour est salué par une recrudescence des chants d'*esani*.

Owona Ngo Ndum s'avance de nouveau dans la cour. Même silence que plus haut. Il recommence à haranguer lafoule. Il s'interrompt et fait venir Fuda Zibi, fils aîné de Zibi Ngomo. Il l'entretient un moment avec lui, puis, il lui crache sur la figure, sur la poitrine et entre les omoplates, une pâte d'écorce d'arbre. Fuda va s'asseoir sur l'auvent où étaient déjà d'autres hommes.

Le chef des funérailles ouvre la prison des veuves. Des neveux s'y précipitent. Ils en ressortent traînant Memono, fille de la tribu d'Endongo, propre mère de Fuda Zibi. Elle est exécutée sous les yeux de son fils. Furent également exécutées deux autres femmes, Ada Menenë, de la tribu de mvog Amug, et Ngo Fumbi, de la tribu des Bakoko.

Les yeux se tournent maintenant vers les fils de Zibi. Vous avez, peut-être, participé à la guerre magique qui a tué votre père. Vous allez prouver votre innocence par le poison d'épreuve, *l'elon*. On va alors faire sauter, à coups de pierre, des écorces du terrible arbre pour en faire des boulettes que l'on fait avaler aux prévenus. Assis en pleine air, ils attendent, inquiets le résultat de l'épreuve. Craignant l'issue fatale, Owona Ngo Ndum se leva et dit: *Dzungoo a wuu, ebamekogo a ligi ai mfeg mebel*. Quand le caméléon meurt, le lézard hérite le sac de colas. Coupables ou non, ces jeunes gens doivent vivre pour perpétuer le sang de Zibi. Qu'on leur administre des antidotes. On donne un vomitif à chacun et le poison est évacué.

A la nouvelle de l'exécution de leur soeur, les frères de Memono en portent la plainte devant le Gouvernement. Le capitaine Dominik, alors chef de poste de Yaoundé, fit venir tous les chefs et leur interdit, sous peine de mort, les exécutions de tout genre.

Toutes les exécutions à la mort du notable ne se passaient pas de la même façon. Parfois les "neveux" s'arrêtaient en route et envoyaient dire au chef des funérailles: *Be zaag bia kad foe"*, qu'on vienne nous dire la nouvelle. On leur apportait alors des gens à exécuter. Ils passaient les esclaves, hommes et femmes, au fil de l'épée, et pendaient les femmes libres. Arrivés au village, ils mettaient à l'épreuve du poison tous ceux qui étaient suspects d'avoir coopéré" à la mort du défunt. Ceux qui sortaient victorieux de l'épreuve, recevaient, pour dénonciation calomnieuse, le montant de la dot moyenne d'une femme.

Certains notables étaient ensevelis à *esam-so* périmètre d'initiation au rite so. Les esclaves qui y portaient le cadavre ne devaient plus retourner au village. Dès qu'ils déposent leur charge, ils sont immédiatement saisis et taillés en pièces. C'est sur leurs corps, dans la tombe, qu'on dépose le cadavre du notable.

Les exécutions à l'enterrement, avaient plusieurs buts:

1) fournir des serviteurs et des femmes au notable qui descendait au séjour des morts. Au jugement des anciens, la vie d'outre-tombe était sensiblement pareille à celle de la terre.

2) punir ceux qui avaient fait le mal au défunt.

3) inspirer, par la crainte, au personnel domestique, le respect pour leur patron.

4) Prouver que le défunt a laissé derrière lui des braves. Il arrivait aussi qu'on masserait en offrande les captifs de guerre sur la tombe des êtres chers ou qu'on y déposait la tête de leurs pires ennemis tués en représailles. C'est ainsi qu'on avait déposé sur la tombe de Mebada Mesomo, chef des Mvog-Onamenye la tête d'Ebono Bela, chef des Tom, qui avait tué Mbene Elumbele, fils de Mebada.

L'opinion d'un prêtre camerounais sur la dot, par l'Abbé Théodore Tsala

(on a communiqué récemment à ce prêtre, qui est le doyen des abbés du pays, le texte d'un projet d'arrêté fixant par régions le taux de la dot. Voici la réponse très réfléchie et autorisée de quelqu'un qui connaît bien la question.)

Monsieur,

J'ai l'honneur de vous accuser réception de votre lettre du 13 juin 1953 et du projet d'arrêté déterminant par Région du Cameroun des taux de la dot au-delà desquels il y a exigences excessives. Je vous en remercie.

Vous avez bien voulu demander mon opinion. Je suis heureux de vous l'exposer en toute franchise.

La pensée aux taux de la dot doit entraîner celle des pénalités contre les délinquants. Ce maximum de dot avait jadis été arête. Les avaricieux en ont fait un minimum et un tremplin pour arriver à ces sommes fantastiques dont nous sommes aujourd'hui les témoins ahuris. Nos juges voyaient sans réaction cette montée en flèche des dots. Pis encore, ils s'y sont vite conformés. Ils vont jusqu'à écrire à l'état-civil des pauvres paysans des dots dont le montant a de quoi effrayer un bourgeois rentier. C'est pourquoi, je suis inquiet. Une loi sans sanction est une loi morte, presqu'une invitation à la transgresser. Le fruit défendu a quelque chose de tentant. Il importe donc de prévoir avant tout une sanction contre les exigences excessives, contre les dots de marché noir. Seule la perspective d'une rude sanction peut prévenir les contraventions.

Processus de la dot
Avant de fixer les taux des dots, le législateur devra se rendre exactement compte de ses différents échelons. La dot peut être concluante, concomitante ou subséquent. La dot concluante est celle que les parents de la femme jugent suffisante à conclure

un mariage, à faire établir l'état-civil de mariage ou à livrer la fille au prétendant. La dot concomitante se fait pendant qu'on accompagne les jeunes mariés à leur domicile. Après les cérémonies religieuses, les deux époux en costume nuptial se rendent à leur demeure. A l'entrée, le cortège s'arrête devant la belle-mère couchée à plat ventre en travers sur le passage. L'enjamber ou la contourner constitue un crime de lèse-maternité lourd de conséquences pour le jeune ménage. Il faut la relever vite par une dot substantielle. La laisser longtemps dans cette posture risqué d'aggraver la situation. Il arrive parfois que des beaux-parents refusent de prendre part au festin ou de s'asseoir tant qu'on ne leur a pas encore fait amende honorable d'une coquette somme.

La dot subséquent renferme tous les biens qu'on donne après le mariage. Je ne voudrais m'arrêter que sur le côte le plus odieux. Les parents à court d'argent invitent leur fille et la retiennent au village pour obliger le mari à apporter un supplément de dot, par eux déterminé. La femme peut passer ainsi des mois, voire des saisons. Si le mari ne se presse pas, on peut parler sans vergogne de le remplacer.

J'allais oublier les accessoires de la dot. Tel frère veut des pagnes, tel autre une paire de souliers. Il ne faut pas oublier cet oncle influent à quoi il faut un complet à la mode, etc. ... Enfin, il faut à toute la famille un repas copieux et abondamment arrosé. Danse se but, on réclame des cabris engraissés, sinon un boeuf, et des dames-jeannes de vin rouge.

On le voit, la dot a plusieurs courants. Si l'on ne canalise ou l'on ne bouge que le principal, l'un des secondaires passera au premier rang et nous voilà in statu quo.

Détermination de la dot

La détermination du maximum de la dot se fait en faveur des prolétaires. Elle devra donc se baser sur leurs revenues et leurs économies possibles, de façon qu'on jeune homme dans le commun de people puisse trouver la dot nécessaire à son mariage dans l'espace de moins de cinq ans. Or, les revenues d'un prolétaire, dans notre région, dans les temps actuels sont de trente mille francs l'an. Sa solde mensuelle oscille entre deux et trios mille francs. En économisant le tiers ou la moitié de son gain, il peut totaliser 10.000 à 15.000 Fr + 10 cabris fait en tout 70.000 Fr. Le prix moyen d'un cabri est de 2.000 Fr., ici, à Atéga, peut-être aussi ailleurs. Il faudra alors au fiancé 10 ans d'économie si l'on pense aux frais divers. C'est trop fort. Les régions les plus riches ont des taux maximum inférieurs aux nôtre. Ex. Wouri, Bamiléké, Dja et Lobo, etc. Qu'on prenne aussi des moyens énergiques pour boucher toutes les autres issues de la dot.

La dot et les mariages d'autrefois

Nous nageons en pleinpis aller. Tous ces compromis ne servent qu'à commercialiser un ancien geste d'alliance. La dot d'autrefois était beaucoup plus simple, plus amicale. Un voyageur arrive. On l'héberge. On le nourrit. On le soigné de son mieux. On mettait un point d'honneur à l'hospitalité gratuite. Satisfait, il dit à son départ: "Je vous remercie d'avoir été aux petits soins avec moi. Je vous donne ma fille ou ma soeur en mariage pour cimenter cette amitié dont vous venez de me donner des preuves". Parfois, on a remarqué des bonnes manières d'un passager. On l'invite. On l'interroge sur son origine. "Mon enfant t'a aimé et nous avec lui. Nous te greffons sur notre famille. Nous te donnons cette fille en mariage. L'homme s'en va avec la femme sans bourse délier. On pouvait également aller donner à domicile sa fille ou sa soeur à un grand chef ou à un grand guerrier dont on cherche de bonnes grâces.

Le mari devait aux parents de sa femme un respect révérentiel. Les Proverbes ewondo encore aujourd'hui en cours le prouvent abondamment. Exemple: "Bakakak nkiè-ngon okpal." On ne promet pas aux beaux-parents une perdrix qui court encore la brousse, autrement si on ne réussit pas à l'attraper, on passé pour un homme sans aveu. Celui qui a reçu une femme comme nous venons de la dire devait prouver sa générosité en donnant en retour sa fille ou sa soeur. C'est ce qu'on appelait mariage, par échange. C'était le cas pour ma mère. A défaut d'autre femme, on offrait des présents dont la quantité se mesurait sur la magnanimité du donateur.

Déviation de la dot. Ses méfaits

La dot actuelle est une déviation de l'ancienne. C'est un fléau social. Elle rompt l'un des principaux buts secondaires du mariage coutumier. Par le mariage, on se créait des amitiés. On s'assurait des soutiens dans le famille de la femme. On se greffait dans un nouveau clan qui jusque-là était fermé. Pour décline, jadis, son identité en cas de malheur, on indiquait non seulement les principaux personnages de sa famille mais aussi ceux de la femme. Actuellement entre le mari et la famille de sa femme, il n'y a guère que des relations entre le client et les employés de la boutique. La dot est réellement le prix d'achat de la femme. La femme dotée devient propriété l'héritage et peur être attribuée à tel ou tel héritier. Elle ne possède rien en propre. Tous appartient à son acheteur, même ses enfants. Le quatrième article de la déclaration universelle des droits de l'homme interdit l'esclavage et la traite des esclaves sous toutes leurs formes. La dot viole cet article et fait de la femme une esclave authentique, un article de commerce et mercuriale officielle. On peut l'acheter et la revendre avec un bénéfice exhorbitant. La nommée Alphonsine Akounga, veuve, dotée 2.800 Fr. et 1 cabri a été revendue 15.000 Fr. Par l'héritier de son mari défunt, Charles Ekoto, chef p.i. groupement Mvogo-Niengué Akonolinga 2 juillet 1953. Convention entre africains N° 2 TCA.

La dot, hypothèques des jeunes filles. — On donne un acompte de dot pour une fille dans ses plus tenders années, parfois même à la mamelle de sa mère, pour lier d'avance sa volonté et l'obliger d'accepter plus tard un homme de l'âge de son père ou de son grande père. Une sanction contre cet abus est de rigueur. Il est à souhaiter que la date du premier versement de dot marque enmmême temps celle des fiançailles et soit notée par le secrétaire de l'état-civil lui-même.

La dot freine la liberté de pouvoir se marier dès l'âge nubile et selon ses amours. Les jeunes gens passent les meilleurs temps de l'âge du mariage à chercher la dot et finissent par tendre la main non à la fille qu'ils aiment mais à celle dont le prix leur est abordable. Souvent les parents poussent leur fille à n'accepter que celui qui paraît de taille à donner une grande dot. Le mois dernier, je suit allé en tournée. Une fille que savait que je devais passer par son village vint me dire en route: "Je voudrais me marier à D. Mais mes parents me pressent." Je la renvoie avec promesse d'examiner son cas sur place. J'arrive au poste. J'interroge les parents. Ils se fâchent. "Ce sont là, dissent-ils, des calomnies. Notre fille aime éperdûment. T. C'est elle-même qui l'a choisi." Je pose la question à la fille. Elle se tait. De grosses larmes qui baignent ses joues me dissent assez qu'elle se fait a été réellement donnée à T, plus âgé de dix ans qu'elle. Un mariage malheureux de plus. Voulez-vous mariage à dot? La voici:

Au village d'A..., du groupement de Mbidambani, Subdivision de Mbalmayo, le nommé Jules E. a acheté une fille de 15 ans pour son fils. Arrivé avec elle dans son village, il en expropria son fils. Il revendiquait lui-même sur elle les droits maritaux et la mettait à la bastonnade pour briser ses hésitations. La fille s'en fuit. E. saisit le tribunal, à Mbalmayo, qui la lui remit. La situation de la fille empira. Nouvelle évasion de la fille à la Mission catholique dAtéga. Nouveau recours d'E. à Mbalmayo pour qu'on lui remette "sa femme" avec laquelle il n'a pas fait d'état-civil. Le 24 juin 1953, deux gardes régionaux sont venus la prendre avec sa mère. Cette fois, le tribunal de Mbalmayo assigna à la fille une résidence obligatoire chez l'Assesseur à Mbalmayo jusqu'à ce qu'elle trouve quelqu'un qui puisse l'acheter pour rembourser E...

La fille ainsi mise en demeure pour trouver un acheteur doit accepter le premier qui se présente pour le délivrer de ce lieu pénitential. Il est d'une clarté fulgurante que le libre consentement de la femme est une utopie.

Dans l'espoir d'une dot majeure, les parents repoussent par système les premiers prétendants ou en acceptant plusieurs à la fois et par un véritable tour d'adresse contentent tout le monde sans rien céder à personne. Survint un malotru cossu, c'est lui qui emporte le morceau. Evidemment la fille n'y trouvera pas de satisfaction. On devine le reste. Il est nécessaire de veiller à cette vente aux enchères des filles. Il n'y a rien de plus efficace à ce sujet que l'application pure et simple du décret Jacquinot qui autorise le mariage sans dot de filles majeures et des femmes dont le premier mariage a été légalement dissous. Il n'est pas rare de voir des parents faire rompre le mariage de leur fille pour pouvoir la donner à donner un autre qui promet une dot supérieure à celle du premier.

La dot asservit la femme

La dot asservit la femme et aggrave son esclavage après la mort du mari. Le mari l'appelle couramment "dzom", la chose, la res mancipi des Romains. Le mariage dans le vrai sens du mot est une union conjugale de l'homme et la femme selon des lois d'une autorité compétente pour constituer une vie de communauté inséparable des deux conjoints. Dans une communauté de mariage, quand l'un est mort, l'autre le remplace automatiquement en tout. La dot écarte la femme de cette succession et en fait plutôt une pièce d'héritage, res mancipi, comme l'était jadis les esclaves à la traite officielle des noirs. La dot, somme toute, n'est qu'un camouflage de la traite des négresses. La femme héritée voit, surtout quand elle ne se paie pas de mine, sa situation aggravée. Son titre deservante a été renforcé avec ses servitudes. La dot évapore les décrets Mandel et Jacquinot. – "Même dans les pays, dit le décret Art. 2, où la dot est une institution coutumière, la fille majeure de vingt-et-un ans et la femme dont le précédent mariage a été légalement dissous, peuvent librement se marier sans que quiconque puisse prétendre à en retirer un avantage matériel, soit à l'occasion des fiançailles, soit pendant le mariage." – Les juges des tribunaux dits coutumiers ont escamoté ce décret avec la complicité de tous les ennemis de l'équilibre social, de la réelle évolution de notre pays. Le Maître devient parfait quand il met à la portée de ses disciples les moyens de l'imiter. Or, la loi française interdit la vente des femmes et la polygamie. Elle doit les interdire aussi pour les mineurs que nous sommes, si effectivement elle veut faire honneur à son engagement de nous acheminer vers la majorité. Les hommes dissolus: chefs abrutis, fonctionnaires dévoyés, commerçants sans aveu, etc. unis aux nombreuses bacchantes dont ils partagent la vie et les manières vénériennes, comptant sur leur richesse grâce à laquelle els rentent de taille à forcer sous la pression des parents cupides, les coeurs des jeunes filles qu'ils ne peuvent gagner par leurs propres charmes, prônent le maintien de la dot. Ce sont les arriérés, les esclavagistes égarés dans le siècle atomique, laudatores temporis acti, soucieux de soutenir les cadres vermoulus de leur bon vieux temps. Ils ne méritent pas d'être pris au sérieux. Ils sont inconséquents. Ils revendiquent les mêmes droits que les Français: droits de vote, droits de syndicat, d'associations, du code de Travail. Ils repoussent leurs devoirs: devoirs de renoncer à la polygamie à la vente des femmes. Ce sont des monstres avec les bras inégaux pour l'acceptation des droits et des devoirs, devoirs qui font l'homme de caractère et de civilisation.

Chaque missionnaire, chaque homme bien pensant peut présenter des cas de réclamations stupides de la dot. Vicaire à la Mission catholique de Yangben, sans las Subdivision de Bafia, j'ai remarqué un lépreux qui vivait en concubinage avec une lépreuse.

Leur maladie faisait de tristes progrès et commençait à les mutiler. L'un et l'autre avaient perdu l'espoir de guérison. J'ai pensé régulariser leur situation par un mariage religieux. Mis au courant du projet, les parents de la lépreuse opposèrent leur veto à la célébration religieuse de ce mariage tant qu'ils n'avaient pas touché de dot pour cette morte à la vie sociale. Le lépreux n'avait rien. J'ai dû les abandonner dans leur triste sort pour éviter les ennuis de la part de l'Administration d'un mariage sans état-civil.

La dot est un ferment de désordre dans le ménage. Quand un jeune homme saigné à blanc par des beaux-parents s'est marié, il vit dans un dénûment voisin de la misère. Ses premiers gains passent à payer les dettes contractées à l'occasion de mariage. La belle-famille est toujours là en quémandeuse. La femme veut être entretenue. L'homme n'a rien. Du broutille dans le ménage pouvant se solder par l'évasion de la femme ou par le divorce. O dot! O dot! O dot désastreuse! Que de conjoints elle a disjoints.

Toutes ces funestes conséquences de la dot plaident éloquemment pour sa suppression. Ses défenseurs, désireux de nous maintenir dans la stagnation, se retranchent derrière la coutume. Ces illogiques maintiennent la coutume de donner la dot et abandonnent celle de la rembourser aux taux qu'elle a été donnée. Une femme qui quitte celui qui l'a dotée ou son héritier est tenue à rembourser. Le terme est mal choisi, à se racheter par une somme 5, 7, 10 fois plus grande que son premier prix d'achat. J'ai cite plus haut un exemple typique. D'ailleurs aucune coutume si vieille, soit-elle, ne vaut contre le droit naturel. Les femmes sont des personnes et ont naturellement droit à la liberté dont les prive la dot. Bien des coutumes ont disparu irrémédiablement. L'anthropophagie de certaines tribus, les ordalies, des rites sociaux très importants, tells que le "so" chez les Yaoundé, le Ngwé chez les Bakoko, le Nga Kolo chez les Manja de l'Oubangui.

On n'avait pas demandé l'avis des bénéficiaires pour les supprimer. On a constaté leurs méfaits dans la vie individuelle ou sociale, et l'on a décrété la suppression. Les polygames, partisans irréductibles de la dot, sachant qu'elle leur fournit une main-d'oeuvre servile, la défendent avec l'âpreté des Sudistes à la guerre de Sécession. Nous comptons sur la justice. Nous savons qu'en acceptant notre Tutelle, la France s'est engagée envers l'ensemble des Nations Unies à favoriser progressivement au niveau des pays évolués. Elle devra veiller avec une manifestations, les élaguant, les émondant et les étayant selon le besoin. On ne civilise bien que dans la mesure où l'on sait reformer et transformer les coutumes retranchant celles qui sont démodées ou nuisibles et suscitant les meilleures.

L'élite du pays, à laquelle je m'associe, nous regardons d'un oeil inquiet cette cristalisation de nos tares: codification des taux des dots. Nous ne pouvons pas reconnaître que la France veut notre progrès si elle conserve par système, chez nous, ce qui est une honte dans les pays évolués. L'abolition de la dot s'impose

Daignez agréer, Monsieur, mes salutations distinguées.

Signe: Abbé Théodore TSALA
Directeur de la Mission cath., Atega.

Appendix C
Translation of Appendix B: Aspects of Traditional Beti Society, by Abbé Theodore Tsala

Beti Government

The Beti had a democratic government. People expressed their will in assemblies. All citizens had, with adaptations to circumstances, the same rights and responsibilities. They were well-disciplined. Each collectivity, small as it might be, had its chief. He who headed the first unit of the society was called the *mie-dzala*, or shaper of the village.

The word *dzal* (or *dzala*), which we improperly translate here as "village," signifies an isolated domicile, even reduced to a single room inhabited by a single man. The inhabitant is a *mie-dzala*, the creator of a village. All those who came afterwards were under him. He exercises a mitigated paternal authority over them. One could not escape his control without abandoning the setting. In certain respects, he will remain dependent on his *mie-dzala* of origin.

The *mie-dzala* who presided over a clan or tribal assembly took the title of *mie-nnama*. He was elected by the council that did not make its choice except on the good conduct demonstrated by the governing of his family, his impartiality, his courage, in a word, by the qualities of a good chief. The *mie-nnama* in charge could also, in accord with the council, appoint his successor. He would make him his assistant.

Despite what Karl Atangana said in his *Jaunde-Texte*, this title was not hereditary to the point of always passing from father to son or whoever held the post. He also did not have the right to impose any tax. Taxation did not exist. There is not even a word for it in the Beti language. The word *toya*, by which we refer to it, is a neologism, the deformation of the German word for tax, *Steuer*. Besides, taxation is made to provide for the expenses of the state and the Beti did not have any state. All communal works demanded communal labor.

The Council

There was a closed circle and an open circle. The first played the role of the court of conciliation; the second dealt with important business and made decisions. They judged without appeal. When the interests of the tribe were before the court,

N.B. This is an informal translation by the book's author of the original texts by Abbé Theodore Tsala.

all the *mie-dzala*, under the presidency of *mie-nnama* had to present themselves before the council if not at least in person, then through representation. In these kinds of meetings the orator, also called judge in the sense that it is he who proclaims the judgments of the clan, has the right to a certain retribution called *akon ntol*, which is dependent on the plaintiffs.

When the presence of a specific orator is desired in a meeting where all have the right to speak and his absence is feared, he is taken to the meeting place a few days in advance, a present called *ebodosi* or traveling expenses is given to help him decide to come at all costs. In certain cases, a small meeting of the elders imposed sanctions endorsed by the clan.

Sanctions

1) Restitution of the contested object with, if it is necessary, repairs of damages;
2) Organization of a fetishist rite. Certain ones, like the *Sso*, were very costly.
3) Honorable amends (*ekpaa-nnam*) to the offended superior (*metunena*). A young man from *kon* (today a suburb of Yaoundé) in hiding eats the pangolin (anteater) meat, reserved for the elders. Discovered, he was condemned to pay five kid goats. In Beti society, it was not advantageous to enter into judgment with one's superior, for one was always obliged to pay him something to make honorable amends if he is right, or to raise him from his downfall, if he is wrong.
4) Beating, imprisonment, shackling, reduction in captivity.
5) Exclusion from the clan or *Ekud-bikob*.
6) Death penalty. This punishment was only applicable to foreigners. We cite only one case of a death penalty of an indigenous person, by drowning.

Special Courts

Only resorted to as a last resort, especially when the defendant was from another tribe with difficult access. They are divided into three kinds:

1. *Mimboug* or *saisie*

The creditor or anyone else acting in his name would seize an object belonging to his debtor or to someone from his community until payment of the claimed debt was made. At this time, the individual was considered a simple element, an ethical person, and member of the community. It was sufficient when those involved could not be reached to take on any member of his clan. When a person was arrested, a shackle (*mbog*) was placed around his foot. The family of the arrested person would apply pressure on the debtor to complete payment of the debt.

2. The *ayanga* or *asan ayanga*

These two words come respectively from the word *san*, to cut (up), *yanga*, to wait, and has for primary meaning, he waits, he cuts-he waits.

When a debtor threatened to not pay his debt, the creditor could go to a powerful person's house, and, without saying anything, cut his plants or kill his animals.

When asked for an explanation, he answered: "I am furious at someone that owes me something and doesn't want to pay me." The powerful man moves to the talking drum and would resonate these words, "Me ne a tsigi, tsigi, a sana, sana" (I am all cut up, cut, cut, all cut, cut). His people would arrive armed to their teeth. He has them record the damages and reimburse the debt. If he could not, he was taken captive.

3. *Evuson*
Evuson (from *vui*: to take away the dirt, and *son*: to fall) is a plea in the name of one or of the dead. A disturbed creditor was going to say to a strong man, "Ma vu wa son ve" (I implore you in the name of ... to pay back this or that debt). The pleader goes with his people to the debtor's house to demand payment of the debt as well as for his traveling expenses.

In the *asan-ayanga* and in *evuson* if, after the investigation, it is proven that the plaintiff is wrong, all the expenses are his own responsibility. There are still other possible penalties.

Toward the end of the nineteenth century, an individual had come to find *Ngema, mie-nnama* of *Mvog-Manze*, at *Minlaba*, the actual administrative subdivision of *Mbalmayo* and told him, "Ma vuwe son ve ebol esoa" (I implore you in the name of the remains of your father, to go bring me the debt of a rebellious debtor). *Ngema* said to the plaintiff, "You came to call me at my home, you must drive me back there." Once arrived in the village, the chief told him, "How did you dare insult the remains of my father when we did not owe you anything? Today you will tell him that he left a son on the ground that is eager to honor him." On this, he hangs him without any other form of proceedings.

Judicial Organization

1. *Details on power*
The judicial organization of the Beti people is different than the French organization, since the Beti have a different social structure. Thus, certain Beti terms, in this order of ideas, do not have French equivalents. I am forced to use these terms in this report. I will attempt, however, to explain them by resorting to their etymology, as the need arises, to better understand the meaning.

The court did not have police, a clerk, a set building, or an appointed assessor. The court would come together wherever it was needed. Those involved were called together by the sound of the *nkul* or talking drum. The ruling cost nothing. Only the judge could receive a certain compensation called *akon ntol* or send out the oldest or throw out judgment, the *ntol* signifying one or the other. All the men who attended court had an advisory voice. When an influential person, for one reason or another, did not want to come to the meeting, one of those involved would go offer him compensation for his transportation called *ebodosi* (in other words, the instrument that kicks up dirt). The value of this *ebodosi* was proportional to the person's dignity and to the distance traveled.

There was little distinction between the civil and the criminal. However, the natural and the supernatural, more precisely, the preternatural were so confused that they were seen together everywhere. The Beti people firmly believed in *mgbel* (closer to the *amgbe*: chrysalis). The *mgbel* is a spell, the war of witches, the war of men transformed into other beings. It is a force from another dimension. To detect the effects, it was necessary to resort to a power from the same dimension. This power was called *ngam*, the *mygale*, the queen of spiders supposedly possessed by a kind and omniscient spirit. The worshippers found answers through clever ways. He who incriminates the *ngam* was presumed guilty even though his innocence had not been proven by appeal to the ordeals of which the most important is the *elon*, the poison of proof.

2. *Holders of power*

The holders of power in the Beti clan are:

(1) The *miedzala* (*mie* or *me*, to shape, to mold; *me mvie*, to mold a pot of clay. *Dzala*, of *dzal*, village, hamlet). Thus, the *miedzala* is the modeler of the village, the Roman *pater familias*, the first person responsible for the village. The word *dzal* does not have a correspondent in French. We translate it roughly as "village." It indicates isolated habitation composed of a group of huts or not. It can even be limited to a single room hut. A *dzal* had only one *miedzala*. The other occupants married or not, were the *bongo de dzal*, the children of the village, minors in a word. That is why every man with any self-respect liked to leave one abode aside where he was *miedzala*.

(2) The *miennama*. From *mie* (see above) and *nnam* (country, territory, and locality). It is the modeler of his clan or his tribe, of his country. He watches over the conservation and the population growth of his community.

(3) The *ntsig ntol* (*tsig* to cut, to sever/cut up, and *ntol*, from tol, to collect in masses; in the division of inheritance, the oldest son took the lion's part). The *stig ntol* resolves the palavers (disputes). The *ntsig ntol* needs to be a skilled orator, instructed in the jurisprudence of the country and having the truth for his best friend, *magis amica veritas*. He was often confused with the *miennama*. Among the Bakoko people he is called *mut mbog*. To be worthy of this title it was necessary to cite, in an assembly of experts, cases where judgment was given, reported in several series of nine.

(4) *Ngenga mod* (from *nga*, to be raised, and *mod*, man) is a superman, a hero. Others derive this word from *ngan ngan mod*, which is to say, a man full of magical recipes.

(5) *Mbege-mfeg* (holder of the sack, implying a sack of fetishes) is the chief of initiations in fetishist associations.

(6) The *mengi-mengi* (literally, gorillas-gorillas) is an allusion to the belief from the country from which respected dead people transformed themselves, willingly, into gorillas. The *mengi-mengi* were "the elders of the country, closer to the tomb than the cradle," the link between the living forces of the country and the disappeared ancestors. They formed the senate of the clan. They had a prominent voice.

(7) *Etogan nnam* (the council of the clan) judged without appeal that the *miedzala* and the *miennama* had more of a disciplinary power. This one from the last was mitigated but strengthened by those from the *mengi-mengi*. The *mbege-mfeg* resolved the disputes between the members of his association.

A Meeting of the Council

The night before the council's meeting, the plaintiff or his representative goes up to the talking drum to summon the people for the meeting. Cf. *Nkul adzo*.

The next day everyone gathers together at the indicated place because it's the duty of every good citizen to be present at the secluded place to deliberate. The council is essentially made up of the judge, one or two representatives from each party, and a few men not directly associated in the affair. At the return, the judge resumes the recitation of the facts, condemns the bad, and gives his decision.

The council is always held outside. The judge speaks standing up, holding in one hand a spear, *akon ntol* (any other orator does not have the right to hold spears), and in the other hand a fly-swatter, *akpaag nnam*, or only one of these two objects. He is excessively expressive through gestures. He employs multiple gestures, and moves about the court, assuming appropriate positions, to convey the impressions he feels or that he wants to challenge with the others. If one of the assistants finds an argument that confirms his theory, he rises and asks him to speak by these words: "Ma tsing wa baa a minken" (I put *baa* on your poles). *Baa*, red mahogany powder, is the emblem of victory.

A very good orator is offered presents with spears on broken poles to signify that his eloquence disarms those most determined. We shout to him, *o nga vaa mimbim a son*, "You will take out the cadavers from the tombs. You will dig up the cadavers without anyone's reprisal; because [everyone is] won over by your eloquence."

Occasionally the orator wakens the audience's attention by expressions such as these: "Yebegana ma a!- Heee" (Approve with me! – This as well), "Bi ne kin a!" (We agree, what? – Perfectly).

The disagreement is examined in all ways. If there is still some shadiness, it is moved back to a later date. Consequently, it was said of a confusing case: "Binke bia kobo a meba mebaa" (We will speak about it during multiple meeting).

The Penalties

There were two types of penalties: disciplinary penalties and judicial penalties. There was not, however, a strict division between the two. The first that were especially physical were reserved to *miedzala* and *miennama*. They are *ebom* (beating), removal of the ears (for slaves), *ngadag* (binding), and *mibog* (being placed in shackles).

The judicial power was:

Eyian (restitution). It is the talion law (the law to punish the offense at the same level as the original offense) on objects. For the stolen object, another replaced it of the same value or something else equivalent in value.

Ntan (compensation). The stolen object was restored to the owner, who was compensated at the same time for the worries that the loss caused him. A proverb read, "Eyian e se ntan" (Restitution is not compensation). Restitution of the object can be asked for without necessarily ending a friendship.

Ekpee akan (condemnation to organizing a fetishist rite). Certain ones like the *Sso*; the complaint requires several dozens of kid goats without prejudice of [adding] divers other objects.

Ekud bikob (deprivation of citizen rights).
Metunena (the honorable fine). A young man from Kon went elsewhere to eat the meat of the pangolin (anteater) that only the *mengi-mengi* of his clan had the right to eat. At his return, he was condemned to pay to them a fine of five kid goats.

Capital punishment was rarely employed.

According to popular belief, he who sheds the blood of a relative or of a close relative brought upon himself ipso facto the *tsoo*, a disease of the chest and other areas. But in a clan, with the exclusion of slaves and married women, everyone is related. If a stranger to the clan commits a crime that deserves death, his condemnation is sure. At the burial of a great person, women and slaves were killed so that he would not go alone. We speak however, among the lakeside residents of Sanaga, of some condemnations by drowning or hanging.

Ekud-bikob

The expression *ekud-bikob* literally signifies percussion of the skins. When a man rebels against the clan's decision or the judges' decision, he receives a visit from the *mengi-mengi*. They summon him to obedience. If he still resists, they tell him, "By disobeying the judge or the clan you have ignored us. We will ignore you as well. Against you we shake off your dust that was attached to our skins (we wore skins)." After this, they stand up, shake their skins, and disappear. From then on, no one from the clan goes to the rebel's house nor receives him. If he is attacked, no one goes to his aid: "Wem night zu raten ist, der mist nicht zu helfen," as the Germans say. He who doesn't listen to counsel does not deserve to be helped. In a country where the individual does not live his life alone, but with the clan, being separated is like a long death. Therefore, the exiled did not stay long under this pain. He would quickly go find one of the *mengi-mengi* to announce his plan to conform to the sentence he had received. He would bring the elder, in order to win his kindness, a rooster, and a bunch of bananas called *elad-ekon*, unified bananas. In more serious cases, a kid goat was given instead of a rooster. All the *mengi-mengi*, now well-informed of the prodigal son's return, assemble, bring him in, and impose on him the fine they deem necessary. The penitent must accept himself now as a submissive son, for even a little pout on his part could ruin the whole affair.

The Lifting of a Curse

To release a curse from a cursed son, he is placed in the middle of the court. His father or another man in that place stands up, holding an *akpaag* (fly-swatter) in his hand. He recites the cause of the curse brought upon him; he then shows the signs of sincere repentance that plead in favor of the guilty one. He declares that he believes the man to be well-mannered enough to be worthy of forgiveness. He asks all the assistants if they share his view. All answer with a unanimous "yes." Then, he scrapes some bark from a tree and divides the bark into three parts. The first part he places on his right hand, then applies it to the penitent's forehead and pulls it down to the nape of the neck. He soaks the second piece in water that he makes the penitent drink. He takes the third and divides it into as many parts as there are *mengi-mengi* members in the whole assembly. He puts his own in his mouth, chews it, and spits it onto the penitent's forehead. All the others do the same. Everyone, extending their hands out to help him, stand up and pronounce together the formula of absolution:

E mongo wan a toa nyo, A a ngleg bele
Ki fee tom ye bia a ! – Heee.
Bi man ya lad ye nye a ! – Heee.
Amana ya bia tuni a ! – Heee.
Mod a vege nye mbe dzam, Emen a dugan ye nye a ! – Heee.
E nye biatie a si nyo a ! – A maas.
Our child who is here,
Has no more talk with us, right? – Exactly.
He has made honorable amends, right? – Exactly.
We are reconciled with him, right? – Exactly.
He who is preparing to trap him,
Let him be caught in his own trap, right? – Exactly.
Here is he that we raise from the ground. – With wonderful ease.

The Death of Zibi Ngomo and Human Sacrifices

Around the year 1900 died at Nkon-Abog, village of the Mvog-Fuda, a great one named Zibi Ngomo. The next day, a tributary of men in his village came to render condolences. The *ban kal*, that is to say the men born from a daughter of the Mvog-Fuda, do not come. They stay on the road near the village and wait for each other. At the end of the day they show up in a gloomy procession. Some of them hold in their hands a large rope with a lax knot at the end (a *l'ekoe*). They throw it in front of the assistants and withdraw to a corner of the village. They do not want to participate in the mourning until they desire to. The funeral chief, escorted by his own, stands up and goes toward them. "Nephew, here is your share," he tells them, pointing to the man he pushes in front of him, a slave of the deceased. A ferocious grimace crosses the saddened faces. They surround the slave and begin to dance the *esani* with the drums beating louder and louder. At some time the eldest orders the slave to withdraw. As soon as he turns his back, he strikes him a deadly blow with a knife. The others imitate him. The slave collapses. The blows continue to rain down upon him. Each nephew is eager to give him his own. Then they gather the torn up cadaver and the strips of flesh and go to bury them in a pit in the backwoods.

Owona Ngo Ndum, chief of the clan, moves forward in the court to speak. Complete silence prevails. He harangues the crowd on the deceased's virtues and on the maliciousness of the evil witches who took from them a man so dear.

Zibi is not the only man who has descended to stay with the dead. For this woman he was everything. "Ebobom ki, eton ki." The fall of the palm tree results in the fall of the house. There are also other women who gave him a lot of troubles. They dreamed of nothing but his death. Without a doubt, they cooperated in it. Will we let them watch Zibi descend to his tomb? We cannot tolerate such an offense. After his harangue the great ones withdrew with him to deliberate. Their return is greeted by a new outbreak of singing of *esani*.

Owona Ngo Ndum moves forward again in the court. The same silence as before. He starts again to harangue the crowd. He interrupts himself and makes Fuda Zibi come over, the oldest son of Zibi Ngomo. He converses with him for a moment, then, he spits on his face, on his chest and between his shoulder blades, a paste of tree bark. Fuda goes and sits down on the awning where there were already other men.

The funeral chief opens the widows' prison. The nephews hurry over there. They come back out dragging Memono, daughter in the tribe of Endongo, the mother of Fuda Zibi. She is executed before the eyes of her own son. Two other women are executed, Ada Menene, from the tribe of Vod Amug, and Ngo Fumbi from the tribe of the Bakoko.

The eyes turn now toward the son of Zibi. "You have, maybe, participated in the magic war that killed your father. You are going to prove your innocence by the poison test, the *elon*." By throwing small rocks we are going to therefore gather bark from the terrible tree to make pellets that we force those who are charged to swallow. Sitting outside, they wait, worried about the test's results. Fearing the fatal outcome, Owona Ngo Ndum stood up and says: "Dzungoo a wuu, ebamekogo a ligi ai mfeg mebel" (When the chameleon dies, the lizard inherits the sack of colas [an African stimulant fruit]). Guilty or not, these young men must live in order to carry on the blood of Zibi. Let us administer to them the antidotes. Let us give an emetic to each one to make the poison leave.

With the news of the execution of their sister, the brothers of Memono bring complaint before the government. Captain Dominik, the [German] chief of post in Yaoundé, assembles all the chiefs and forbids them, under penalty of death, any executions of any kind.

All the executions at the great one's death did not happen in the same way. Sometimes the "nephews" stopped along the way and sent word to the funeral chief: "Be Zaag bia kad foe" (that we come to tell the news). People were therefore brought to them to be executed. They put slaves, men, and women under the knife, and hung free women. After having arrived in the village, they put all those suspected of having cooperated in the death of the deceased through the poison test. Those who emerged from the test victorious received the minimum amount of a woman's dowry for the false accusations against them.

Certain great ones were buried at *esam-so*, a perimeter of the *Sso* initiation rite. The slaves that took the cadaver there must not come back to the village. As soon as they lay down their charge, they are immediately seized and carved into pieces. It's on their bodies, in the tomb, that the great one's cadaver is laid.

The executions at the burial site had several objectives:
(1) To supply servants and women to the great one who was descending to the dwelling place of the dead. On the elders' judgment, life beyond the grave was noticeably similar to the one on earth.
(2) To punish those who had wronged the deceased.
(3) To inspire, by fear, the household personnel, to respect their boss.

(4) To prove that the deceased had left behind him brave men. It was also possible that we would bring the captives together in a war offering on the tomb of the dear ones or that there we would lay the head of their worst enemies killed in retaliation. That is the way that we laid on the tomb of Mebada Mesomo, chief of Mvog-Onamenye, the head of Ebono Blea, chief of the Toms, who had killed Mbene Elumbele, son of Mebada Mesomo.

A Cameronian Priest's Opinion on the Dowry, by the Abbé Theodore Tsala

[This article was written for a French Roman Catholic journal, the citation of which the author is unable to locate.]

(We communicated recently with this priest, who is the dean of the clergy of that country, about the text of a government decree fixing the dowry [bride-price] rates by region. Here is the authorized and well thought-out answer from someone who really understands the question.)

Dear Sir,
   I have the honor of acknowledging receipt of your letter of the 13th of June 1953 and of the government decree determining rates of dowry in regions in which there are excessive demands. I thank you. You asked for my frank opinion. I am happy to provide you with it.
   The concept of dowry rates should also lead to the one of penalties against offenders. This maximum dowry of former times is no more. The greedy misers set a minimum and a springboard to obtain these enormous sums of which today we are the stunned witnesses. Our judges witnessed without reaction this rising increase in dowries. Even worse, they quickly adapted to it. They are going as far as to allow poor peasants' to pay dowries the amount of which could frighten even an easy-living bourgeoisie. That is why I am worried. A law without penalties is a dead law, providing almost an invitation to break it. The forbidden fruit is tempting. It matters then to anticipate above all a penalty against excessive demands, against black market dowries. Only the prospect of a severe penalty can anticipate infractions.

The Dowry Process

Before fixing dowry rates, the legislature will need to come to an exact knowledge of the different dowry grades. A dowry can be *conclusive, concomitant*, or *subsequent*. A conclusive dowry is one that the woman's parents judge sufficient to conclude a marriage, to establish the legitimacy of marriage, or to leave the daughter to the suitor. The concomitant dowry is made when the young couple is accompanied to their home. After the religious ceremonies, the two spouses in nuptial apparel go to their home. At the entrance way the procession stops in front of the mother-in-law who is laying flat down on her stomach sideways across the passage. To step over her or walk around her constitutes a crime of wronging motherhood, heavy with consequences for the young household. One must pick her up quickly with a substantial dowry. Leaving her for a long period in this position risks aggravating the situation. Sometimes the parents-in-law refuse to take part in the feast or to sit down as long as the couple have not yet made honorable amends with a nice sum.

As for the subsequent dowry, I would only like to emphasize the most unattractive aspect. Parents that are hard on cash invite their daughter to return to the village to force the husband to bring an addition to the dowry, determined by them. The woman can stay like this for months, even seasons. If the husband does not hurry, one can speak shamelessly of replacing him.

I almost forgot the accessories of the dowry. This brother wants a loincloth, another one a pair of shoes. One must not forget the influential uncle to whom a fashionable suit is due, etc. ... And lastly, a large meal with an abundance of drinks for all the family. For this purpose, fattened up kid goats are called for, or else an ox and demijohns of red wine.

The dowry is viewed at different levels. If we do not contain it or if we only address the principal, one of the secondary figures will move up to first rank and we will find ourselves once more in the status quo.

Determining the Dowry
Determining the maximum dowry favors the working class. It should be based on their income and possible savings, in such a way that a young man of the common people can find the necessary dowry within the space of at least five years. But the income of a working-class citizen in our region these days is thirty thousand francs a year. His monthly salary range is between two and three thousand francs. In saving a quarter or a half of his gains, it can total 10,000 to 15,000 francs plus ten kid goats, which in all makes 70,000 francs. The average price of a kid goat is 2,000 francs, here in Atega, and maybe elsewhere as well. The fiancé would then need ten years of saving if we keep in mind other expenses. That is too much. The richest regions have maximum rates lower than ours. For example, Wouri, Bamileke, Dja and Lobo, etc. We should also take different drastic measures to block other dowry issues.

The Dowry and Marriage in Former Times
It is getting worse and worse and we are in over our heads. All these compromises only serve to commercialize an old gesture of alliance. The dowry in former times was a lot simpler, friendlier. A traveler arrives. He is accommodated. He is fed. He is taken care of as best as possible. Free hospitality was considered a point of honor. Satisfied, at his departure he says: "I thank you for having taken care of all my little needs. I give you my daughter or my sister in marriage to bind this friendship that you have proven." Sometimes, the good manners of a traveler are noticed. He is invited. He is questioned on his origins. "My child loved you and us along with him. We call you one of our family. We give you this girl in marriage. The man leaves with the woman without paying a penny. It is just as possible to go to someone's home and give a daughter or sister to a great chief or great warrior from whom one seeks a special favor.

The husband owed a reverent respect to the parents of his wife. The *ewondo* proverbs still in use today thoroughly prove this, for example: "Bakakak nkie-ngon okpal." "One does not promise his parents-in-law a partridge that still lives in the backwoods," or else if one is not able to trap it, he is seen as a man without means. He who has received a woman like the ones we have hereto mentioned had to prove his generosity by giving in return his daughter or sister. This is what was called exchange marriage. This was my mother's case. For want of another woman, presents were offered the quantity of which was measured against the magnanimity of the donor.

Deviation of the Dowry: Its Wrongdoings
The current dowry is a deviation of the old one. It is a social plague. It breaks one of the main secondary objectives of customary marriage. Through marriage, friendships were created. The wife's family was ensured support. We became a part of a new clan that until then had been closed. In olden days, a man might decline or refuse his identity in case of misfortune. [This affected] not only the main people of his family but also those of the wife. Currently between the husband and his wife's family there are only connections like those between the client and the employees of a boutique. The dowry is really the price for buying a woman. The woman with a dowry becomes part of an estate and may be awarded to this or that inheritor. She does not possess anything of her own. Everything belongs to her buyer, even her children. The fourth article of the Universal Declaration of the Rights of Man forbids slavery and the treatment of slaves in all forms. The dowry violates this article and makes the woman an authentic slave, an article of business and bargainable merchandise. She can be bought and resold with a nice profit. The named Alphonisine Akounga, widow, was with a dowry of 2,800 francs and one kid goat, and was resold for 15,000 francs by her dead husband's inheritor, Charles Ekoto, p.i. chief of the group Mvogo-Niengue Akonolinga the 2nd of July 1953. An agreement among Africans # 2 TCA [citation of official document].

The dowry, the mortgage of young girls. A down payment on the dowry is given for a daughter in her most tender years, sometimes even from her mother's breast, to bind her in advance of her making a decision, and obliging her to later accept a man the same age as her father or grandfather. Sanctions against this abuse are rigorous. It is best that the day of the first dowry payment be that of the engagement and at the same time that the transaction be noted by a civil official.

The dowry curbs the right to marry from the age of consent and a marriage based on love. Young men spend the best times of their youth (at the age of marriage) hunting for the dowry and end up proposing not to the women they love but to those whose price is affordable. Often parents push their daughter to only accept those who seem to have the means to give a large dowry. Last month, I went on tour. A girl who knew that I was supposed to pass through her village came to me and said: "I would like to marry D. But my parents are pressuring me." I sent her away with a promise to look into her case. I arrived at the post office. I interrogated the parents. They got angry. "These are lies," they said. "Our daughter is madly in love with T. She is the one who chose him herself." I asked the question of the daughter. She kept quiet. Big tears covered her cheeks and told me enough – that she had really been given to T, ten years older than her. An unhappy marriage too. Do you want a marriage with dowry? Here it is:

The village of A ... the group of Mbidambane, subdivision of Mbalmayo, the man named Jules E. bought a 15-year-old girl for his son. Arriving with her in his village, he claims her instead of his son. He demanded the marital rights from her for himself and would beat her for shattering his expectations. The girl escaped. E. submits his case to the court, in Mbalmayo, who gave her back to him. The girl's situation worsened The girl escaped again to the Catholic Mission of Atega. Another appeal from E. in Mbalmayo so that "his woman" would be returned to him [even though] he did not legitimately have a civil marriage. The 24th of June 1953, two regional guards came to take her with her mother. This time, the court of Mbalmayo assigned the girl to an obligatory residence at the assessor's home in Mbalmayo until someone could buy her to reimburse E....

The daughter, therefore, is placed in a home to await a buyer, and must accept the first one who presents himself to deliver her from this penitential place. It is with striking clarity that free consent by a woman is a utopia.

In the hopes of a greater dowry, the parents, pushed again by the wealth of the first suitors, or by accepting several at the same time, and by a real clever trick satisfying everyone without giving up anything to anyone. An affluent lout arises, and it is him who will take the choice piece. Evidently the daughter did not find satisfaction in this. We can guess the rest. It is necessary to watch over this auction-like selling of girls. There is nothing more efficient in this subject than the pure and simple application of Jacquinot's decree that authorizes marriage without dowry for daughters of age and for women whose first marriage was legally dissolved. It is not rare to see parents break up the marriage of their daughter to give her to another who has promised a greater dowry than the one given by the first.

The Dowry Enslaves the Woman

The dowry enslaves the woman and aggravates her slavery after the death of the husband. The husband commonly calls her "*dzom*," the thing, the *res mancipi* of the Romans. Marriage in the true meaning of the word is a conjugal union of a man and a woman according to the laws of a competent authority [allowing them] to constitute an inseparable life between the two persons. In the marriage union, when one is dead, the other replaces him/her automatically in everything. The dowry dismisses the woman from this succession and makes of it/her instead an item of inheritance, *res mancipi*, like slaves were in former times during the slave trade. The dowry, in short, is nothing but a camouflage for the slave trade of Negro women. The inherited woman sees, especially when she does not pay a deposit, her situation worsen. Her deserving title has been strengthened with her servitude. The dowry evaporates the Mandel and Jacquinot decrees. – "Even in the countries," says Article 2 of the decree, "where the dowry is a customary institution, the twenty-one year old girl and the woman whose first marriage had been legally dissolved, can freely marry without anyone being able to claim to take away material benefits, either during the engagement or during the marriage." – The customary court judges skirted around this decree with the complicity of the enemies of social balance, [affecting] the real evolution of our country. The Master becomes perfect when he makes accessible to his disciples the means to imitate him. But French law prohibits the selling of woman and polygamy. [French law] should also prohibit them for the minors, which we are, if it wants to effectively honor its commitment to help us move toward full maturation. The dissolute men: foolish chiefs, civil servants lead astray, dishonorable merchants, etc. ... united in ways in which they share life and their sexual manners. Counting on their riches, they give into pressure from greedy parents, and advocate upholding the dowry, [thus allowing them access to] the hearts of young girls they cannot win through their own charms. It is the backward people, the slave traders lost in the atomic century, *laudatores temporis acti*, preoccupied with sustaining the age-old structures of their good old times. They are not worthy of being taken seriously. They are inconsequential. They claim the same rights as the French: the right to vote, union rights, association rights, of the labor code, etc. They reject their obligations: obligations to renounce polygamy and the sale of women. They are monsters with arms uneven enough to accept rights and obligations, obligations that make a civilized man of character.

Every missionary, every well thinking man can describe stupid dowry cases. While vicar of the Catholic Mission of Yangben, in the Bafia subdivision, I noticed a leper that was cohabiting with another leper. Their disease was making bleak progress and was beginning to mutilate them. Both of them had lost hope of being healed. I thought of putting their situation in order by a religious wedding. Being informed of the possibility, the parents of the leprous woman forbade the religious celebration of this marriage as long as they did not receive a dowry for this living-dead. The leper had nothing. I had to abandon them in their sad situation to avoid annoyances with the Administration over an illegitimate marriage.

The dowry is a presence of disorder in the household. When a young man cleaned out by his parents-in-law was married, he lives in utter destitution. His first earnings are used to pay the debts that were incurred upon the marriage. The in-laws are always there begging. The wife wants to be taken care of. The man has nothing. Mere trifles in the home can result in the woman leaving or in divorce. Oh dowry! Oh dowry! Oh disastrous dowry! How many unions can she split?

All these catastrophic consequences of the dowry eloquently plead for its elimination. Its defenders, desirous of keeping us in stagnation, hide behind tradition. This illogicality upholds the tradition of giving the dowry and abandons the one of reimbursing it at the rate it had been given. A woman who leaves him who gave her a dowry or her inheritor is expected to provide reimbursement. The term is badly chosen, to make amends by a sum of 5, 7, 10 times greater than the original buying price. I cited above a typical example. Besides no other tradition so old, as it may be, goes against natural rights. Women are people and thus naturally have rights to freedom of which the dowry deprives them. Many traditions have irretrievably disappeared. The anthropology of certain tribes [shows the loss of] ordeals, extremely important social rites, such as the [*Sso*] of the Yaoundé, the Ngwe of the Bakoko, the Nga Kolo of the Manja from Oubangui.

The opinions of the beneficiaries were not asked in order to do away with them. Their wrongdoings have been noted in individual and social life, and elimination of [the rites] was ordered. The polygamists, diehard supporters of the dowry, knowing that it provides them subservient labor, defend it with the harshness of the Southerners during the war of secession. We count on justice. We know that by accepting our guardianship, France committed itself to the full position of the United Nations in gradually making preferences toward developed countries. She (France) would watch over them with a careful eye, pruning them and backing them up according to need. One only civilizes well to the extent where we know how to reform and transform the traditions, rejecting those that are out-dated or harmful and favoring the best ones.

The country's elite, with whom I associate myself, we look with a worrisome eye at this crystallization of our defects and the codification of dowry rates. We cannot acknowledge that France wants our progress if she retains this system, in our country, [a system that] would be shameful in developed countries. The abolition of the dowry is necessary.

Please accept, Monsieur, my distinguished greetings.

Signed: Abbé Theodore TSALA
Director of the Catholic Mission, Atega

*"With the Abbia game it is like this:
... reasonable people do not play it, only those who are out to steal.
For when somebody has lost all his possessions
in the Abbia game, then his heart thinks only about stealing.
That is the reason why all the other people do not like the game."*
— Paul Messi

ABBIA STONES

FREDERICK QUINN

The Beti are a Bantu-speaking people numbering approximately 500,000 who live in the vicinity of Yaounde, the capital of Cameroon. The land is rainforest for the most part, set on a plateau which is broken by deep ravines and a few hills, and becomes savannah toward the north. Until the Germans arrived in the 1880's, Beti government was characterized by several thousand headmen each acting independently of one another, or bound in alliances by ties of friendship, kinship or marriage. Each compound was ruled by its own headman and usually contained his unmarried brothers, wives, and their children. The Beti practiced hunting and limited agriculture, including the growing of root crops. Because of the tsetse fly, only household animals were kept.

Few forms of traditional Beti art survive. The Beti once made masks and statues, especially in conjunction with the *Sso* (antelope) initiation rites for young men, but that art disappeared, probably with the outlawing of the *Sso* ceremonies by the Germans about 1910. Several years ago, a Beti informant, at that time in his late seventies, described the masks used in the *Sso* ceremonies by saying: "They were terrible to see." The initiation rite which he had experienced as a young man marked the transformation of the liminal state of adolescence to incorporation as warriors in the rainforest society. Included in his statements on the art and culture of his people was a fairly extensive description of the Beti's highly decorative art of the *Abbia* stone.

Abbia was a very popular game in the Cameroonian rainforest and among the Beti. It was not a game of skill, but almost entirely a game of chance, much like throwing dice. *Abbia* stones *(mvia)* were carved from the hard pits of the Mimusops Congolensis tree. Paul Messi, a Beti who served as assistant for Yaounde languages at Hamburg for several years following World War I, described the gathering of the fruits of the tree, which he referred to as *elan:* "*Elan* is a big tree in the forest. It gives fruit only every second year. *Elan* fruits are poisonous. If somebody eats them, he dies. Therefore, we do it like this: when the *elan* tree has borne fruit and the fruits have fallen to the ground, the women and children go into the forest and pick up the fallen and rotten fruit. Sometimes even adult men go into the forest; however, it is usually the women and children. They do not bring the fruits to the village, but only the hard pits. They do not bring the fruits themselves because they are afraid that the domestic animals, the goats, chickens, and pigs would die from them. If they eat the *elan* fruits, they perish. When they arrive [at the village] with the *elan* pits, they sell them to the *Abbia* players. The *Abbia* player cracks the nut into two parts carefully, and carves the game stones out of them. With these stones they can then play the *Abbia* game. The *elan* tree is indeed very dangerous; the fruits as well as the insides of the pits and the leaves are all poisonous; if somebody eats them, he dies on the spot. That much I know of it."

The stones are about the size of a large button, but elliptical in shape, and dark brown or black in color. The carving is done in such a way that the picture remains in relief forming the brown surface of the pit, while the carved-out background is a lighter color. Players were supposed to carve their own *Abbia* stones, but not all did. Ready-made stones were rarely available for purchase, since *Abbia* stone carving was not considered a profession in itself. Sometimes if a man lost all his possessions and could not continue to play, he would sell his stones. Those who did not know how to carve could go to a good friend or one with a reputation as a skilled carver and ask that a set of stones be made. In such a case, the carver, rather than the player, usually decided the objects to be depicted on each stone. These objects could be divided into three groups: inanimate objects, living beings, and supernatural beings. The second group, living beings, was the most frequently carved. As the carvings served no functional purpose in the *Abbia* game itself, it would appear that they are primarily the result of the Beti's desire for ornamentation. An experienced carver could produce up to five or six stones a day. Every player owned several stones, and some had hundreds. Messi remarked on the carving and symbolism of the stones as follows: "When the women and children used to come to sell the *elan* nuts to the gamblers it was like this: one uncarved stone cost two little iron staffs. One carved stone

---

1. (ABOVE) SMALL ARMADILLO. 2. (OPPOSITE PAGE) MAN SITTING BY A RIVER BANK. 3. A CHIEF, RECOGNIZABLE BY HIS POSTURE. 4. MAN WITH A GUN HUNTING MONKEYS. 5. MAN AND WOMAN CHATTING. 6. WOMAN WEARING LOINCLOTH. 7. HAWK KILLING FISH. 8. POLICEMAN WITH BAYONET. 9. WILD CATS. 10. GORILLA. 11. RAVEN. 12. SIX MONKEYS. 13. BIRD. 14. ANTELOPE. 15. BIRD OF PREY. 16. CHICKEN NESTING ON EGG. 17. LEOPARD. 18. FISH. 19. ANTELOPES' RESTING PLACE. 20. DOG. 21. BIRD OF PREY. 22. BAT. 23. TWO BIRDS. 24. RAT. 25. LEOPARD WITH RAT. 26. FISH.

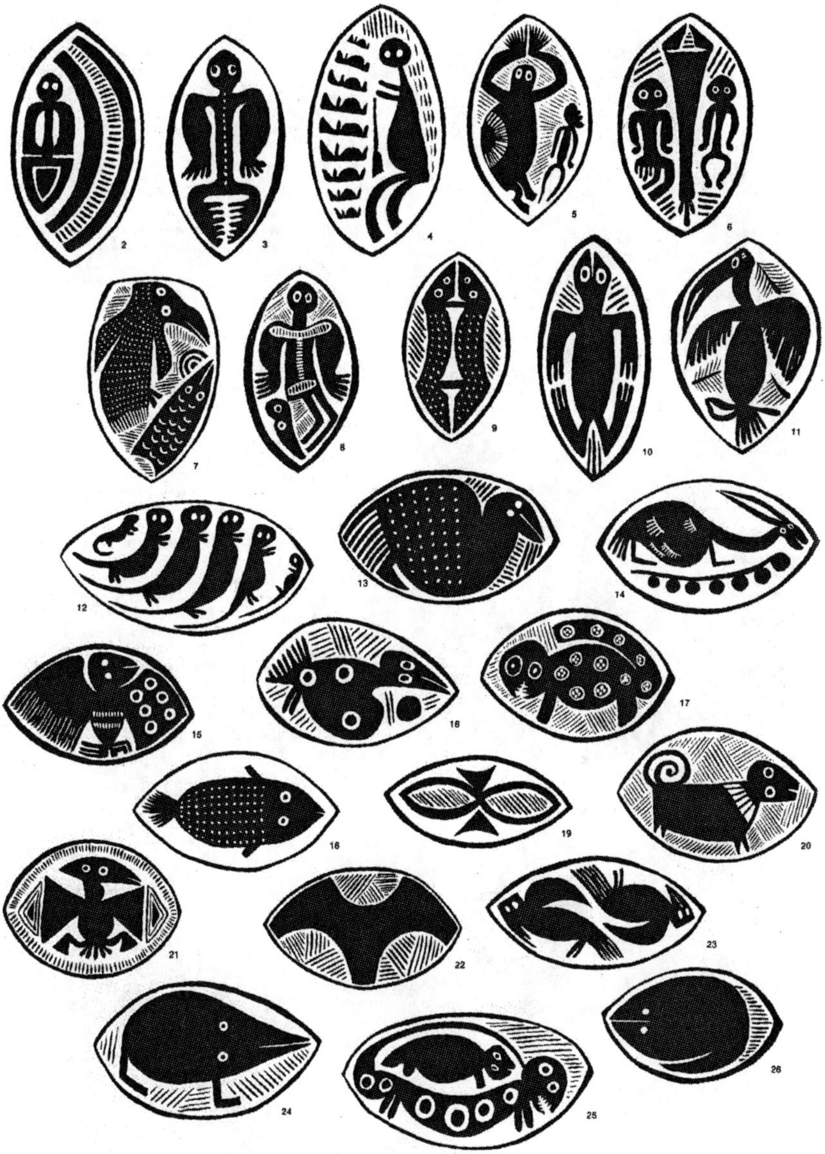
2
3
4
5
6
7
8
9
10
11
12
13
14
15
16
17
18
19
20
21
22
23
24
25
26

cost five staffs. The things carved on the stones do not have any special meaning [the decorations do not have any relation to the game; one could also play with totally undecorated stones], be it man or animal, bird or fish. These things exist in various forms, but nobody carves a particular person or a particular object. They carve like this: a man, an animal, a bird, a chicken—the last two are totally alike. Animals that look like humans, gorillas and chimpanzees, are usually depicted exactly like humans. Parrots can be recognized for what they are only by the way they sit. The same thing is true of the hawk and the raven. All other birds look the same. The horse and the donkey are shown as one animal. Man and woman are also usually the same. Except that a woman is usually depicted with a loincloth of raffia leaves in the back—by this we recognize: this is a woman. If she does not have a loincloth on, we call her only a human, since we do not know what she is, whether man or woman."

The stakes are high in an *Abbia* game; the loss of wives was common in former times, and it was not infrequent for a man to gamble himself into slavery. The game was played by men who sat in a circle around a plate-shaped woven basket and placed their carved stones in the basket, along with undecorated discs (*sa*) cut from the peel of the calabash. Messi described the game itself as follows: "The *Abbia* game is like this: the people come with iron staffs and money and sit in a circle. Every participant has his carved stones, and they also bring a braided grass basket. They put the stones in the basket, and also several other pieces. These are called *sa*, playing discs. One person who is experienced in the game is seated next to the basket and decides all things connected with the game. He lifts the basket and throws it to the ground upside down. With the basket still covering the stones, the players put down their staffs (make their bets). When the basket is removed, the positions of the seven discs indicate who has won. If there are six *Abbia* stones and seven discs in the basket, and two, three, or four of the stones lie with the carving on top, and two or three of the discs also lie with their backs up, then you know that the stones with the carved side up are the winners. The ones with the carved side down have lost. If one stone goes the same way as all seven discs, then it wins. If one stone goes one way and all the other discs and stones go the other way, then you know that the stone that went its way alone has won, and all the others have lost (are dead). If two stones and all of the discs go one way, then you know that just these have lost. When all of the discs and stones lie on their backs, the throw is invalid."

Sets of *Abbia* stones can be found in several German museums. It is also possible to purchase them from the Benedictine Abbey (Yaounde, Cameroon) where Père Lutfried Marfurt, a Swiss monk who has spent many years in Cameroon, has helped restore this art form.

The stones shown here demonstrate the remarkable range of inventiveness and subject matter of the Beti carvers. They are reproduced from the illustrations of an article "Das Abia-Glucksspiel Der Juande Und Die Darstellungen Auf Den Spielmarken" by Otto Reche, in the *Mitteilungen aus dem Museum für Völkerkunde*, Hamburg, Volume 9, 1924.

26. MAN DANCING. 27. TWO WOMEN CHATTING. 28. TWO PEOPLE IN A RAFFIA TREE. 29. TREE. 30 FOUR FISH. 31. THREE MEN WITH A MACHETE. 32. SOLDIER WITH RIFLE AND BAYONET. 33. CALABASH PALM WINE CONTAINER. 34. WOMAN CATCHING FISH. 35. CHIMPANZEE 36. MAN WITH IVORY TUSK. 37. CALABASH WITH TWO HOLES, FORMERLY USED AS AN INSTRUMENT. 38. DONKEY CARRYING SUITCASE. 39. (OPPOSITE PAGE) MAN PLAYING MUSICAL INSTRUMENTS.

EIGHT BETI SONGS

FREDERICK QUINN

The eight Beti songs which follow show aspects of life, love, death, and warfare in the rainforest. The songs were collected during the summer of 1967 for a history I was writing about the Beti. They were recorded by Pierre Betene, a researcher, and translated by him from Ewondo, the Beti language of the Yaounde region, into French. In presenting the songs in English, I have shortened the texts, eliminating some refrains and repetitions, while attempting to retain the narrative line.

Most of the songs were sung in the evening by the women, who often performed as both soloists and chorus. Accompaniment could be a drum, flute, xylophone, or *mvet*, a long piece of bamboo from which two or three long, thin strands were cut and tightened over a bridge. The strings terminated in half-gourds, placed on each end of the bamboo stick, thus providing resonance. These were not the songs of the professional praise-singers, also known as *mvet* (*African Arts/Arts d'Afrique*, Vol. II, No. 4, page 17).

NO WAR SINCE THE WHITE MAN CAME

"No war since the white man came."
My mother, no one can do this to me;
Atana Odi will kill me,
Enyege Abene will kill me,
That is not something I desire;
My mother, how can I sleep tonight?
The son of Mfege will kill me,
My mother, what can I do?
Refrain: *"No war since the white man came."*

A young Beti warrior complains that he cannot fulfill his natural inclinations toward combat, and that his enemies can easily kill him. The chorus answers that since the white man has come, for better or for worse, they have sought to keep peace among the tribes. One of the first interests of the Germans, after they arrived in the interior of Cameroon in the late 1880's, was to put an end to Beti warfare.

MINSANGALI, OPEN THE DOOR FOR ME

"Minsangali, lovely lady, open the door for me."
"Who is there that I should open the door?"
"It is I, the Panther, the most gallant in the forest."
"Panther, go quickly back from where you came...
It is Minsili-Ebana-Zene who is my fiancé.
I do not think of anyone but him for whom my hair is well-dressed."
"Aie, Aie! Look at me, rejected by a woman!"

The panther as a trickster is a familiar rainforest image.

HOW DID YOU GET IT IN YOUR HEAD?

How did you get it in your head...?
You, Ovugvugu, that you are a lord?
The sparrow has been killed,
The sparrow's throat has been cut
Because of what the wren did.
How did you get it in your head that you were a chief?
You, Ovugvugu, how did you get it in your head?
The sparrow has been killed and the other bird killed...

"Ovugvugu" is what the Beti called the first German to come to that part of central Cameroon circa 1887. Perhaps "Ovugvugu" is how the Beti heard his name. "Sparrow" and "Wren" were his unfortunate companions in this ironic song of the first encounter between the Beti and the colonizers.

DEATH

Death, having taken my father, also took my mother
And I went out on the roads, crying:
"Is it I that have brought death?"
Death, having taken my mother, also took my brother,
Death, having taken my brother, also took my husband's father,
Death, having taken my husband's father, also took my father's father
And I went out on the roads, crying:
"Is it I that have brought death to earth?"

The Beti considered misfortunes such as crop failures, sickness, and death as coming to earth because the ancestors were displeased with the conduct of their living successors. Diviners determined the cause of the misfortune, and a council of those concerned, men and women, met and offered a sacrifice to propitiate the ancestors.

WAR SONG

Wife of Nkodo Embolo, wife of Zoa Anaba, whose maternal uncle is Ondoa Akumu,
Come, help us.
The enemy gathers in large numbers and small,
War will break out.
Come, help us.
My children, bring guns and all your arms and come.
Will our brother Owona Ada be left to die like a pig?

Traditional Beti warfare was largely feuding with other Beti groups. Bands of combatants could range from twenty to one hundred participants, usually composed of kinsmen or neighbors. The use of European rifles, or those made by coastal tribes, was fairly widespread by the late nineteenth century.

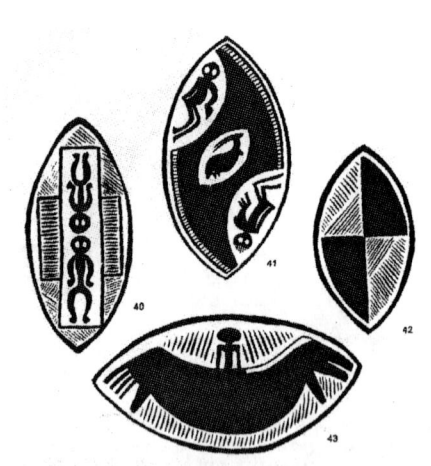

ATANGANA NTSAMA, THE WAR IS OVER

Atangana Ntsama, the war is over...
Hè! Atangana Ntsama, the war is over!
The cannon are broken,
Go tell it to the son of Ndono Edoa,
To the great man who is the son of Ndono Edoa,
Run quickly, why do you languish there?
All you Ewondo, come and run quickly,
Come and run quickly, brothers;
Go tell it to Mindili Ebulu, son of Ndono Edoa.
How is it that you would like me to leave so many goods behind?
Hè! They will surprise you in your greed!
Such richness. I should take some!
You others, move off, what are you doing there?
Friend, there were as many goods as in a market;
Friend, we have marched through all of that without taking anything!

This is a song the Beti women sang at the end of World War I. Charles Atangana, (Atangana Ntsama in the song) was a Beti headman whom the Germans named *Oberhauptling*, or Chief of all the Beti, shortly before the war broke out. He is also referred to as Mindili Ebulu, or the man whose house is so large that it had a roof divided into nine sections instead of the two sections of an ordinary dwelling. (*Mindili* = roof sections in Ewondo; *Ebulu* = nine, a number with powers above all numbers.)

On January 1, 1916, Atangana and seventy-two other chiefs, several thousand Beti, and the Germans began a two-month exodus to Equitorial Guinea. This song announces the end of the war. It also relates an incident which took place on the march: some of the women wished to seize the departing Germans' goods, which they compared to those in a market; but others urged the women to leave the goods and march south without them.

40. TWO EUROPEANS IN A HOUSE. 41. TWO MEN CATCHING AN ANTELOPE IN A NET. 42. DOOR. 43. MAN ON HORSEBACK. 44. PATH BETWEEN TWO HILLS. 45. TWO MONKEYS.

MY MOTHER, DO NOT CRY FOR ME

The child sings this song to its mother shortly before its death.

Do not bury me in a dunghill,
For there people pour anything,
Leave anything,
Throw anything.
Do not bury me in the courtyard,
For there anyone can walk,
And anyone can sit.
Do not bury me under the footpath,
Where anyone can pass.
Do not bury me in the forest,
Where there is too much noise,
Where people cut anything,
Where they hack trees down.
Bury me among the raffia grass
For there the frogs will cry,
The frogs will cry a lot...
My mother, do not cry!

Death was no stranger to the rainforest. The average life expectancy was under forty years, and infant mortality was high. Consequently, many Beti songs deal with death, and some of them show a great dignity and stoicism. The child's plea against an inconsequential burial is not far-fetched, because funeral rites among the Beti were usually limited to elders.

THE PYGMIES KILLED NBARGA MSUDU

The Pygmies have killed Mbarga Nsudu,
And with our spears we bat his head about,
And make a mosquito net of his small intestine;
His nose will serve us as a whistle,
His eyes are mirrors for us,
And his teeth our combs;
The Pygmies have killed Mbarga Nsudu.

This song is sung by the chimpanzees in the rainforest who have a cynical joke about the fact that the Pygmies have killed a certain Mbarga Nsudu. The Pygmies were the original inhabitants of the part of central Cameroon into which the Beti eventually migrated, and were renowned for their ability to move through the rainforest undetected. Chimpanzees and gorillas figure in many Beti songs and proverbs, usually as symbols of strength or age. ■

Bibliography

I Unpublished Sources

1. Archival materials: The major source of archival materials for this study was the Cameroonian National Archives, Yaoundé, in particular reports in the six thousand series labeled "Préfecture de Yaoundé." Most of these were compiled after 1917 and included the following folders:

6139	—Fiches personnelles de nominations de chefs.
6148	—Rapports de tournées effectuées dans les groupements Minta et Nguen, subdivision de Nanga-Eboko par le chef de subdivision.
6151	—Tableaux pour rapport annuel 1952.
6152	—Correspondance de chef de région.
6166	—Photos actualités du journal des villages.
6177	—Des elections municipales de Okola 1959.
6183	—Rapport annuel 1951–1952.
	—Haut Commissaire de la République Français au Cameroun; Messieurs les Chefs de Région et subdivision, "Marriage-Dot-Liberation de Veuves," 21 June 1954.
6193	—Photos actualités des villages.
6204	—Fiches avec photos.
6206	—Syndicats.
6207	—Commandement Indigène, Bulletin des Notes, Année 1948 et 1949, Abega Atangana Martin (individual report cards on several chiefs).
6210	—Subdivision de Yaoundé, Rapport Politique, août 1945.
6210	—Subdivision de Yaoundé, Rapport Politique, janvier 1947.
6210	—Affaires politiques et administratifs; 5, Régime de l'indigénat – suppression 46–51; 9, Rapport politique juillet–novembre 1945; 10, ONU.; 11, Activités Musulmanes.
6210.5	—Abega Atangana Martin.
6210.5	—Le Ministre de la France d'outre-Mer à Monsieur le Haut-Commissaire de la République au Cameroun; Suppression du région de l'indigénat, Paris, 8 avril 1946.
6210.6	—Delavignette aux Chefs de régions, enquête sur Missions Réligieuses, Yaoundé, 10 fevrier 1947.
6210.8	—Martin Abega au President du Conseil de Tutelle de l'ONU., 29 novembre 1949.
6213	—Région Nyong et Sanaga, Rapport Annuel 1939.
6213	—1. Rapports mensuels – Yaoundé 1916–1917. 2. Administration provinciale – Nanga-Eboko, 1925–1929. 3. Semestrials Nanga-Eboko 30, 31, 32, 33. 4. Tournées, Nanga-Eboko, 1932. 5. 1939 Nyong et Sanaga, rapport annuel. 10. Nyong et Sanaga – 1951.
6214	—a. Subdivision d'Akonolinga – 1948 Rapport Annuel. b. Subdivision d'Akonolinga – 1950 Rapport Annuel. c. Renseignements Généraux (SAA) Subdivision de M'Balmayo Rappel Historique 1951.
6214	—Contains several hand-sketched maps of ethnic groups in the Yaoundé area, ca. 1951. Similar maps are contained in folders 6292 and 6514.

6217	—Le Gouverneur des Colonies à Chef de la Circonscription de Yaoundé, Douala, 6 January 1917.
6217	—Rapports annuels – population Nyong et Sanaga 1952.
	—"Synthèse UPC. – UDE, FEC. – JDC." (Nyong et Sanaga et Lobo), Mbalmayo, 22 janvier 1957.
	—Région Nyong et Sanaga – Rapport Annuel 1956 – Subdivision de MFOU.
6219	—Rapports annuels 1953.
6220	—Yaoundé subdivision 1951.
6237	—Populations.
6293	—Rapports annuels 1951–1952.
6294	—Affaires économiques.
6295	—Situation Politique, Yaoundé, 1922.
6295	—Situation Politique, Yaoundé, 1923.
6295	—Situation Politique, Yaoundé, 1924.
6295	—Cameroun, Région de Nyong et Sanaga, Subdivision de Yaoundé, Commandement indigène, Bulletin de Notes, Année 1936. (Individual notes on several chiefs).
6295	—Yaoundé à chef de la subdivision d'Akonolinga, "Construction Village des Chrétiens." 2 mars 1933.
6295	—Circonscription de Yaoundé, Rapport Semestriel, 1er semestre 1933, situation politique.
6296	—Subdivisions.
6296	—Rapport annuel, subdivision Akonolinga, 1939.
6299	—Subdivision.
6301	—Rapports politiques mensuels.
6312	—Mbalmayo, Akonolinga, Nyong et Sanaga 1952.
6322	—Correspondance.
6324	—Élevage.
6330	—Agriculture, Santé.
6352	—Journal des villages.
6373	—Rapport annuel 1949.
6392	—Nyong et Sanaga.
6401	—APA/AE Dossiers d'associations diverses.
6402	—Rapports annuels subdivisions.
6404	—Nyong et Sanaga, Santé Publique.
6405	—APA – Activités des Partis Politiques U.P.C. Affaires Musulmanes: Arrivé à Yaoundé de Marabout Ould Cheick Sidie Youssouf et de sa suite.
6408	—Commandement African, Bulletin de Notes, 1952 (on several chiefs).
	—Procès-verbal de la Réunion de l'Association Amicale des Chefs Traditionnels du Cameroun, Mvolye, 23 November 1952.
	—Région de Nyong et Sanaga. Décision Régionale No. 910, 24 December 1952.
6408	—30 oct.–1 dec. 1931 – Chef de subdivision Nanga-Eboko Chefferies africaines – Primes rendements des chefs – allocations des chefs.
6412	—Nyong et Sanaga – Dossier: Mission d'Inspection de colonies, 1951.
6425	—RNS Réorganization de l'Etat-Civil indigène.
6435	—APA – Rapports politiques mensuels.
6439	—Rapports politiques, 1946–1947.
6443	—Tourné à Nanga-Eboko.
6448	—Service géographique – Populations.
	9. Coutumes et moeurs.
6478	—Propagande Allemande, 12 December 1940.
6496	—Archives du Commandement indigène.
6500	—Affaires sociales: Hygiène publique, travail et main d'oeuvre, Code de travail, Affaires militaires, enseignements, sports.
6501	—La Réunion sur la dot, le marriage et le divorce.
6510	—Caisse centrale de la France d'outre-mer, Service des Etudes Générales, Graphiques de l'Evolution Economique de L'A.E.F. (Monnaie, Prix, Commerce Extérieur, Budgets, Investissements), 1952.
6516	—1937/39 affaires militaires – mobilisation administrative.
6518	—Mission Catholique, Rapport succinct sur l'oeuvre des Missions Catholiques dans le vicariat apostolique du Cameroun, 3 septembre 1924.
6519	—Rapport d'ensemble de la circonscription de Yaoundé 1925 – Nanga-Eboko 1921.
	—Circonscription de Yaoundé, Rapport du 1er Trimestre 1931, situation politique.

6524 —Rapport annuel de Service de Santé, 1951-1952.
6548 —Articles parus au "Journal des Villages de Nyong et Sanaga," 1956-1957.
6590 —Correspondances.
6813 —Rapport politique du 1er Trimestre 1954.

Also consulted were a set of annual reports of government services, numbered as follows:

10.010 —Exposé Général de la situation dans les Territoires Occupés de l'Ancien Cameroun (undated, probably 1920).
11.181 —Rapport annuel PTT 1925.
10.020 —Rapport annuel PTT 1926.
11.165 —Rapport annuel PTT 1936.
10.098 —Rapport annuel PTT 1941.
11.121 —Rapport annuel du Service de Santé 1925.
10.022 —Rapport annuel du Service de Santé 1926.
10.028 —Rapport annuel du Service de Santé 1928.
11.665 —Rapport annuel du Service de Santé 1936.
11.381 —Rapport annuel du Service de Santé 1937.
10.012 —Rapport annuel Chemin de Fer 1918, 1919, 1920.
10.025 —Rapport annuel Chemin de Fer 1925.
11.181 —Rapport annuel Enseignement 1925, and
11.803/A —Rapport sur le Secteur-Est, Yaoundé, 14 July 1938.
11.819 —Charles Atangana à la chef de la région de Nyong et Sanaga, Mvolye, 23 August 1938.
—Rapport de la tournée effectuée du 31 août au 8 septembre 1938 par Monsieur Aimont, Chef de la Subdivision de Yaoundé, dans la Région du Chef de Groupement Martin Abega.
11.828 —Exposé de la politique Générale, attitude des chefs-Esprit des populations (1918).
—Rapport de tournée effectuée par la sous/lieutenant Roussell du 15 au 26 avril 1918.
—Administration générale, Affaires Politiques, Chef de la Circonscription de Yaoundé, juin 1919.
2305 —Région de Yaoundé, 1 à 66, Procès-Verbeaux de déclarations des indigènes a/s massacres, tuerie, meurtres commis par les Allemands (1918).
2949 —Chef de la Circonscription de Yaoundé à Commissaire de la République; "Objet Impôt de Capitation de 1923" (16 July 1932).
—Rapport sur les modifications proposées par les chefs de circonscription au sujet d'une refonte de l'assiette de la taxe de capitation (1922), Territoires du Cameroun, "Depuis l'occupation du Territoire ..."

The Cameroonian National Archives also contain a series of French translations of German reports or articles dealing with Cameroon, listed as TA (traduction allemand), most of which are numbered in the one thousand series. Where possible, I have used the original German source, but in some instances, the papers are missing or the original was incompletely identified, in which case the translation is used and identified "TA" with its archive number.

The Institut de Recherche du Cameroun (IRCAM) contains a valuable collection of documents of anthropological and historical interest from the French period. Most of these documents were answers to specific queries sent to administrators in different prefectures, or were culled from other government reports. Those concerning the Beti are mostly contained in Files I and J in the librarian's office, IRCAM. Some of the most useful of these archival reports are listed below:

Atangana, Charles. "Signification des Mots Politiques." IRCAM, File I. 27 September 1929.
Bertaut, Maurice. "Notes sur les coutumes de indigènes de la subdivision d'Ebolowa." IRCAM, File N, N.D.
_____. "Circonscription d'Ebolowa, étude sur le marriage indigène." IRCAM, File N, 1934.
Chef de la subdivision de M'balmayo au chef de la Région de Nyong et Sanaga. "Tribu des Mvog-Atangana Mballa." IRCAM, File I, 1938.
"Chez les Etons, les coutumes-conception-grossesse-accouchement." IRCAM, File I, 1933.
Cournarie, P. "Note sur les Coutumes des Populations de la Région du Nyong et Sanaga par Cournarie." CNA (Director's office), Yaoundé, December 1933.
"Coutumes Pahouines de la subdivision d'Ambam." IRCAM, File N, 1933.

Delteil, P. "Etude des coutumes des populations de la Subdivision d'Akonolinga." IRCAM, File J, 1933.
Dominik, H. "Rapport du Capitaine Dominik rel. à l'expédition Yebekolle-Maka 1906." CNA 923, 1 May 1906.
Dugast, M. "Documents recueilles en pays Mangisa par M. Dugast communiqués par Mme. Dugast." Yaoundé, N.D., IRCAM, File I.
"Enquête sur l'Alimentation des Indigènes." Mbalmayo, IRCAM, File I, 1939.
"Extraits des Dossiers et des Rapports rel. à la Station de Yaoundé depuis 1885." CNA TA 39.
"Généalogie et Origine des Races dans la Subdivision d'Akonolinga d'après les renseignements recueillis par M. Tremesaygues durant les années 1929 et 1930." 1944. IRCAM, File I.
Guillon, Médécin-Lieutenant. "Habitation, Tribu-Eton-Ouest." IRCAM, File I.
"Note sur la coutume dite 'Bilaba.'" 1937 (?). IRCAM, File N.
Otyam, Martin. "L'Institution du 'Bilaba' chez les Boulous." 1934, IRCAM, File N.
"La Région de Nyong-et-Sanaga." 1949. IRCAM, File I.
"La Situation Politique, Nanga-Eboko." 1934, IRCAM, File I.
"La Situation sur la Station Yaoundé et la Région de la Sanaga Supérieur." CNA TA-60, 1895.
"Sondage démographique effectué dans la subdivision de Saa." N.D. IRCAM, File I.
Stoll, A. "Le Tambour d'Appel des Ewondo." 1942, IRCAM, File I.
"Traduction d'un Document Allemand contenant les Prescriptions du Lieutenant Von Hogen, Commendant du District Ebolowa." CNA 1526, 1915.
"Troubles dans le Sud-Cameroun de 1904–1906." CNA TA-37.
Zoeller, H. "Voyages d'Exploration dans la Colonie Allemande du Cameroun." CNA TA-59, 1885.

II Unpublished Manuscripts (in private possession)

Atangana Amengue, Henri. "Mevoungou." April 1968.
_____. "Le Tam-Tam ou 'Nkoul.'" April 1968.
Betene, Pierre. "Le Chant dans la Vie Traditionnelle du Beti." Yaoundé, July 1967.
_____. "D'Une Génération à une Autre, Étude des Changements Survenus dans Notre Société depuis 25 Ans." Torrok, Chad, 7 January 1968.
_____. "Enquête sur les Beti." Yaoundé, 1967.
Bikoa, Materne. "Origine des Beti." Yaoundé, 1967.
_____. "La Musique Traditionnelle en Pays Beti." Yaoundé, 1967.
De Thé, M. S. "Influence des Femmes sur l'évolution des structures sociales chez les Beti du Sud-Cameroun." Université de Paris, Ecole Pratique des Hautes Etudes, VIe section, Paris, 1965.
Ebogo, Apollinaire. "Les Beti." Yaoundé, 1967.
_____. "Les Beti, Supplement aux Recherches Sociologiques." Yaoundé, 1967.
_____. "Remarques sur les notes sur les coutumes des populations de la region du Nyong et Sanaga par Cournaire, December 1933." Yaoundé, 1968.
Embolo, Laurent. "Rapport à l'Enquête sur les Beti." Yaoundé, 1968.
Esomba, F. "Réligion Traditionnelle." Mbalmayo, 14 March 1968.
Foudda, Max Abe. "Histoire des Beti (Ewondo)." Typescript of six pages prepared by the last living Beti *chef supérieur* of French times, copied 17 December 1967. Max Abe Foudda, whose middle name is not a clerical title, was born ca. 1872 at Nkolbewa, south of the Nyong, son of an Ewondo headman.
Onana, Ambroise Alfred Marzavan. "Généalogie des Beti." Yaoundé, March 1968.
_____. "Généalogie Générale de la Tribu Mvog-Amugu." Yaoundé, March 1968.
_____. "Je veux savoir comment la tribu Beti est venue de l'Orient...." Yaoundé, March 1968.
_____. "Les Rites Fétichistes Anciens des Ewondo." Yaoundé, 1968.
Owona Nde, Cyprian. "Généalogie Général de la Tribu Mvog Amougou." Mbalmayo, 14 March 1968.
Tjamag, Louis. "Le Fétichisme et la Guérison en Pays Bassa." Yaoundé, 1968.
Tsala, Théodore. "L'Abbé Tobie Atangana. L'un des huit premiers prêtres Camerounais." Mvolye, May 1968.
_____. "Bénédictions et Malédictions." Mvolye, May 1968.
_____. "Charles Atangana Ntsama." Mvolye, 20 August 1968.
_____. "Curriculum Vitae de l'Abbé Théodore Tsala Etono." Mvolye, 1968.
_____. "Géographie et Population." Mvolye, 1 June 1968.
_____. "Le gouvernement des Beti." Typescript in French. 1968.
_____. "La Guerre des Esele, Tribu Eton, et des Kolo (Yaoundé)." July 1968.
_____. "Interdits." Typescript in French and Ewondo. 1968.
_____. "Monseigneur Francois Xavier Vogt." Typescript with carbon copy in French. 1968.

_____. "Grammaire Ewondo par l'Abbé Théodore Tsala, prêtre diocesain de l'arcdiocese de Yaoundé (Cameroun)." Mvolye, N.D.
_____. "La Mort de Zibi Ngomo et les Sacrifices Humaines." Mvolye, 26 March 1968.
_____. "Nlam Mesin." Mvolye, 21 September 1969.
_____. "Les Noms des Jours." Mvolye, April 1968.
_____. "L'Opinion d'un Prêtre Camerounais sur la Dot." September 1953.
_____. "L'Organization Judiciaire." Mvolye, 2 March 1968.
_____. "Les parents et les enfants: Bebonde ai bon." Typescript with carbon copies in French. 1968.
_____. "Principales Valeurs Sociales des Beti." Mvolye, June 1968.
_____. "Regles de vie sacredotale." Typescript with copies in French. 1968.
_____. "Seigneur Angongo Woo." In *Oeuvres inédites de l'Abbé Tobie Atangana*. Mvolye, April 1968.
_____. "Des Vedettes de l'évangélisation du Cameroun." Mvolye, 1 April 1968.
Vieter, Heinrich. "Erinnerungen aus Kamerun 1890–1903." Typescript of Bishop Vieter's journal, in possession of Pére Frederick Koster, O.P.M. N.D. Yaoundé.
_____Vincent, Jeanne-Fancoise, and Théodore Tsala. "Mort, Revenants et Sorciers d'après les Proverbes des Beti du Sud-Cameroun." July 1968.

III PUBLISHED SOURCES

1. Books, Pamphlets

Barbier, J., ed. *Femmes du Cameroun: Méres pacifique, Femmes rebelles*. Paris: Karthala, 1985.
Beti, M. (Alexandre Biyini) *La Pauvre Christ do Bomba*. Paris: Éditions Robert Laffont, 1956.
_____. *Mission Terminée*. Buchet-Chastel: Éditions Corrêa, 1957.
_____. *Remember Ruben*. Washington, D.C.: Three Continents Press, 1980.
Billard, P. *La Circulation dans Le Sud Cameroun*. Lyon: Imprimerie des Beaux-Arts, 1961.
_____. *Le Cameroun Physique*. Lyon: Imprimerie des Beaux-Arts, 1962.
Binet, J., and P. Alexander. *Le Groupe dit Pahouin (Fang-Boulou-Beti), Monographies Ethnologiques Africaines publiées sous le patronage de l'Institut International Africain*. Paris: Presses Universitaires de France, 1958.
Deane, S. *Talking Drums from a Village in Cameroon*. London: John Murray, 1985.
DeLancey, M., and V. DeLancey. *A Bibliography of Cameroon*. New York: Africana Publishing Company, 1975.
DeLancey, M. and H.M. Mokeba. *Historical Dictionary of the Republic of Cameroon*, 2nd edition, African Historical Documents, No. 48. Metuchen, N.J.: The Scarecrow Press, 1990.
DeLancey, M., and M.D. DeLancey. *Cameroon*, World Bibliographical Series, No. 63, revised edition. Oxford, England: Clio Books, 1999.
Dominik, H. *Kamerun, Sechs Kriegs-und Friedansjahre in deutschen Tropen*. Berlin: Ernst Siegfried Mittler und Sohn, 1901.
_____. *Vom Atlantik zum Tschadsee Kriegs-und Forschungsfahrten in Kamerun*. Berlin: Ernst Siegfried Mittler und Sohn, 1908.
Dugast, I. *Inventaire Ethnique du Sud-Cameroun*. Memoires de l'Institut Francais d'Afrique Noire (Centre du Cameroun, Yaoundé), 1949.
Dussercle, R. *Du Kilima-Ndjaro au Cameroun, Monseigneur F. –X. Vogt. (1870–1943)* Paris: Editions du Vieux Colombier, Paris (ca. 1950).
Fitzner, R. *Deutsches Kolonial-Handbuch*. Band I. Berlin: Herman Paetel, 1901.
Gardinier, D. *Cameroon, United Nations Challenge to French Policy*. New York: Oxford University Press for the Institute of Race Relations, 1963.
Geertz, C. "Religion as a Cultural System." In W. Lessa and E. Vogt, eds., *Reader in Comparative Religion: An Anthropological Approach*. New York; Harper & Row, 1965, pp. 204–216.
_____. "Religion-Anthropological Study." In D. Sills, ed., *International Encyclopedia of the Social Sciences*. Vol. 13. New York: The Macmillan Company & The Free Press, 1968, pp. 398–406.
Gluckman, M., and F. Eggan. *Political Systems and the Distribution of Power*. A.S.A. Monographs, 2. New York: Frederick A. Praeger, 1965.
Gorges, E. *The Great War in West Africa*. London: Hutchinson & Co., N.D. [c. 1920].
Greenberg, J. "The Languages of Africa." *International Journal of American Linguistics* 29, no. 1, part II (January 1963).
Guyer, J. "The Provident Societies in the Rural Economy of Yaoundé, 1945–1960." Boston University African Studies Center, Working Papers, Series, No. 37. Boston, 1980.
_____. *Family and Farm in Southern Cameroon*. Boston University African Research Studies, No. 15. Boston, 1984.

_____. "From Seasonal Income to Daily Diet in a Partially Commercialized Rural Economy (Southern Cameroon)," in *Seasonal Variability in Third World Agriculture*. David E. Sahn, ed. Baltimore: Johns Hopkins University Press, 1989.
_____. "The Value of Beti Bridewealth," in *Money Matters, Instability, Values and Social Payments in the Modern History of West African Communities*. Portsmouth, N.H. Heinemann, 1995.
Guthrie, M. *The Bantu Languages of Western Equatorial Africa*. London: Oxford University Press, 1953.
Heepe, M. *Jaunde-Texte von Karl Atangana und Paul Messi, nebst Experimentalphonetischen Untersuchungen über die Sprache*. In *Abhandlungen des Hamburgischen Kolonial-Instituts Band XXIV*. Hamburg: L. Friedrichen & Co., 1919.
Kuczynski, R. *The Cameroons and Togoland: A Demographic Study*. London: Oxford University Press, 1939.
Laburthe-Tolra, P. *Les seigneurs de la forêt Minlaaba I, essai sur le passé historique, l'organisation sociale et les normes éthiques des anciens Bëti du Cameroun*. Paris: Publications de la Sorbonne, 1981.
_____. *Initiations et sociétés secretes au Cameroun, Essai sur la religion Beti, Les mystères de la nuit, Minlaaba II*. Paris: Editions Karthala, 1985.
_____. *Vers la Lumiere? Ou le Desir d'Ariel, à propos des Beti du Cameroun, Sociologie de la conversion, Minlabba III*. Paris: Editions Karthala, 1999.
Laburthe-Tolra, P. and C. Falgayrettes-Levera. *Fang*. Paris: Musée Dapper, Editions Dapper, 1991.
Leach, E. "Lévi-Strauss in the Garden of Eden: An Examination of Some Recent Developments in the Analysis of Myth." In W. Lessa and E. Vogt, eds., *Reader in Comparative Religion, an Anthropological Approach*. New York: Harper and Row, 1965, pp. 574–81.
_____. *The Structural Study of Myth and Totemism*. A.S.A. Monographs, 5. London: Tavistock Publications, 1967.
Le Vine, V. *The Cameroons from Mandate to Independence*. Los Angeles: University of California Press, 1964.
_____. *The Cameroon Federal Republic*. Ithaca: Cornell University Press, 1971.
Lévi-Strauss, C. "The Story of Asdiwal." In E. Leach, ed., *The Structural Study of Myth and Totemism*. A.S.A. Monograph, 5. London: Tavistock Publications, 1967, pp. 1–47.
_____. *Structural Anthropology*. Garden City, N.Y.: Anchor Books, 1967.
_____. *Tristes Tropiques*. New York: Atheneum, 1968.
_____. *The Savage Mind*. Chicago: The University of Chicago Press, 1968.
Mandrou, R. *Introduction à la France Moderne, Essai de psychologie historique, 1500–1640*. Paris: Editions Albin Michel, 1961.
Middleton, J. *The Effects of Economic Developments on Traditional Political Systems in Africa South of the Sahara*. Vol. VI. International Committee for Social Sciences Documentation. The Hague: Mouton & Co., 1966.
Nash, M. *Primitive and Peasant Economic Systems*. San Francisco: Chandler Publishing Co., 1966.
Ndongo, J. "L'esthétique Romanesque de Mongo Beti: essai sur les sources traditionelles de l'écriture modern en Afrique." Paris: Présence Africaine, 1985.
Nekes, P. *Vier Jahre im Kameruner Hinterland*. Limburg: a.d. Lahn, Kongregation der Pallottiner, 1912.
Ngoa, H. "Le Mariage Chez les Ewondo." Doctoral thesis, Universitie de Paris, Faculté des Lettres et Sciences Humainies (Sorbonne), Paris, 1968.
Ngoué, F. *Implantation des Organismes Cooperatifs dans la Zone Cacaoyere au Cameroun Oriental 1960–1961, Rapport Provisoire*. Yaoundé: IRCAM, N.D.
Ngwa, J. *An Outline Geography of the Federal Republic of Cameroon*. London: Longmans, 1967.
Oyono, F. *Le vieux nègre et la médaille*. Paris: Editions Julliard, 1956.
_____. *Une vie de boy*. Paris: Editions Julliard, 1960.
Pichon, P. *Petite Grammaire Ewondo Avec Exercises Appropries*. Yaoundé: Mission Catholique, 1950.
Puttkamer, J. *Gouverneursjahre in Kamerun*. Berlin: Georg Stilke, 1912.
Quinn, F. "African Studies, A Bibliography for Teachers." New Jersey Urban Educational Corps, 1969.
_____. "The First World War and Beti Reactions to the Imposition of French Rule in Cameroon." In Melvin E. Page, ed., *Black Men in A White Man's War: African Manpower Questions in World War I*. London: MacMillan, 1986.
_____. "Charles Atangana and the Beti People." In Martin Njeuma, ed., *Introduction to the History of Cameroon*. London: MacMillan, 1989.
Rapport Annuel du Gouvernement Français sur l'Administration sous mandat des territoires du Cameroun pour l'année 1923. Paris, 1924.
Rudin, H. *Germans in the Cameroons 1884–1914: A Case Study in Modern Imperialism*. New Haven: Yale University Press, 1938.

Sahlins, M. "The Segmentary Lineage: An Organization of Predatory Expansion." In R. Cohen and John Middleton, eds., *Comparative Political Systems, Studies in the Politics of Pre-Industrial Societies.* Garden City, N.Y.: The Natural History Press, 1967, pp. 89–119.
_____. *Tribesmen.* Englewood Cliffs, N.J.: Prentice-Hall, Inc., 1968.
Schnee, H. *Deutsches Kolonial-Lexikon Herausgebeben von Dr. Heinrich Schnee, Governeur.* 3 vols. Leipzig: Quelle & Meyer, 1920.
Service de la Statistique Générale, *Résultats du Recensement de la Ville de Yaoundé (1957) Population Authochtone.* Yaoundé, 1957.
Skolaster, H. *Die Pallottiner, 25 Jahre Missions Arbeit in Kamerun.* Limburg a.d. Lahn: Kongregation der Pallottiner, 1924.
Smith, M. *Government in Zazzau, 1880–1950.* International African Institute. London: Oxford University Press, 1960.
Stoecker, H. "Cameroon 1906–1914." In *German Imperialism in Africa,* Helmuth Stoecker, ed.; Bernd Zölner, trans. Atlantic Heights, N.J.: Humanities Press, 1986.
Tessman, G. *Die Pangwe Völkerkundliche Monographie eines Westafrikanischen Negerstrammes.* 2 vols. Berlin: Ernst Wasmuth, 1913.
Vaast, P., H. Bala, and R. Gineste. *La Republique Federale du Cameroun, Geographie a l'usage des Ecoles Primaire, des Colleges et des Candidats aux concours Administratifs.* Bourges: Imprimerie Andre Tardy, 1962.
Von Laue, T. *The Global City: Freedom, Power and Necessity in the Age of World Revolutions.* New York: J. B. Lippincott Co., 1969.
Weber, M. *The Sociology of Religion.* Boston: Beacon Press, 1968.
_____. *The Theory of Social and Economic Organization.* New York: The Free Press, 1968.
Zimmerman, O. *Durch Busch und Steppe vom Campo bis zum Schari, 1892–1902.* Berlin, 1909.
Zoa, J. *Pour un Nationalisme Chrétien au Cameroon.* Yaoundé, 1957.

2. Periodicals

Abega, C. "La bru tueuse." *Journal des Africanistes,* vol. 62, no. 1 (1992): pp. 95–106.
Atangana, C. "Aken so (le Rite Sso) chez les Yaoundés-Banes." *Anthropos,* 38–40 (1942–45): pp. 149–57.
Bois, P. "Le chant de cantefable chez les Evuzok du sud Cameroun." *l'Ethnographie,* vol. 89, no. 1 (1983): pp. 43–67.
Champaud, J. "L'Économie cacaoyère du Cameroun." In Cahiers O.R.S.T.O.M., *Sciences Humaines* (Paris), vol. III, no. 3 (1966): pp. 105–24.
"Der Handel der Duala." *Mittheilungen aus den Deutschen Schutzgebieten* (Berlin), 2 Heft (1907): pp. 85–90.
"Deutsch-Ostafrica, Kamerun, Togo, Deutsch-Sudwestafrica-Neu-Guinea, Karoliner, Marshall-Inseln und Samoa für das Jahr 1907–1908." *Medizinal-Berichte über die deutschen Schutzgebiete* (Berlin) (1909): pp. 155–249. "Dreimal 25 Jahre, Die Kirchen-Geschichte Kameruns." *Pallotis Work,* no. 3 (September 1965): pp. 40–44.
L'Effort Camerounais (newspaper, Yaoundé). No. 254, 11 September 1960; no. 256, 18 September 1960; no. 257, 2 October 1960; no. 272, 15 January 1961; no. 275, 5 February 1961; no. 289, 14 May 1961.
Essomba, J-M. "Le fer dans le dévelopment des sociétes traditionelles du Sud Cameroun." *West African Journal of Archeology,* vol. 16 (1986): pp. 1–24.
"Expedition von Hauptmann Kund." In F. von Dankelman, ed., *Mittheilungen von Forschungsreisenden und gelehrten aus den Deutschen Schutzgebieten* (Berlin) (1889).
Fouda, B. "Philosophical Dialogue and the Problem of Evil amongst the Beti (Southern Cameroun)". *Journal of African Religion and Philosophy,* vol. 1, no. 2. (1990): pp. 43–52.
Franqueville, A. "Le Paysage urbain de Yaoundé." *Les Cahiers d'Outre Mer* (Bordeaux), no. 82 (April–June 1968): pp. 113–54.
Geertz, C. "The Cerebral Savage in the Work of Claude Lévi-Strauss." *Encounter* 28, no. 4 (April 1967): pp. 25–33.
Guyer, J. "The Food Economy and French Colonial Rule in Central Cameroon." *Journal of African History* (London), vol. XIX, no. 4 (1978): pp. 577–97.
_____. "Female Farming and the Evolution of Food Production Patterns amongst the Beti of South-Central Cameroon." *Africa* (London), vol. 50, no. 4 (1980): pp. 341–56.
_____. "The Administration and the Depression in South-Central Cameroon." *African Economic History* 10 (1981): pp. 67–79.
_____. "Head Tax, Social Structure and Rural Incomes in Cameroon, 1922–37." *Cahiers d'Études africaines* (Paris) 79: pp. 305–29 (1980).

_____. "Indigenous Currencies and the History of Marriage Payments: A Case Study from Cameroon." *Cahiers d'Études africaines* (Paris) 104: pp. 577–610 (1986).
_____. "The Iron Currencies of Southern Cameroon." *Symbols* (December 1985): pp. 2–5, 15–16.
Hermann-Weilheim, R. "Statistik der farbigen Bevölkerung von Deutsch-Afrika." *Koloniale Monatsblätter, Zeitschrift für Kolonialpolitik, Kolonialrecht und Kolonialwirtschaft*, no. 6 (June 1914): pp. 249–63.
Laburthe-Tolra, P. "Le so des Bëti selon M. Hubert Ondana." *Annales de la Faculté des Lettres et Sciences Humaines* (Yaoundé), no. 1 (1969).
_____. "Yaoundé d'après Zenker." *Annales de la Faculté des Lettres et Sciences Humaines* (Yaoundé), no. 2 (1970).
_____. *A travers le Cameroun du Sud et du Nord.* Traduction et Commentaire de l'ouvrage de Curt von Morgen. *Annales de la Faculté des Lettres et Sciences Humaines* (Yaoundé), no. 8 (1972).
_____. "Un tsogo chez les Eton." *Cahiers d'Études africaines* (Paris), no. 59, VX-3 (1975).
_____. "Charles Atangana." *Les Africaines* (Paris), vol. V, edition *Jeune Afrique* (1978).
_____. "Martin-Paul Samba." *Les Africaines* (Paris), vol. X, edition *Jeune Afrique* (1979).
_____. "Essai sur l'histoire des Beti." *Actes du Colloque sur la Contribution de l'ethnologie à l'histoire du Cameroun* (Paris), C.N.R.S., 1981.
_____. "Christianisme et overture au monde"; le cas du Cameroun, 1895–1915." *Revue Française d'Histoire d'outre-mer*, vol. 75, no. 279 (1988): pp. 207–21.
_____. "Inventions missionaries et perception africaine: quelques données camerounaises, *Civilizations*, vol. 41, nos. 1/2 (1993): pp. 239–55.
Mohamadou, E. "For a History of Central Cameroon: Historical Traditions of the Vute or 'Babuti.'" *Abbia* (Yaoundé), no. 16 (March 1967): pp. 59–127.
Nekes, H. "Jaunde und sein Bewohner (Sudkamerun)." *Kolonialen Rundschau* (Berlin), Heft 8 (August 1912): pp. 468–84.
_____. "Totemistische Manistische Anschauungen der Jaunde in ihren Kultfeiern und Geheimbunden." *Kolonialen Rundschau* (Berlin, 1913): pp. 134–52, 207–21.
Ngoa, H. "Situation Historico-Genealogique des Ewondo. Etude Critique." *Abbia* (Yaoundé), no. 22 (1969): pp. 65–88.
Passarge, S. "Die Geschichte der Erforschung und Eroberung Kameruns." *Zeitschrift für Kolonialpolitik, Kolonialrecht und Kolonialwirtschaft* (Berlin, 1908): pp. 557–75.
Quinn, F. "Charles Atangana and the Ewondo Chiefs, A Document." *Abbia* (Yaoundé), no 23. (1969).
_____. "Mardi Soir Vers 7 Heures." *African Arts* (Los Angeles), vol. II, no. 3 (spring 1969).
_____. "Abbia Stones." *African Arts* (Los Angeles), vol. IV, no. 4 (summer 1971).
_____. "Eight Beti Songs." *African Arts* (Los Angeles), vol. IV, no. 4 (summer 1971).
_____. "The Beti and the Germans." *Afrika and Übersee* (Hamburg), Bnd LVI, Heft 1/2 (1973).
_____. "World War I in Cameroon." *Cahiers d'Études Africanes* (Paris), vol. XIII, no. 4 (December 1973).
_____. "French and German Rule in Cameroon." *Tarikh*, vol. 4, no. 4 (March 1974).
_____. "Beti Society in the 19th Century." *Africa* (London), vol. 50, no. 3 (1980).
_____. "Charles Atangana of Yaoundé." *Journal of African History* (London), vol. 21, no. 4 (1980).
_____. "A Beti Song Cycle." *Griot: A Journal of African and AfroAmerican Culture* (Berea College, Berea, Ky.) (March 1998).
_____. "Abbia Stones." *Griot: A Journal of African and AfroAmerican Culture* (Berea College, Berea, Ky. (fall 1998).
Reche, O. "Das Abia-Glucksspeil der Jaunde und die Darstellungen auf den Spielmarken." *Mitteilungen aus dem Museum fur Volkerunde in Hamburg* (Hamburg) (1924): pp. 3–15.
"Reise von Lieutenant Tappenbeck von der Jaunde-Station über den Sannaga Nach Ngila's Residenz." *Mittheilungen von Forschungsreisenden und Gelehrten aud den Deutschen Schutzgebieten* (Berlin) (1890): pp. 109–25.
Smith, M. "Segmentary Lineage Systems." *Journal of the Royal Anthropological Institute* (1956): pp. 39–80.
Tsala, T. "Moeurs et Coutumes Ewondo." *Etudes Camerounaises*, no. 56 (1958): pp. 8–113.
Zenker, G. "Jaunde." *Mittheilungen von Forschungsreisenden und Gelehrten aus den Deutschen Schutzgebieten* (Berlin), no. 8 (1895): pp. 36–70.

IV ORAL INTERVIEWS

Ahanda Ayissi, Etienne; age ca. 40; deputy. Ngomedzap, 18 March 1968.
Alima Etoundi, Charles; municipal counselor. Ngomedzap, 18 March 1968.

Alogo, Messie; age ca. 80; healer. Mfou, 4 April 1968 and 12 April 1968.
Atangana, François; age 46. secretary to cocoa grower's cooperative. Yaoundé, 2 May 1967.
Atangana, Katerina; age ca. 55; daughter of Charles Atangana, *chef supérieur* of Beti. Yaoundé, 11 December 1967.
Atangana Amengue, Henri; age ca. 50. Mfou, 4, 12, 18 and 26 April 1968.
Ateba, Philibert; age ca. 59; secretary to Albert Ateba, *chef supérieur* of Etons. Obala, 19 April 1968.
Ayissi Nsimi, Laurent; age 41. Ngomedzap, 18 March 1968.
Bétéyéne, Jean F.; former foreign minister and business entrepreneur. Yaoundé, 17 June 1968 and 8 July 1968.
Bindzi, Benoit; age 44; former foreign minister. Yaoundé, 26 May 1968.
Bisso Medza, Gotfried; age ca. 55; son of Paul Medza, former Mbidambane chief. 18 March 1968 and 26 March 1968.
Elon, Peirre; musician in Charles Atangana's band. Mvolye, 1 July 1968.
Eloudon, Abe Thomas; age 50; son of Max Abe Foudda, an important chief. Nkolbewa, near M'balmayo, 23 December 1967. ("Abe" was a proper name for both informants.)
Essomba, Frédéric (Abbé); Beti priest who has written about traditional religion. Mbalmayo, 14 March 1968.
Essono, Joseph; age ca. 90; former public health worker for Germans and French; various interviews with Pierre Mebe, Yaoundé, 1967 and 1968.
Fouda Ngono, Jean; age 73; brother of *chef supérieur* Max Abe Foudda. Ngomedzap, 18 March 1968.
Foudda, Max Abe; age ca. 96; Ewondo *chef supérieur honoraire*, last known living close associate of Charles Atangana in German administration. Nkolbewa, near Mbalmayo, 23 December 1967 and 7 January 1968.
Mballa Foe, Martin; age 42; son of an important chief of French times. Mbalmayo, 14 March 1968.
Mbida, André-Marie; age ca. 50, former prime minister. Yaoundé, 28 July 1968.
Mebe, Pierre; age ca. 75; Ewondo family head and former catechist and school teacher in German and French times. Yaoundé, various interviews in 1967.
Okah Mbana, Fabian; age ca. 60; retired medical worker. Ngomedzap, 18 March 1968.
Ondana, Hubert Mbida; age ca. 90; family chief who signed his letters "Doyen de connaissances spécifiques des myths." (Dean of the Specific Knowledge of Myths), Ayéné-Ngomedzap, 5 August 1967 and 2 March 1968.
Ondoua Awomou, Laurent; age 41; Ewondo family chief. Ebogo (near Mbalmayo), 14 March 1968 and 31 March 1968.
Owona Nde, Cyprian; age 67; kinsman chief of Frédéric Foe, during French times. Mbalmayo, 14 March 1968.
Tsala, Théodore; age ca. 70. Numerous interviews at Mvolye, 1967 and 1968.
Ze, Daniel; age ca. 50; former census worker, secretary to two chiefs. 13 April 1968.
Ze, Marie-Jean; age ca. 50; chef du groupement. Ebogo, 4 April 1968.

V REGISTER OF THE EUGENE FREDERICK QUINN PAPERS, 1882–1991

Stored in the Hoover Institution Archives
Stanford University
Stanford, California, 94305–6010
Phone: (650) 723–3563
Fax: (650) 725–3445
Email: archives@hoover.stanford.edu
Internet access: Online Archive of California>Hoover Institution>Eugene Frederick Quinn Papers.
Collection Prepared by:
Harold P. Anderson.
Date Competed: 1976

Descriptive Summary:
Title: Eugene Frederick Quinn Papers, 1882–1991

Creator:
Quinn, Eugene Frederick, 1935

Extent:
16 ms. Boxes, 3 microfilm reels, 2 envelopes, 1 expanding folder, 4 phonotapes

Abstract:
Research notes and drafts, lists, writings, interviews, copies of government documents, printed matter, tapes of tribal chants, and photographs relating to the Beti society in Cameroon. Used by E.F. Quinn as research material for his dissertation entitled "Changes in Beti Society, 1887–1960" (University of California, Los Angeles, 1970). Entire collection available on microfilm (7 reels).

Administrative Information
Access
Open for research.

Publication Rights
For copyright status, please contact the Hoover Institution Archives.

Preferred Citation
[Identification of Item] Eugene Frederick Quinn papers [Box no.], Hoover Institution Archives.

Access Points
Beti (Bantu tribe).
Ethnology-Cameroon.
Africa.
Cameroon.
Cameroon – History.
Cameroon – Social life and customs.

Series Description

Project File for Beti Society Study, 1966–1974.
Boxes 1–2

Correspondence, drafts, research notes, outlines, resumes, and bibliographies related to Frederick Quinn's project to write a history of Beti society in the nineteenth and twentieth centuries. The history is an unpublished dissertation entitled Changes in Beti Society – 1887–1960 (University of California, Los Angeles, 1970).

Categories:
General
Tsala, Abbé Theodore, 1968–1971
Zoa, Jean, Archbishop of Yaoundé, Cameroon, 1967
Drafts (incomplete) of Beti Society in the Nineteenth Century by Frederick Quinn
Notes: General, Notecards, Notebooks
Bibliographies
Resumes
Outlines, chronological and topical
Miscellaneous

Chronological Series, 1822–1961.
Boxes 3–9

Photoprints, photocopies, and typewritten transcripts of documents in the Public Record Office, the Cameroonian National Archives, and the Institut de Recherches scientifiques du Cameroun, and photoprints and photocopies of selected pages of French and German publications, collected by the author during the 1960's, arranged chronologically by date of document or publication with undated documents in folders marked undated. A partial list of documents and publications contained in the 1916–1950 folders, prepared by the author, is contained in the first folder.

Categories:
1822
1827–1828

1829–1830
1832–1833
1885
1889–1890
1892(?)
1894–1900
1901
1902–1921(?)
1922–1923
1924–1933
1933: Chef de Region Cournaire. Note sur les coutumes des populations de la region du Nyong et Sanaga. Typewritten transcript.
1934–1945
1946–1951
1952–1961

Undated, General:
Dugast, I., Documents recueillis en pays Mangisa (Documents collected in the Land of the Mangisa) Photoprint of typescript.
Six Months Ago...Sheikh al-Islam. Photocopy of untitled manuscript in North African Arabic with English translation attached.
Talinde. Quelques fetiches des Ewondo (Fetishes of the Ewondo), undated. Photoprint of typescript

Collected Unpublished Writings, 1903–1968.
Boxes 10–12

Holographs, typescripts, transcripts, photoprints, photocopies, and carbons of unpublished writings in English, French, and Ewondo, for the most part prepared or collected in response to queries made by the author among the inhabitants of the Yaoundé region, and arranged alphabetically by author or title.

Categories:
Atangana, Charles. Discussion of the Evolution of the Role of Chiefs in the Yaoundé region. Typewritten transcript with photocopy and carbon copies in French with an introductory note entitled Charles Atangana and the Ewondo Chiefs, a Document, by Frederick Quinn, 1968.
Atangana, Amengue, Henri. Definitions of Forms of Sorcery among the Beti, 1968. Holograph and typescript in French.
_____. Le tam-tam ou 'Nkoul' (The Tom-Tom), 1968. Holograph and typescript with carbon copy in French.
Atangana, Abbé Tobie. Nti Angono Woo (Zee) (The Leopard Nbamed Zee), undated. Typewritten transcript in Ewondo with French translation by Abbé Theodore Tsala, 1968.
Benediction nuptiale de la jeune fille par ses parents (Nuptial Blessing of a Young Girl by her Parents), undated. Typescript in Ewondo and French.
Betene (also Beteyene and Beteyne), Abbé Pierre. Le chant dans la vie traditionnelle du Beti (Song in the Traditional Life of the Beti), ca. 1967–1968. Typescript in French.
_____. D'une génération à une autre: étude des changements survenues dans notre société depuis 25 ans (From One Generation to the Next: A Study of the Changes Occurring in Our Society Over the Past Twenty-Five Years) 1968. Typescript in French.
_____. Enquete sur les Beti du Sud-Cameroun (An Investigation of Beti Society in the southern Cameroon), 1967. Typescript in French and Ewondo.
Bikoa, Matherene and Pierre Betene. La Musique Traditional en Pays Beti. (Traditional Music in the Land of the Beti), 1967. Typescript with carbon copy and photocopy in French and Ewondo with an introductonary note by Frederick Quinn, undated.
Bikoa, Materene. An Investigation of the Evolution of Beti Society, 1967. Transcript in French.
Biographie de Charles Atangana Ntsama, Chef supérieur des Ewondo (Biography of Charles Atangana Ntsama, Chief Superior of the Ewondo), ca. 1968. Typescript with carbon copy in French.
Chant (Les Ewondo pleurent Atangana Ntsama) (Chant: The Ewondo Weep for Atangana Ntsama), undated. Carbon copy: typescript in Ewondo and French.
Chilver, E.M. and P.M. Kaberry. Draft notes on the Kingdom of Kom (West Cameroon) in the 19th Century. 1964. Photocopy of typescript.

Les croyances des Beti à travers la semantique et les maxims (Religious Beliefs of the Beti as revealed in their Semantics and Maxims), undated. Carbon copy of typescript in French and Ewondo.
Ebogo, Abbé Apolllinaire. Les Beti (The Beti), 1967. Typescript in French and Ewondo.
_____. Les Beti, supplement aux recherches sociologiques sur les Beti de Nnanga (The Beti: Supplement to the Sociological Research on the Beti of Nnanga), 1968. Typescript in French with a letter, list of questions, and a list of project expenses attached.
_____. Remarques sur les 'Notes sur les coutumes des populations de la region du Nyong et Sanaga,' par Cournaire, decembre 1933 (Remarks on the 'Notes on the Customs of the People of the Nyong and Sanaga Region,' by Cournaire, December 1933). Typescript in French.
Embolo, Abbé Laurent, Rapport à l'enquete sur les Beti (Research on the Inquiry about the Beti), 1967. Typescript in French.
Essomba, Abbé Frédèric. Religion traditionnelle (Traditional Religion), 1968. Mimeograph in French.
Le fétichisme et la guerison en pays Bassa (Fetichism and Healing Medicine in the Land of the Bassa), undated. Typericpt in French.
Foudda, Max Abe. Histoire des Beti (Ewondo) (History of the Ewondo Beti), 1967. Typescript with carbon copy in French and Ewondo.
Généalogie générale de la tribu D'Enoa (Genealogy of the D'Enoa Tribe), 1968. Typescript in French and Ewondo.
Genealogy of the Nda-Bod Mvog Amougui Mbezele or Mvog Elomo, undated. Typescript in French.
Laburthe-Tolra, Philippe. Essai de synthese sur l'histoire des populations dites 'Beti' de la region de Minlaba Region [Sous le Nyong]), 1973. Mimeograph of a communication in French.
Le marriage des Beti et ses differentes sortes (The Variety of Marriages among the Beti), undated. Typescript in French and Ewondo.
Mballa, Foe, Martin. Généalogie générale de la tribu Mvog Amougou (Genealogy of the Mvog Amougu Tribe), 1968. Typescript with carbon copy in French; notes of an interview.
Owono Nde, Cyprien, attached.
Mvondo, Marcel, II. Une image de l'Afrique précoloniale (A Description of Precolonial Africa), 1968. Carbon copy of typescript in French.
_____. De la poésie camerounaise (Cameroonian Poetry), 1968. Typescript in French and Ewondo.
Onana, Ambroise Alfred Marzavan. Généalogie des Beti (Genealogy of the Beti), 1967. Typescript with carbon copy in Ewondo; holograph and typescript with carbon copy. French translation by Onana.
_____. Généalogie générale de la tribu Mvog-Amugu (Genealogy of the Mvog-Amugu Tribe), 1967–1968. Typescript with carbon copy in Ewondo; holograph and typescript with carbon copy. Translation by Onana.
_____. Minkana/Paraboles (Proverbs), 1967–1968? Typescript of carbon copy in Ewondo and French, and partial holograph in Ewondo and French.
_____. Les rites fétichistes anciens des Ewondo (Fetish Rites of the Ewondo), 1967–1968? Photoprint of holograph in Ewondo, holograph and typescript with carbon copy. French translation by Onana.
Open Letter to Pope Jean XXIII from the Diocesan Clergy of Yaoundé, Cameroon, October 6, 1960. Carbon copy of typescript.
Principaux instruments de musiques des Beti (Principal Musical Instruments of the Beti), undated. Typescript in French.
La procedure du marriage au sein de certaines families côtière en Cameroun – La dot (The Marriage Customs of Certain Coastal Families of the Cameroon – the Dowry), undated. Typescript in French.
Situation sociale de la femme chez les Beti (The social Status of Women among the Beti), undated. Carbon copy of typescript (incomplete) in French and Ewondo.
The, M.S. de. Influences des femmes sur l'évolution des structures Situation sociale chez les Beti du Sud-Cameroun (The Influence of Women on the Evolution off the Beti of the Southern Cameroon),March 1965. Typescript with carbon copy of a thesis presented to the École Pratique des hautes Études, VIIe Section, University of Paris.
Tjamag, Louis. Le foot-ball au Cameroun. (Soccer in the Cameroon), 1968. Typescript in French.
Tsala, Théodore. "Bénédictions et Malédictions." (Bendictions and Maledictions) Mvolye, May 1968.
_____. "Charles Atangana Ntsama." Mvolye, 20 August 1968.
_____. "Curriculum Vitae de l'Abbé Théodore Tsala Etono." (Biography of Abbé Theodore Tsala, an Eton), Mvolye, 1968.
_____. "Géographie et Population." (Description of Beti Society) Mvolye, 1 June 1968.
_____. "Le gouvernement des Beti" (The Government of the Beti), 1968. Typescript in French.
_____. "La Guerre des Esele, Tribu Eton, et des Kolo (Yaoundé)." N.P., July 1968.
_____. "Interdits" (Interdictions), 1968. Typescript in French and Ewondo.
_____. "Monseigneur Francois Xavier Vogt." 1968. Typescript with carbon copy in French.

_____. "La Mort de Zibi Ngomo et les Sacrifices Humaines." (the Death of Zibi Ngomo and Human Sacrifices), Mvolye, 26 March 1968.
_____. "Nlam Mesin." Mvolye, 21 September 1969.
_____. "Les Noms des Jours." (The Names of Days), Mvolye, April 1968.
_____. "L'Opinion d'un Prêtre Camerounais sur la Dot." September 1953.
_____. "L'Organization Judiciaire." (Organization of the Judiciary), Mvolye, 2 March 1968.
_____. "Les parents et les enfants: Bebonde ai bon" (Parents and Children), 1968. Typescript with carbon copies in French.
_____. "Principales Valeurs Sociales des Beti." Mvolye (Principal Social Values of the Beti), June 1968.
_____. "Regles de vie sacredotale" (Rules of the Priestly Life), 1968, Typescript with copies in French.
_____. "Des Vedettes de l'évangélisation du Cameroun." (Prominent Figures in the Evangelizing of the Cameroon), Mvolye, 1 April 1968.
Vieter, P. Erinnerunger aus Kamerun, 1890–1903 (Recollections of the Cameroon), ca. 1903. Photocopy of typewritten transcript in French.
Vincent, Jeanne-Francoise and Abbé Theodore Tsala. "Mort, revenants et sorciers d'après les proverbs des Beti du Sud-Cameroun" (Death, Ghosts and Witches, based on Proverbs of the Beti of the Southern Cameroun), 1968. Photocopy of typescript in French.
Wars among Beti Tribes, ca. 1968. Untitled typescript in French and Ewondo.

Miscellaneous. Partial manuscripts in French and Ewondo.

Oral Interviews, 1967–1968
Box 13

Handwritten and typescripts, notes, and correspondence related to oral interviews conducted, for the most part, among Beti elders, by the author, arranged alphabetically by name of interviewee.

Categories:
Atangana, Francois. Near Mbalmayo, 2 May 1967.
Atangana Amengue, Henri Mfou. 5, 18 April, 26 May 1968.
Ateba, Albert and Philibert. 19 April 1968.
Bétéyene, Jean Faustin, Yaoundé, 1968. Conversation Concerning Colonial occupation and the Independence Movement on Cameroon.
Binzi, Benoit. Near Yaoundé, 14 and 26 May, 1968.
Bissome Dza, Paul (Bisso Medza Gotefried). 18 and 26 March, 1968.
Brunschweg, Henri. 1 June 1968. Notes on Conversation.
Essomba, Abbé Frédèric, Mbalmayo, 14 March 1968.
Foudda, Max Abe. Nkolbewa, 23 December 1967; January 1968.
Mballa, Foe, Martin and Owona Nde Cyprian. Mbalmayo, 14–15 March 1968.
Mbida, Mr. And Mrs. Andre Marie, Yaoundé, 28 July 1968.
Mbida, Mbelle, 15 February 1968.
Mebe, Pierre. April?, 10 May, 30 June, 7, 12, 14, 20, 22, 26 July, 1, 8, 16 Nov., and 21 Dec., 1967; 8, 22 Feb., 1968.
Messsie, Alongo. Mfou, 4, 12 April 1968.
Okah Mbana Fabian, Fouda Ngono Jean, Ayissi Nsimi Laurant, Ahanda Ayissi Etienne, and Alima Etoundi Charles, Ngomedzap, 18 March 1968.
Onana, Mbida, Hubert. Ngomedzap, 19 March, 5–7 August 1968
Ondoua Awoumou, Laurent. Near Mbalmayo, 14, 31 March 1968.
Tsala, Abbé Theodore. Mvolye, 13, 15, 17, 22, 24 February, 2, 12, 19, 26 March; 2, 7, 22, 24 April; 1, 5, 14, 30 May; 6, 10, 14 July; 1 August 1968.
Ze, Daniel. Yaoundé. 13 April 1968.
Ze, Marie-Jean. 4 April 1968.
Zoa, Archbishop Jean. Yaoundé. 30 November 1967.

Published Matter, 1893–1970
Boxes 13–16

Transcripts, photoprints, photocopies, offprints, resumes, and translations of periodic literature, books, and other printed matter in English, French, German, and Ewondo, collected by the author, in part from the London Library of the Royal Geographic Society, arranged alphabetically by author or title.

Categories:
Alexandre, Pierre. Proto-histoire du groupe beti-bulu-fang: de synthese provisoire (Proto-History of the Beti-Bulu-Fang Group: An Essay), 1962–1963. Photocopy.
Atangana, Charles. Aken Sso (le Rite Sso) chez les Yaoundés-Banes (The 'Sso' Rite among the Yaoundés-Banes), *Anthropos*, 38–40 (1942–1945). Typewritten transcript in French and Ewondo.
_____. Lebenslauf Karl Atangana/Curriculum Vitae de Charles Atangana (Life of Charles Atangana), selection from Heepe (ed.) *Yaoundé-Text*, 1919. Photocopy in German; typescript in French.
Avec Charles Atangana: Une page d'histoire camerounaise (With Charles Atangana: A Page from Cameroonian History), *L'Effort Camerounais*, 10 May, 1958. Photocopy.
Binet, Jacques. Budgets familiaux des planteurs de cacao au Cameroun (Family Budgets of Cocoa Planters in the Cameroon), in L'Homme d'outre-mer (The Man Overseas) series of the Conseil supérieur de la Recherché sociologique outre-mer (Council on Overseas Sociological research), 1956. Photocopy.
_____. Groupes socio-professionnels au Cameroun (Socio-Professional Groups in the Cameroon) *Cahiers Internationaux de Sociologie*, XXIV (1958). Photocopy.
Bot Ba Njock, Henri Marcel. Préeminences socials et systems politico-religieux dans la société traditionnelle Bulu et Fang (Social Preeminence and the Political-Religious System in the Traditional Society of the Bulu and Fang) *Journal de la Société des Africanistes*, 1961. Offprint.
Buell, Raymond Leslie. *The Native Problem in Africa*, 1928. Photocopy of selected pages.
Chilver, E.M. Nineteenth Century Trade in the Bamenda Grassfields, Southern Cameroon, *Afrika und Übersee* (photocopy).
Chilver, E.M. and P.M. Kaberry, From Tribute to Tax in a Tikar Chiefdom, *Africa*, XXX (Photoprint).
_____. Traditional Government in Bafut, West Cameroun, *The Nigerian Field*, XXVII (undated) Photocopy.
Dark, Philip. Notes on the Eton of the Southern French Cameroons, *Man*, LV (1955). Photocopy.
Dominik, Hans. *Vom Atlantik zum Tschadee: Kriegs-und Forechungsfahrten in Kamerun* (From the Atlantic to Lake Chad: Voyages and Discovery in Cameroon) 1901. Photoprint of selected pages with English translation.
_____. *Kamerun: sechs Kriegs-und-Friedensjahre in den deutschen Tropen* (Cameroun: Six Years of War and Peace in the German Tropics), 1901. Photoprint of selected pages with English translation.
Dankelmann (ed.) *Mittheilungen von Forschungsreiden Gelehrten aus den Deutschen Schutzgebieten* (Information on Explorers and Scholars in the German Protectorates), 1889. Photocopy of selected pages.
Dussercle, Roger. *Du Kilima-Ndjaro au Cameroun: Monseigner F.-X. Vogt, 1970–1943)* (From Kilimanjaro to the Cameroin, Monseigneur F.-X. Vogt, 1870–1943), 1950. Photoprint of selected pages.
Franqueville, A. Naissance et analyse d'un payasage urbain: Yaoundé (Birth and Analysis of an Urban Landscape: Yaoundé, 1967. Photocopy of typescript.
Heberer. D. Jaunde (the Ewondo) *Kamerun*, undated. Photoprint of selected pages.
Heepe, M. ed.) *Jaunde-Texte von Karl Atangana und Paul Messi* (Ewondo Texts of Charles Atangana and Paul Messi) in *Abhandlungen des Hamburgischen Kolonialinstituts* (Transactions of the Hamburg Colonial Institute), 1919. Photoprint in German and Ewondo; manuscript and typescript with carbon copies and French translation.
Institut Géographique Nationale (Yaoundé) Service Géographique (Brazzaville) Map of Yaoundé, République du Cameroun.
Kaberry, Phyllis M. Retainers and Royal Households in the Cameroons Grassfields. *Cahiers d'Études Africaines*, 10 (196–). Photocopy.
_____. Traditional Politics in Nsaw, *Africa*, XXIX (1959). Photocopy.
Kaberry, P.M. and E.M. Chilver. An Outline of the Traditional Political System of the Bali-Nyonga. Southern Cameroons. *Africa* (1961) Photocopy.
Morgen, Curt von. *Durch Kamerun von Süd nach Nord, Reisen und Forschungen im Hinterlande 1889 bis 1891* (Across the Cameroon from South to North: Travels and Studies in the Interior from 1889 to 1891), 1893. Photoprint of selected pages; typescript of French translation.
Nekes, Herman. Jaunde und seine Bewohner (Sudkamerun) (Yaoundé a ses Inhabitants [Southern Cameroun], *Koloniale Rundschau* (1912). Photoprint of selected pages. Photoprint with English translation.
_____. Totemistische manistische Anschauungen der Jaunde in ihren Kultfeiren und Geheimbunden (Some Views about Death-Worship and Totemic Symbols in Ewondo Cult: Religion and secret Societies), *Koloniale Rundschau*, 9 (1913). Photoprint with French and English resumes.

_____. *Vier Jahre im Kameruner Hinterland* (Four Years in the Cameroonian Hinterland), 1912. Photoprint.

Passarge, S. Die Geschichte der Erforchung und Eroberung Kameruns (History of the Exploration and Conquest of the Cameroun), *Beitschrift fur Kolonialpolitik, Kolonialrecht und Kolonialwirtschaft* (Note on Colonial Policy, Colonial Law, and Colonial Economy) edited by the Deutschen Kolonialgesellshaft (German Colonial Society), 1908. Photoprint with French translation.

Pogge von Strandmann, H. The German Role in Africa and German Imperialism: A Review Article, *African Affairs*, 69. (1970) Photocopy.

Die politische Organisation der Eingeborenen und ihre Verwendung fur Verwaltung und Rechtsprechung in Schutzgebiet Kamerun (The Political Organization of the Natives and Its General Administration of Justice in the Camerounian Protectorate), *Amtsblatt fur die Schutzgebiet Kameroun* (Official Gazette for the Cameroonian Protectorate) 1910. Photocopy.

Puttkamer, Jesko von. *Gouverneursjahre in Kamerun* (The Governor's Years in the Cameroun), 1912. Photoprint with French resume.

Rechte, Otto. Das abia-Glucksspiel der Jaunde und die Darstellungen auf den Spielmarken (The 'Abia' Game of the Ewondo with a description of the Game Pieces), *Mitteilungen dem Museum fur Volkerkunde im Hamburg* (Communication of the Folklore Museum in Hamburg), IX (1924). Photoprint.

Rudin, Harry R. *Germans in the Cameroons, 1884–1914: A Case Study in Modern Imperialism.* 1938. Photocopy.

Schnee, Heinrich, ed. *Deutsches Kolonial-Lexikon*, 1920. Photoprints of selected articles.

Skolaster, Hermann. *Die Pallottiner in Kamerun. 25 Jahre Missions-arbeit.* (The Pallotiner Fathers in Cameroun. Twenty five Years of Missionary Work), 1924. Photoprint.

Tessman, G. *Die Pangwe Völkerkundliche Monographie eines Westafrikanischen Negerstrammes.* (The Pangwe, Ethnological Monograph of a West African Tribe), 1913. Photoprint with French translation.

Tsala, Théodore. "L'Abbé Tobie Atangana. L'un des huit premiers prêtres Camerounais" (Abbé Tobie Atangana, One of the First Eight Cameroonian Priests), *Spiritus* 8, 1961). Typewritten transcript with carbon copy.

Zenker, G. "Jaunde." *Mittheilungen von Forschungsreisenden und Gelehrten aus den Deutschen Schutzgebieten* (Information from Explorers and Scholars in the German Protectorates). Photoprint with English translation.

Zimmerman, O. *Durch Busch und Steppe vom Campo bis zum Schari, 1892–1902* (Through Bush and Savannah, 1892–1902), 1909. Photocopy of selected pages with French translation.

Zoa, J. *Pour un Nationalisme Chrétiene au Cameroon.* (For a Christian Nationalism). 1957. Pamphlet

Microfilm Series
Microfilm cabinet.

Microfilm (negative) strips of handwritten and typewritten archival documents, unpublished writings, periodical literature, and portions of books in English, French, German, and Ewondo, dealing with African history and, in part, reproduced in other series of this collection.

Phonotapes
Tape cabinet

Four tapes of Beti tribal chants.

Memorabilia
Memorabilia cabinet

Thin piece of market cloth used by the Beti.

Photographs
Photo file

See photo card catalog for description.

Index

agriculture, 15, 17, 90, 114
Ahidjou, Ahamadou, president of Cameroon, 105, 110–114
anciens combattants (returned veterans), 101, 103
Atangana, Karl (later Charles, under French) *chef supérieur* under French, 80–82
  decline of, 82–84, 108
  during World War I, in Spain for peace talks, 75–78
  Oberhäuptling (Superior Chief) under Germans, 56–59
  as tax collector, 52–53
Aujoulet, Dr. Louis-Paul, French medical missionary, political figure of 1950s, 111–112

Banë, related to Beti, 18, 109
Basa, neighboring group, 16–17, 20, 35, 45–48, 61–62, 65, 111
Beti
  bride-price, 32–33, 38, 54, 59, 71, 96, 107, 117
  bridewealth, 19, 25, 32–33, 36, 61, 65, 78–79, 91–92, 95, 103, 107–108
  description of compound, 21–22
  genealogy, 17–18
  geographical setting, 15–16
  headmen, 19–21
  ivory trade, 63–64
  lineage councils, 30–32
  lineage structure, 18–19
  marriage alliances and bridewealth, 32–33, 107–109
  myth of origins, 13–14
  as plantation, caravan, and railroad workers, 65–65
  polygamy, 71, 107

potlatch, 36–37
regulatory groups, 24–26
role differentiation, 22–23
self-concept, 14–15
social norms, 26
traditional religion, 23–24
warfare, 34–35
wrestling matches, 31, 37
Beti, Mongo (Alexandre Biyidi), Beti author, 104–105
Biya, Paul, Bulu civil servant, Cameroon's prime minister, president since 1982, 105, 113–114
British role in World War I, 68–77
Bulu, neighboring group, 17, 25, 46, 91, 113

chiefs
  appointed by Germans, 53–54
  decline of, 80–84
  further decline in post–World War II period, 108–110
  role of in collecting taxes, 79–80
  recruiting laborers, 88–89
cocoa, 45
  French-era cash crop, 80, 84, 88–92, 103–104

Dominik, Major Hans, Jaunde station chief (1895–1898, 1902–1910), 50–52, 57, 62–69
Duala, coastal population, 15, 44, 49, 61–65, 84, 111

évoluées (the evolved class), 102–103, 109

Foudda, Max Abe, Beti chief, 76–81, 88

– 174 –

French presence in Cameroon, after World War I
  local administration, 78–79
  tax collection, 79–80
  role of chiefs, 79–80, 82–84

German presence in Cameroon, 1887–1916
  arrival, 43–45
  Beti reaction to and perceptions of Germans, 46–47
  Beti-German armed conflict, 47–50
  caravans move inland, 62–63, 66–67
  chiefs as tax collectors, 53–54
  compound "mayors," 52–53
  German civil administration, 50–52
  messengers, 55
  police, 54–55
  relations with chiefs, 79–80

Hausa, northern neighbors to Beti, 16, 44, 63, 94

Islam, minimal influence among Beti, 15, 44, 94, 107

justice, administration of
  in traditional society, 20, 24–26
  under French, 78–79
  under Germans, 55–56

League of Nations Mandate in Cameroon, 77–78, 110–112

Mbida, André-Marie, Beti school teacher, Cameroon's first prime minister (10 May 1957), 111–117
Mbidambane, neighboring group, warfare with Germans, 49

Oyono, Ferdinand, Beti writer, 104–106

political parties, 110–113

railroad
  adverse health conditions, 87–88
  Beti songs about, 87–88
  chiefs' roles as recruiters, 88–89
  inland, 86–87

religion, Roman Catholic among Beti
  German era
  arrival of missionaries, 67–68
  Beti Pallottiner School in Kribi, 69
  Msgr. Henri Vieter, 68–69
  Pallottiner Sisters, 69
  French era
  African bishops, including Beti prelates Paul Etoga and Jean Zoa, 107
  African priests, 96–97
  "Cameroonian Pentecost," 92–93
  lay African catechists, 94–96
  Msgr. Francis-Xavier Vogt (1922), 93–94
  Msgr. René Graffin (1931), 96, 107

Sso (antelope) initiation rite, 37–41, 69–71

trade, inland, 16–17, 20–21, 26, 33, 41, 44–49, 53, 62–67
Tsala, Théodore, Beti scholar-priest (ordained 8 December 1935), 14, 18, 19, 25, 29–31, 97–99

Vute, northern neighbors of Beti, 16–17, 49

World War I and Beti, 67, 71, 74–77
World War II and Beti, 84, 90, 95, 104–105, 110–111

Recent Titles in the Series

"... it is worth saluting Berghahn, the publisher that produces the Cameroon Studies series. This undertaking ... is a wonderful resource for English-speaking students of Cameroonian history. Not only are these books well produced with plentiful illustrations, but they are also reasonably priced. They will form some of the canonical texts for Camerooon studies for years to come, and Cameroonists are very lucky to have such a supportive publisher ... Cameroonists now have a whole group of newly available primary sources, elegantly set in context and ready for interpretation. " –African Affairs

MEMOIRS OF A MBORORO
The Life of Ndudi Umaru: Fulani Nomad of Cameroon
Henri Bocquené
Translated from the French by Philip Burnham

"This books has the advantage of being an enumeration of rich detail about a Fulani nomad society and a skillfully told personal narrative, a rearity in the literature of disappearing societies."
–International Journal of African History

Praise for the French edition:

"Dear Father Bocquené, Your Mbororo are certainly very different from mine (except perhaps in their taste for self-ornamentation). But that hasn't prevented me from reading your book with enchantment: this is life, this is the reality. Without belonging to the profession, you have produced one of the masterworks of ethnographic literature. Rich and precise information, accompanied by penetrating insights, emerge from each page - not in the form of arid data but integrated with the unfolding of an individual existence. One feels a little bit Mbororo after having read your book." –Claude Lévi-Strauss

"This work has certainly considerably advanced our knowledge of African culture." –Radio Vatican

"This is a document of rare human density; an account like this one, one does not read but devours it." –La Croix - L'Evènement

"This book is an extraordinary history, unlike any other ethnological work." –Ouest-France

2002. 320 pages, 30 photos, 1 map, glossary
ISBN 1-57181-844-8 Hb $39.95/£25.00
Volume 5, Cameroon Studies

LELA IN BALI
History through a Ceremony in Cameroon
Richard Fardon

Lela in Bali tells the story of an annual festival of eighteenth-century kingdoms in Northern Cameroon that was swept up in the migrations of marauding slave-raiders during the nineteenth century and carried south towards the coast. Lela was transformed first into a mounted durbar, like those of the Muslim states, before evolving in tandem with the German colonial project into a festival of arms.

Reinterpreted by missionaries and post-colonial Cameroonians, Lela has become one of the most important of Cameroonian festivals and a crucial marker of identity within the state. Richard Fardon's recuperation of two hundred years of history is an essential contribution not only to Cameroonian studies but also to the broader understanding of the evolution of African cultures.

Richard Fardon is Professor of West African Anthropology in the University of London and has been editor of the journal AFRICA since 2001.

Autumn 2006. 176 pages, 45 ills, bibliog., index
ISBN 1-84545-215-9 Hb $65.00/£37.50
Volume 7, Cameroon Studies

Berghahn Books, Inc. 150 Broadway, Suite 812, New York, NY 10038, USA

Berghahn Books, Ltd. 3 Newtec Place, Magdalen Rd. Oxford OX4 1RE, UK

orders@berghahnbooks.com   www.berghahnbooks.com